THE ARMY AND THE CROWD
IN MID-GEORGIAN ENGLAND

THE ARMY AND THE CROWD IN MID-GEORGIAN ENGLAND

Tony Hayter

ROWMAN AND LITTLEFIELD
TOTOWA, NEW JERSEY

THE LONDON SCHOOL OF ECONOMICS
AND POLITICAL SCIENCE

First published in the United States 1978 by
ROWMAN AND LITTLEFIELD, Totowa, N.J.

Library of Congress Cataloging in Publication Data

Hayter, Tony, 1938–
  The army and the crowd in mid-Georgian England.

  Bibliography: p.
  Includes index.
  1. Great Britain. Army – History. 2. Riots –
England – History. 3. Riot control – England – History.
4. England – Social conditions – 18th century. I. Title.
UA649.H38   1978   354'.41'00756   77–26288
ISBN 0–8476–6034–6

Printed in Great Britain

TO MY MOTHER AND FATHER

Contents

Preface

The subject of the army and society has come under the notice of historians and political scientists, but their researches have chiefly been into recent history, and there is little published material on this interesting relationship for the eighteenth century. This book, which began life in the form of a doctoral thesis in the University of London, is intended as a contribution to one aspect of the subject, that of the army acting in aid of the civil power, in a century when there was only a very rudimentary force of civil police, and many riots. As students of the eighteenth century are aware, there are a number of books about the crowd, and a good many more about soldiers. Here the relation between them is examined. The workers in the first of these two fields so far have told us how and why crowds collected, and sometimes how they behaved, but we have not been told in much detail how they were suppressed. Similarly, military historians have concentrated on the primary role of soldiers in foreign war, and we lack information as to how they occupied their time at home.

In the usual sense of the terms this book is not a piece either of military history or of working-class history. It occupies ground at the meeting-point of the two, and is best described as a study in administrative history. As such, it has to take account of political, social, constitutional, legal and military factors which impinged upon the army's role in peace-keeping.

Other authors whose work will be found helpful to the student of this subject should be mentioned. Professor Beloff's useful book *Public Order and Popular Disturbances, 1660–1714* is about an earlier period, and the nineteenth century is served by F. O. Darvall, *Popular Disturbances and Public Order in Regency England*, and F. C. Mather, *Public Order in the Age of the Chartists*. The fourth volume of Professor Radzinowicz's *A History of English Criminal Law* explains the legal and constitutional implications of the use of the military as a police. The most recent contribution is Professor Shelton's *English Hunger and Industrial Disorders*, a useful companion to this book, but one which, as with the work of E. P. Thompson and George Rudé, is more concerned with the causes than with the suppression of riots. To all these authors I have incurred a debt I am glad to acknowledge. Also I am grateful to the staffs of the London Institute of Historical Research, the British Museum, and the Public Record Offices of London and Ipswich, whose courtesy and kindly help always seems unaffected by difficult working conditions. Professor J. H. Plumb, Professor I. R. Christie, Professor John Shy, Geoffrey Cleare, Michael Collinge and John

Sainty made useful suggestions and criticisms, and Alice Clare Carter of the London School of Economics was a never-failing source of ideas and encouragement, as well as an identifier of errors. Some mistakes must remain: they are my responsibility. A grant from the Bequest to the University of London of the late Isobel Thornley was a timely and generous help towards publication, which I and the publishers gratefully acknowledge. Finally should be mentioned Michael Howard of All Souls College, who when he was at King's College, London, first compellingly drew my attention to the importance of military factors in history. In acknowledging this last heavy debt I take my place in the ranks of a numerous society.

A. J. H.

Abbreviations

Ann. Reg.   The Annual Register (from 1758).

Cavendish, *Debates*   John Wright, *Sir Henry Cavendish's Debates of the House of Commons, During the Thirteenth Parliament . . . Commonly Called the Unreported Parliament . . . 1768–1771*, 2 vols (1841–3).

Clode   C. M. Clode, *The Military Forces of the Crown*, 2 vols (1869).

C.J.   *Journals of the House of Commons.*

D.N.B.   *Dictionary of National Biography.*

Fortescue   Sir John Fortescue, *A History of the British Army*, 13 vols and 6 atlases (1899–1930).

Fortescue, *Correspondence*   Sir John Fortescue (ed.), *The Correspondence of King George the Third from 1766–December 1783*, 6 vols (1927–8).

Gent. Mag.   *Gentleman's Magazine*, 302 vols (1731–1907).

H.M.C.   *Historical Manuscript Commission Reports.*

P.H.   William Cobbett (ed.), *Cobbett's Parliamentary History of England*, 36 vols (1806–20).

Shute Barrington   Shute Barrington, *The Political Life of William Wildman, Viscount Barrington* (1814).

State Trials   T. B. Howell, *A Complete collection of State Trials and Proceedings for High Treason and other Crimes and Misdemeanors*, 21 vols (1816), continuation by T. J. Howell, 12 vols (1817–26).

Generally quotations are rendered in modern English, that is to say 'ye', 'yt' and such archaisms are converted, bizarre spelling is modernised and unnecessary capitals suppressed. Punctuation is also modernised in appropriate cases, e.g. the prolific commas in which some eighteenth-century correspondents delighted have been removed.

Page references are given for books and for most documents. In cases where documents are foliated, the folio number is given and the right or left page indicated by the initials r or v: where the folio number alone appears this indicates both sides, or recto and verso. In cases where documents are unfoliated, or the foliation is on the face of it unreliable, no number has been given.

Introduction

The eighteenth and early nineteenth century was the high noon of mob disorder in England. Apart from the Jacobite attempts, rebellion had become a thing of the past, but with its disappearance riots increased considerably. This was also a period when Britain, for reasons connected with its social, political and military development, had an almost perversely ineffective system of police.

The wretched lot of the poor in the eighteenth century and their propensity to riot is well known. At times the apparent stability of Georgian society was clearly balanced on a knife-edge. Archenholtz's often-quoted remark, that he could not understand why the poor did not enter into a conspiracy to rise up in a body and plunder their betters, must have seemed to be coming true in riotous years such as 1766 and 1780. The annals of the darker side of Georgian life, while posing interesting problems for the historian today, nevertheless make sorry reading. The indifference (with few exceptions) of one class was as noteworthy as the turbulence and desperation of the other. The habits of working-class deference, even in the country village, clearly went no more than skin-deep, as may be seen from their slogans in riotous times. The glaring inequalities of wealth and power that existed were of the sort which in other times and other societies have needed an elaborate system of terror and repression to maintain. Yet the governments of the age seemed curiously casual about security, and we find an odd dual system of police, in which reliance was placed on an uneasy partnership between the magistrate and the army. The methods of the first were primitive and inefficient. The latter on the other hand was diffident about its right to intervene at all, slow and cumbersome in its operations, and yet armed with deadly weapons.

Sometimes magistrates showed that riots could be dealt with without calling in troops. There were even occasions when the reading of the proclamation in the Riot Act was enough to disperse a mob. But such successes were rare, and the use of the army appeared to most contemporaries to be inevitable. It is the purpose of the book to examine the employment of the British army in this way, with all the problems its use created, from the middle of the eighteenth century until the time of the Gordon riots, when it was put to its harshest test.

It is not my purpose to write much about the historical crowd and its characteristics. They have been well described by several historians and I have little to add. Similarly I have written little about the magistrates, seeking only to show why it was that riots so often and so quickly passed beyond their control. Besides, their role also has been dealt with in published works. With soldiers it is a different story; in fact the eighteenth-century army is only beginning to be properly examined as to its structure and function. There exist many operational studies describing particular campaigns, some biographies of great captains, and a few works on the development of the art of war and on the new theories of warfare in the period. A good many of these books are about Europe, and there is not much published work on the British Army of the eighteenth century, its recruitment, training, the expansion of forces in wartime, planning, supply systems and relations with other government departments. Many other social and constitutional factors connected with the maintenance of a standing army during the century need to be researched. New workers in the field unavoidably continue to take as their starting-point a very few books written many years ago, such as Clode and Fortescue.

A further difficulty arises from gaps in the source-material. The great tragedy of the War Office records, as M. A. Thompson showed, is the paucity of in-letters (the series known as W.O.1). Some unknown hand, probably in the early nineteenth century, consigned most of the letters written before 1756 to oblivion, and what is left is only a small fraction of the total. To some extent the story can be pieced together by examining the records of other government departments, e.g. the Treasury, the Office of the Secretaries of State, the Admiralty, or even the Crown, but many letters from Lords Lieutenant, provincial magistrates and other local sources are irretrievably gone.

A great lack of eighteenth-century military memoirs, diaries and letters constitutes a further gap, and there is little else available to supplement the bald official version of events. Such memoirs as do exist usually fail to tell the modern historian what he wishes to know. Their concern is with campaigns and notable events, and they are of little use in a study of administration or function. The following is a fair example of this tantalising blank in our knowledge:

> I have a mass of letters and correspondence on this campaign [Portugal, 1762]; but I do not propose going into details, for no general actions were fought, and so I do not think that it would interest the public in general to go into matters of commissariat and supply, or dry accounts of marching and counter-marching.[1]

Regimental histories, of which there are many, share this view, usually being little more than calendars of notable battles. These gaps force the cautious researcher into an unfortunate but necessary etherealising of some of his conclusions, and much of the military background of the time remains a mystery. Neither can we expect to find much information about the doings and attitudes of the ordinary soldiers. Professor Rudé has complained of a similar problem with members of eighteenth-century crowds. Neither the man in the ranks nor the man in the street wrote memoirs or correspondence, and our information has to be made up from many scattered and oblique sources.

In the eighteenth century Britain, although aware of her martial traditions, remained in the strict use of the term essentially unmilitaristic, and its stunted army, the natural product of an insular maritime society, was unfitted for many of the tasks it was called upon to perform. Contemporary opinion preferred the navy and the militia: the former was the traditional guardian of the shores, the latter the 'constitutional force'. The army on the other hand was regarded with deep suspicion by the public, and its demeanour was carefully and often unfairly scrutinised in parliament and the press. Attempts to increase it in size were jealously curtailed, as tending towards setting up military government. As Britain's continental commitment declined in the years after Queen Anne's reign so the army's numbers were reduced, so that under George I the total force was scarcely equal to an army corps in more modern times. Needless to say, a good deal was expected from this army in wartime; and at home, scattered piecemeal throughout the country, it was often the only effective police force of a government faced with serious problems of public order. During the middle years of the century the army increased in size in response to the demands of fresh wars, and there are signs that its discipline, reliability and the professionalism of its officers improved. But it remained socially isolated and apologetic about its very existence. This adversely affected its relations with magistrates and its efficiency in dealing with riots. Even without this difficulty the basic problems of riot control were serious enough. As will be shown, the army, apart from obvious shortcomings in equipment or special training, had the further drawback that it found the riot-duty distasteful. The officers cordially detested it and frequently objected to it. Soldiers have been used from time to time to combat civil disorder since the days of the empires of the ancient world, but they have seldom accepted it as part of the military task. Even in modern times a commander in Northern Ireland can be heard to hope that a peace-keeping operation may soon end so that 'the men can get back to some real soldiering'. But the soldiers of the twentieth century have at least been trained for a police role. In the eighteenth century no guidance was given to officers as to techniques of mob-breaking or, more important, as to what the extent of their powers was. As a result their response was at best cautious, at worst fumbling, until exasperation led them into over-reacting with tragic results. The social background and training of officers in most periods of history probably predisposes them to dislike and distrust mobs, and careful instructions about the use of force are essential. In the absence of them, mob-breaking tactics in eighteenth-century England were usually hasty and sometimes drastic improvisations.

The daily running of the army in England was the care of the Secretary at War, a somewhat shadowy figure whose office still needs much investigation. His part in dealing with rioting was crucial, for the marching orders that moved the units of the army from place to place proceeded from his office. From this simple cause developed an elaborate machine for maintaining the public peace, with the Secretary at War as its head as a chief of police, at least for riot-suppression. He received the accounts of rioting from local magistrates, sometimes directly, sometimes after they had passed through the hands of the Secretary of State. In the War Office he formed a strategic picture of the riots, which might at times be one of great complexity. And from his office went the carefully-worded orders that moved the troops, and the letters that carried explanation, encouragement and censure.

The ultimate responsibility for domestic peace belonged to the Secretaries of State, but increasingly during the century they left the task to the War Office. The Secretary at War, no doubt aware that he was permanently committed to the task, began in the early years of George I's reign to take the opinion of the Law Officers of the Crown on the legality of using the military at all, and then on the limits of their power in a confrontation with rioters. Assurances were given – indeed repeatedly given, for opinion on the same subject was called for at intervals throughout this century and into the next – that the lawful basis of such use of soldiers was not in doubt. The advice about the drafting of orders as to when force would be legal was much less palatable to the Secretary at War, who decided to take his own independent course. Indeed he seems in this, as in other contexts, an unfettered and secretive figure, making his plans in his own way. He had in fact much more control over policy than he was prepared to admit. Most Secretaries at War in the eighteenth century were careful to foster the notion that they were not responsible for policy. That was a matter for the cabinet, who considered the propriety of measures and then handed them on to the War Office to apply the detail and carry them out. In reality the part played by the Secretary at War in planning campaigns abroad and managing police matters at home does not accord with this version of his job. But he preferred to shelter behind this useful screen, being reluctant to be politically responsible to Parliament. Parliament on the other hand was determined to find someone answerable for the army, something they were not able to achieve until 1782, when Burke's Act imposed the sort of tasks upon the Secretary at War that made it impossible for him any more to claim that he was an irresponsible official. But before that date it was much easier for the Secretary at War to claim that if he was responsible to any one it was to the King. Parliament got little information about his activities, including his police work in Britain, and thus found it difficult to control them. The unsuccessful demand for an official inquiry after the riots of May 1768 should be seen in this light.

Many of the problems faced by officials, officers and soldiers in the period of this book disappeared in Victorian times. The development of a more modern police system made reliance on the army less necessary. In any case there was a sharp decline in, though by no means a disappearance of, mob violence in the second half of the nineteenth century. And the settling and publication of proper codes of procedure for riot-duty for magistrates, police and troops made for less mistakes, greater efficiency and more humanity. Deprived as they were of such advantages and beset by great difficulties, the army of two centuries ago nevertheless achieved a great deal. It would not be too much to say that within the limitations discussed in this book it did all that it could. That these limitations were very great, and in some cases derived from problems not capable of solution at the time, is testified to by the many mob-successes. Even the mechanism of forecasting and monitoring social unrest was primitive, unreliable and peculiar to a few officials. In modern times the failure of some highly-organised states to solve the problems of violence and public order should warn us not to be too critical of eighteenth-century governments that failed to understand the chemistry of social disorder, and attempted to deal with it in ways that seem unsubtle and drastic.

PART I
The Problems

1 The Law of Riot

There was in this century a widespread ignorance and bewilderment even in official circles about the law relating to riot. In fact the legal position was not unduly complex, and this ignorance derived from a failure to explain it to those officers, civil and military, who had the task of maintaining public order.[1] Even a public figure such as Sir George Savile, while engaged in riot duty when he was a colonel of militia, could write as late as 1779:

> The nasty service we have been upon here has made me consider the Riot Act more a great deal than ever I did before. We have been in situations which would have been very puzzling and disagreeable if there had been resistance. I could be glad you would turn your thoughts to that subject a little. There are commonly received maxims regarding the military and civil powers, and the right of the former to act offensively and fire etc., etc., which I do not very well understand, nor do I find anybody that does. It seems an unlucky Act; for it has always been looked upon as a stretch of power bearing hard on the people, and I am sure it puts the military to great difficulties too, and is much complained of by them.[2]

Before 1714 the position at common law was straightforward and differed little from that in force today.[3] If three or more persons collected for purposes forbidden by law it constituted an illegal assembly only. It could be dispersed, but great care had to be used, for the members of it were as yet only misdemeanants. If the crowd then proceeded to put into effect an illegal purpose with force and violence its offence was riot and all participants became felons. Any private person could lawfully endeavour to suppress such a riot, even taking up arms to do so. It was a duty as well as a right to give help to a civil officer if called upon; only those excepted by statute could avoid it.[4] Any battery, maiming or killing of rioters in such circumstances was justifiable.[5] In the period before 1714 there were several attempts to make riots appear as 'levying war upon the King', and therefore as treason, but juries regarded them with suspicion and crown prosecutors had little success with them.[6]

The Riot Act (1715)[7] was intended to be helpful, since it made felons all persons to the number of 12 and upwards remaining in the area of the riot after one hour from the reading of the proclamation in the Act. The drawbacks were not at first realised. It was difficult in practical terms to carry out the reading, and magistrates were often insulted, attacked, or merely inaudible.

Much more serious was the legal confusion caused. Magistrates after 1714 behaved as if the Act had submerged the common law right of dealing with rioters, and believed their hands to be tied for one hour after proclamation. In fact the position at common law was still intact as it was before 1714; a crowd could become felons by statute after the expiry of one hour, but could also become felons at common law if within the hour they proceeded to acts of felonious violence, such as pulling down houses. This position was explained in the judgments in the case of *R. v. Gillam* (1768)[8] and again by Lord Mansfield in the House of Lords[9] and by Lord Loughborough in the trials arising from the 1780 riots.[10] The Riot Act has a poor record, and better drafting at the time to make plain the intention of the legislature, or a clarifying statement later, would have saved much difficulty. A great deal of damage was done within the statutory hour on many occasions during the 1780 riots, because the authorities believed themselves unable to interfere. The law was no better understood at the time of the Bristol riots in the next century and further explanation was necessary.[11]

The position at law of the army in this context was even more puzzling. Again the common law was fairly simple: the soldier had the same rights and duties as a civilian in the suppression of disorder, and was subject to the same penalties at law if he refused to obey lawful commands. This maxim was also repeated in judgments during the century. In Gillam's Case the judge quoted

> . . . established authorities, which proved, beyond a doubt, that a magistrate, when there is any occasion to support the laws, has a right to demand assistance from *all* His Majesty's subjects who are capable of bearing arms.[12]

And in 1780, in the debate on the Gordon Riots Lord Mansfield said:

> What a private man may do, a magistrate or peace officer may clearly undertake, and according to the necessity of the case, arising from the danger to be apprehended, any number of men assembled, or called together for the purpose, are justified to perform. This doctrine I take to be clear and indisputable, with all the possible consequences, which can flow from it, and to be the true foundation for calling in the military power to assist in quelling the late riots.[13]

This may have been good law, but outside governing circles there was a loud dissenting body of opinion. The very existence of a standing army was questioned by many and the use of it for political purposes in the past had left a legacy of distrust not easily dispelled. The distrust of the executive, so

much a feature of the age, which had prevented the formation of a proper
force of civil police, also meant that police action by the army would be
jealously scrutinised. As a result many inaccurate statements of the law
were confidently advanced. In 1737 during a debate on the Porteous
murder one speaker, in discussing the indemnity by statute for magistrates
who use force after reading the proclamation, said

> . . . but I doubt much if a magistrate would be indemnified, even by this
> law, should he take the short way of dispersing a mob, by ordering his
> assistants to fire among them, and should thereby kill any person who
> had committed no overt act of resistance; especially if it should appear,
> that he had fired upon the crowd without any necessity for so doing, and
> even without any extraordinary provocation. . . .
>
> I would not advise them to fire, unless they should find themselves in
> very great danger of being overpowered, and perhaps murdered by the
> mob.[14]

The idea that arms were to be used not to disperse a mob but only in the last
resort in self-defence, although perhaps humane in its intent, had no legal
basis and was certainly not part of the intention of the legislature in 1714. It
was commonly expressed however. In 1768 the riots ascended to the
political level because of their association with Wilkes, and the newspapers
carried many more letters than usual favouring the crowd. For mistakes of
law and fact this indignant philippic, printed after the St George's Fields
riot of 10 May 1768, can stand for an example:

> It is to be hoped that it will be enquired into in a proper place, by *whose
> order* any of the military were sent into those Fields, against an unarmed,
> and for aught appears, then, a very peaceable multitude, and by *whose
> order* the soldiers were to furnish themselves with ball. It appears by the
> affidavit, that G——[15] gave the fatal orders to fire, as a Justice of Peace.
> I wonder where that gentleman learnt the duties of his office: not in the
> laws, nor the law books: for the laws of England know of no such remedy
> against a riot, *even where the rioters are armed*. If he had done his duty as an
> *English Magistrate*, he should first have sent away the soldiers, who had
> no business there, and if the people had not dispersed, on his reading the
> proclamation, as it is believed they would, he was then to call in the
> power of the county to his assistance. This is the remedy and the only
> remedy which our laws have provided against riots; for we are not as yet
> under military government.[16]

Such letters struck a familiar chord in 1768 and throughout the century.
The respect for public order and private property was great, the distaste for
the soldier was greater still. Whatever judge-law might say, there was a
widespread conviction that the use of military power in suppressing riots

was no part of the English constitution. Edmund Burke entered the controversy after the St George's Fields riot. His information was better, his opinions less chimerical, but his attitude was clear. In pressing for an inquiry into the riot he objected to the remark of Lord Weymouth, the Secretary of State, that the military 'can never be employed to a more constitutional purpose, than in support of the authority and dignity of the magistracy'.[17] The military, Burke insisted, 'can never be employed to any constitutional purpose at all'.[18] The house rejected his motion. George Grenville, in the same debate, believed that

> As to the relation betwixt the civil and military, it stood on as good ground now as it well could; the civil magistrate could call out the military to his assistance when he wanted it, but . . . if he used them improperly, it was at his own peril.[19]

But for the reasons already examined the meaning of 'improperly' in legal terms was not clear to magistrates.

The government was aware that the legal position was unclear, and at intervals the Secretary at War or the Secretary of State took advice from the Law Officers of the Crown. Copies of some of the opinions they received in the early part of the century were placed at the beginning of a file of the Amherst papers containing correspondence on the 1780 riots, thus clearly showing the army's anxiety half a century later about procedure.[20] In fact throughout the century the War Office is found from time to time to be asking the same question, viz: Is the army acting legally in suppressing riots? – and always receiving the same reassuring answer. The fact that they felt compelled to go on asking it is a powerful testimony to their uneasiness and lack of confidence in this role.

In 1717 the Attorney-General, Edward Northey, was asked to advise after the Tiverton riots of that year. Soldiers, in his view, might act and use arms in so doing.[21]

In 1722 the Attorney-General, Raymond (later Lord Chief Justice), was asked to advise again after the Taunton riots, the circumstances of which did not differ essentially from those of Tiverton in 1717. His opinion was that soldiers might properly assist the civil power in suppressing riots, and added that they should always be guided by the civil magistrates.[22]

Having established this, the Secretary at War was concerned to fix upon a form of words in the orders to soldiers to act which would place any military intervention above suspicion. The Attorney-General, Philip Yorke (later Lord Hardwicke), after studying several precedents used between 1724 and 1732 thought that the part of the order under discussion should be 'but not to repel force with force, unless absolutely necessary'.[23]

Sir William Strickland, the Secretary at War, evidently found the implications of this advice alarming. The decision as to what was 'absolutely necessary' would fall to the military commander present, which would expose riot operations to the criticism of being part of an attempt to set up military government. In spite of the Attorney-General's opinion orders continued to go out to troops on riot duty, ending 'but not to repel force with force unless thereunto required by the civil magistrates',[24] or, more emphatically, 'but not to repel force by force unless the civil magistrates conceive there is an absolute necessity for it and not otherwise'.[25]

In 1735 the War Office (under a new Secretary at War, Sir William Yonge), took the opinion of the Law Officers on orders to be used in the smuggling service, hoping perhaps to get advice more favourable to their viewpoint that the magistrate should take responsibility in a crisis. Yonge in fact suggested that the form should simply be 'unless thereunto required by the Civil Magistrates'. He received no comfort from Sir John Willes and Sir Dudley Ryder (both later to be Lords Chief Justice) who rejected the suggestion and reached the same conclusion about the wording as Yorke.[26]

The War Office was unhappy about this. It is difficult not to sympathise. It was being asked to give military help in a domestic civil context, with all the dangers that this involved, and to do so on its own responsibility. Yonge took so much of this advice as to create a new form,[27] which was continued by subsequent Secretaries at War and frequently used by Henry Fox. The curious form of words he invented was not at all within the scope of the legal advice given, but it was obviously more comforting to the military; it ran 'but not to repel force with force, unless it shall be found absolutely necessary or being thereunto required by the civil magistrates'.[28] The formula, which supposed there to be a friendly co-operation between civil and military officers which was seldom achieved in practice, persisted through Lord Barrington's period in the War Office and afterwards. By 1765 there had appeared the even more cautious form involving the alteration of one word: 'unless in case of absolute necessity and being thereunto required by the civil magistrates'.[29]

The Secretary of State applied again for reassurance on the legality of using the Army after the Leeds turnpike riots of 1753, and the Solicitor-General Murray (later Lord Mansfield) patiently stated the law once more. In the same terms as his predecessors he reminded his correspondent that a soldier was as much a subject as anyone else when civil disorder needs to be suppressed, although he should be careful to act with the magistrate.[30] This last piece of advice was prudent, but it reinforced the already current impression that it was part of the law, and that it was not only advisable to act with the magistrate, it was impossible to act without him. It is interesting to compare Murray's careful opinion with the practice into which Fox had fallen. Officers involved in the Leeds riots (and in several others) were sent orders containing the words: 'I must recommend it to you to take care a civil officer be always present, when the repelling force with force may be necessary, that the proceedings may be legal.'[31]

These orders, which Murray asked to see in order to be able to comment with more accuracy, show that in spite of frequent assurances the War Office never lost its uneasiness on the subject of soldiers acting without magistrates. In the riotous year of 1773 Lord Barrington, notwithstanding his years of experience in the matter, applied once more to the law officers, stating the case as before, but extracting from it some slightly different problems. He recited the precedents of Raymond, Hardwicke, Willes and Ryder, and admitted that the forms now used in the War Office were not in accordance with these. The recent riots had made him examine the whole problem again and he wanted advice on three heads. Firstly, was the Secretary at War, an officer (according to Barrington) unknown before the Revolution, justified in giving orders to troops to assist magistrates, or should such orders come only from the Secretary of State, 'a known officer to signify the King's Pleasure since the time of King Henry VIII'? Secondly, was the form of words currently in use safe and legal? Thirdly, could troops be ordered to assist in some preventive capacity where a riot was merely threatening.[32]

Neither did the army officers lose their uneasiness. The result was most clearly seen in 1780. Unbelievably, further instructions to advise on the same subject were sent to the Law Officers in 1796[33] and 1801,[34] with the same responses.

The uncertainty of the Army in 1780 about the extent of their powers is well known, and need only be briefly mentioned. The determination of the War Office not to allow its troops to act without magistrates coincided with an almost unanimous failure of magistrates to act, or at times even to be found at all. The events of 1768 had frightened them as much as they had the army, the riots were on a scale unheard of before, they feared reprisals against their own property, and some may have had political reasons for not wishing to discourage the mob. Whatever their motives, the important fact for the government was that the partnership of army and magistracy, never a happy one, had broken down and left the mob a clear field. The well-known intervention of the King as chief magistrate on his own responsibility after hearing the advice of Wedderburn, the Attorney-General, resulted in the issue of general orders to the troops to act without magistrates. Its effect is discussed in Chapter 13. It is noteworthy that the position in practice, although temporarily solved by this legally correct though drastic expedient, remained uncertain, and no proper attempt was made to clarify it after June 1780. More than half a century after Sir George Savile's anxious letter, quoted at the beginning of this chapter, the Duke of Wellington, agitated by Irish and Chartist threats, wrote:

It would be a very nice and difficult measure to fix the exact point at which an armed body should initiate its operations by fire or weapons against a mob armed by firearms. . . .

It is difficult for those in authority to prescribe in writing the rule according to which these bodies must be resisted in the different stages of their progress.[35]

Lord Amherst, who handled the troop movements in London during the 1780 riots, naturally approved of the Order in Council which gave rise to the issue of these general orders, and, in a note attached to the legal opinions in his file, mentioned above, proposed that a new Order in Council should issue for the troops to be enabled to act without magistrates in any riots which might occur at any future time.[36] But no steps were taken to carry out this draconian proposal. Necessary as it obviously was in the terrible days of June 1780, the issuing of orders as a permanent arrangement would have been socially and politically objectionable.

2 The Magistrate

It is not part of this study to examine in great detail the part played by the magistrates in suppressing riots, except in so far as it impinges on the part of the military. General remarks on the quality of the magistracy, which is supposed to have improved, especially in London, during the eighteenth century, can be found in standard works.[1] Here it is relevant to consider certain particular factors which contributed to the uncertainty or ineffectiveness of magistrates faced with riots, and to show why, having admitted their failure and sent for troops, they were often reluctant to accompany them and take the responsibility of acting with them.

The fact that a J.P. turned to the War Office at all was a tribute to the dangerous nature of many riots. It is true that some magistrates were merely alarmist. The trading justices in some towns attracted criticism that was justified. But there seems little reason to think of the magistracy as a whole as being more or less firm than the generality of men. There are however two factors upon which we may confidently rely: their jealousy of their local territorial power, and their dislike of the central executive, and of the army in particular. With these attitudes, it was a worried magistrate who asked for military help.

In acting against mobs, whether with or without troops, the magistrate suffered from the same curious lack of guidance already referred to in the case of officers. He had none of the useful guidance nowadays to be found in Stone's *Justices' Manual*. All kinds of didactic books on many subjects were constantly appearing in this century, but no one had taken up the task of instructing the suppressors and peace-keepers, civil and military, in their duty. The many manuals that were available for the J.P. contained little more than bare statemants of the law, and almost nothing about practice. Burn's manual[2] contained a short account of the law of illegal assembly; Nelson[3] and older authorities such as Lambarde[4] were no help at all. The often-quoted Dalton, reprinted many times, was vague:

> Any one Justice of Peace alone may use all good meanes to prevent a Riot or Rout before it be done; and for to stay it whilst it is in doing, and in the doing may take and imprison the Rioters, or binde them to their good behaviour.[5]

For this he might take his servants or the power of the county. But neither Dalton nor any other manual contained any guidance as to what might be meant by the phrase 'all good meanes'. In the eighteenth century servants would mean a small number of constables and peace officers, in many cases accused with justice of encouraging riots themselves. Attempts to raise the *posse comitatus* had occasional success but were more likely to end in embarrassment. The London magistrate Saunders Welch, in offering the following rather defeatist advice, seems more concerned to find good excuses after the attempt to raise the posse has failed:

> . . . as this necessary power of calling in aid is lodged in you, and the execution of it has of late years been treated with contempt by the commonalty; and as your safety is greatly concerned in a ready assistance, you will do well to fix your charge of aid upon some known person; and upon his or their refusal, if the party to be apprehended escape, or you are struck or even resisted, in pursuance of your duty, indict them for the contempt; and I dare promise you, the sessions will support your authority.[6]

With no guidance but his own wit as to how to deal with a mob, the magistrate had other snares set about his feet by the puzzling Riot Act, already referred to. Understandably he felt that his path was a delicate one, and this impression was reinforced by the trial for murder of two magistrates in the middle years of the century.

In June 1757 the forcible suppression of a corn riot in Carmarthen caused the deaths of five colliers. At the trial of John Evans, the magistrate who attended the troops, it appeared from the evidence that before the troops had been ordered to fire he had read the proclamation and several times asked the mob to disperse, that he had offered them grain at a reasonable rate, and that the colliers merely attacked him and the troops with pick axes and other weapons. The jury acquitted him without going out of court.[7]

In 1768 Samuel Gillam, who gave the orders to fire in the much more notorious riot in St George's Fields, was also tried for his life. Again the verdict was not guilty.[8]

Although these two men escaped, the very placing on trial of men who thought they were doing their duty was bound to be discouraging to others. After the case of *R. v. Evans* in 1757 one observer commented bitterly:

> The mayor having thus exerted himself beyond any of the country magistrates, in dispersing these dangerous banditti, it might have been expected, that all persons of property, who had any regard for the constitution, would have thanked him for the service he had done; but instead of that he was prosecuted at the great sessions, and put to a considerable expense to defend himself.[9]

It is possible to find in the records examples of riots where the firmness and courage of a determined magistrate alone dispersed a riot. Some of these are very remarkable. One magistrate wrote during the dark days of 1757:

> I got amongst them as soon as I could, and after some reasoning, and a little strong beer I got them to promise me to disperse, and go home without doing any further mischief. They did not quite keep their words, but went into the town of Whitby – made some people give them a little money for drink, but committed no damage; I was then in hopes we had done with such riotous proceedings.[10]

Sir John Fielding's wise policy of never asking for soldiers if he could help it deserves mention. In 1768 he worked long hours trying to pacify and disperse London crowds determined on mischief and usually drunk. In the same riots an Alderman (probably Beckford) dispersed a crowd, which had already broken many windows, outside the Mansion House by a speech to them, after (significantly) ordering the soldiers at hand to withdraw.[11] John Hewitt, a strong-minded though opinionated justice of Coventry for many years, described a confrontation with the Warwickshire colliers who were rioting about provision prices in 1756:

> I went to the door, which was no sooner opened than my outer room was filled. Without the appearance of surprise, I demanded their business? . . . To convince them I was not afraid of numbers, I admitted as many as my house would contain. That I might recollect myself, I desired their patience whilst I ate my dinner, which they readily admitted, as I had left my dinner at the farm to wait upon them.[12]

Hewitt told them he would always listen to complaints but would punish anyone who broke the law, sent abstracts of the laws against forestalling to the press for printing and distribution the same day, called a meeting of magistrates, and wrote to the Secretary at War for troops, so that 'if I was disappointed in my plan I should, by being prepared against all events, escape the reflection of the town and my brethren'.[13]

Hewitt's account, interesting as being nearest to a practical guide that his colleagues ever received in the period, presents the image magistrates would approve of: resolute, resourceful and cool. The Secretaries of State often wrote appreciatively to such magistrates. Sometimes they treated them with more extravagant marks of favour. Lord Mayor Harley, whose favourite method seems to have been to rush impetuously into a crowd, seize a prominent rioter as an example and bear him off, was publicly thanked by the Speaker of the Commons on 16 May 1768:

> No man . . . can do a more essential service to his country, than a civil magistrate, who, by a prudent, temperate, but at the same time, firm and vigorous exertion of the powers, with which the laws of the land

entrust him, suppresses all riots and tumults, and resolutely resists those lawless and desperate practices, which tend to deprive every individual of the rights and privileges to which he is entitled by our excellent constitution. . . . By your example, every other civil magistrate will be convinced, that he has sufficient power, by the laws, to prevent every disturbance of the public peace.[14]

This was the natural reaction of a harassed government beset by mobs but disliking the use of military force, a policy which was always liable to ascend to the political level and shake a weak administration, as happened in 1768. But no one, least of all magistrates, really put much faith in the moral force argument. Experience showed that although it had some validity, that although there were some magistrates who were exceptional and some riots that were controllable, yet it was more realistic to admit that there were some magistrates who were mediocre, and many riots which were totally beyond the power of any magistrate, however exceptional. His civil supports were often unwilling and unreliable: sometimes they deserted him completely. A J.P. wrote in 1757:

. . . the constables who are the only executive part of the civil power in the country to put a stop to these riotous and unlawful assemblies, were the very persons who appeared at the head of this mob.[15]

Another wrote during the same riot; his account provides a clue in excuse for the constables:

I fear for some time we shall have a total relaxation of justice if something is not immediately done by the government to put a stop to these riotous proceedings, for the gentlemen in these parts cannot do it by the civil power as none of the peace officers will obey us, being intimidated by the threats of the mob to pull down their houses.[16]

The situation was no better in London, where a riot would speedily pass beyond hopes of control by magistrates by reason of sheer numbers. The results of the failure to set up a proper system of police, which had been pressed for by the Fieldings, was seen most forcibly in these metropolitan riots. Sir John Fielding himself had only 80 peace officers for his division, a district with a population of many thousands. The other alternative, so feared by Burke,[17] of encouraging magistrates to call for soldiers at the least alarm, would have been equally objectionable. But in this age, with a government fearful of the results and a magistracy suspicious of the central executive and proud of its local power, this was not likely to happen.

3 The Army

The unpopularity of the British Army at this date is well known. In Europe the writers of the Enlightenment generally regarded armies as a pest; some described them as a state within a state. In Britain the very existence of a standing army was, or was affected to be, regarded with great suspicion by many members of parliament, who kept a close watch for any possible attempt on the part of the government to improve its control over what they regarded as the most offensive sector of the executive. There were fears, more justified, that the army would be put to corrupt use through government patronage. Others were concerned about the cost of keeping up the army, or accused it of Cromwellian ambitions. These arguments united Lockeian Whigs with hard Tories such as William Shippen, who claimed to have attacked the army in parliament on 21 occasions between 1717 and 1739.[1] On many occasions during periods of rioting opinions, whether of honest foundation or not it is difficult to say, were expressed to the effect that there was never any real need to call for troops, and that there was a reservoir of natural force in the state which, if properly appealed to, would be sufficient to quell any disturbance. This opinion is found in newspapers and journals, pamphlets, parliamentary debates, and in letters from ministers.[2] The remark of Alderman Beckford during a debate arising out of the Wilkes riots in 1768 is typical: 'I was always of opinion, that mobs might be quelled without the aid of the military'.[3] Even the dangers of an invasion were brushed aside, as if defence forces were to appear from the ground. Former Secretaries at War such as Yonge and Pulteney were so irresponsible as to play on the fear of military government:

> I hope Sir that we have men enough in Great Britain who have resolution enough to defend themselves against any invasion whatever though there were not so much as one redcoat in the whole kingdom.[4]

At times the arguments touched strange depths of unreality. In the debate on the proposal for an establishment for 1738 of 17,704 men, Sir George Barclay said:

> I have heard it said, Sir, that if we do not keep up a standing-army, everything must run into confusion. Sir, I am one of those who think that a standing-army is worse than the worst confusion.[5]

In the same debate Sir William Yonge, who as Secretary at War had to take a practical view, insisted that the civil government of the country could not go on without an army, and hinted that unchecked riots could easily become rebellions. The government in fact had to keep order and saw no alternative to the use of troops. This itself raised a number of further problems, for the army was not only unpopular in Parliament. Raised, trained and billeted as it was, it could never be regarded as anything but a scourge to society by the public, and its arrival on the scene would frequently provoke a riot or aggravate an existing one. This naturally induced in the War Office a reluctance to send soldiers until the last moment, which robbed an intervention of much of its effectiveness.

The annual as-of-grace passage of the Mutiny Act[6] ensured that the army existed on sufferance, and it was hedged about by custom and statute with many other legal and constitutional demarcations as if to emphasise the country's dislike for, and lack of trust in it. Just as contemporary warfare was canalised and conducted with an apparent consensus of moderation, so that violations of accepted usage would be deplored by all nations, so armies, and particularly the British army, were by common consent disapproved of and placed in a narrow allotted sphere. It was not an efficient, a national, or a particularly happy force; the attitudes of society ensured this. On the other hand there is no doubt that the army often behaved extremely badly in its off-duty dealings with the public: the frequent mention of soldiers in the criminal records is only one proof of this. Equally it is clear that soldier-baiting was a common form of sport. The Secretary at War in 1717 asked a regimental commander to ensure that the officers to be sent on riot duty be careful not to enter into any disputes with the populace, who 'will I fear be too forward to provoke them to some rash and perhaps unwarrantable actions, unless prepared against them'.[7] Years later Lord Barrington warned a commander who was quarrelling with the magistrates of Plymouth that 'from the nature of our constitution the civil power will always in disputes (unless on very extraordinary occasions) have the advantage of the military.'[8] The same distrust of the army was an accompanying feature of the deterioration of the British position in North America. Lord Shelburne felt obliged to remind General Gage 'how desirable it is that every officer should remove as much as possible those prejudices which are apt to prevail amongst the civil part of His Majesty's subjects with regard to the military by promoting a temperate and amicable intercourse'.[9] But in spite of frequent appeals from the War Office to officers to see that the men live peaceably with the inhabitants and give no offence, the complaints about the riotous conduct and serious crimes of the soldiers continued throughout the eighteenth century. Some were frivolous, but many were justified and must have constituted a grave drawback in a force charged with a peace-keeping function. Soldiers and sailors together made a great affray in Plymouth in 1757;[10] soldiers caused a riot in Sudbury in 1761;[11] men of the Coldstream Guards caused a riot in a dissenting meeting house in Swallow Street in London.[12] The examples could be multiplied. Many instances of disorder among troops in quarters could be traced to the long absences of officers from regimental duty. Sometimes their presence produced the same effect: a riot in Bridgwater was started by soldiers, apparently abetted by their officers.[13]

However, with all its drawbacks and the fact that they regarded it as an object of contempt, many people seem to have preferred this small mercenary force to possible alternatives. Adam Smith thought it the cheapest and most effective way of carrying on an activity which was regrettably necessary. At least it provided a sort of outdoor relief for the younger sons of the aristocracy and gentry, besides giving employment as private soldiers to what was regarded as a troublesome sector of humanity. But only those rendered desperate by failures in civilian life enlisted in such a force. Fortescue wrote: 'There was no idea in those days of making a hero of the soldier, not even for a day. When he had served his purpose he was cast aside and went back to his old status of a plague of the nation.'[14]

The composition and equipment of the army has been discussed at length in histories of eighteenth-century warfare, and need no extensive treatment here. Under Walpole the army was small, seldom more than 18,000 in peace,[15] at a time when the French peacetime establishment was 133,000,[16] but increasing during the Austrian Succession War to 74,000.[17] After the 1748 reduction the army at home totalled under 19,000 men.[18] It increased gradually during the Seven Years War, reaching a total of over 67,000,[19] with 27,000 militia.[20] It was felt that Dutch, Hanoverian or Hessian paid levies could always be employed to supply the want of British forces, but the use of these against British mobs could not of course be considered, a fact clearly stated in 1757 by the Secretary at War to a magistrate who advocated it:

> . . . Your present proposal of calling in the Hessian forces to suppress any disturbances is still more embarrassing. I am very glad their behaviour among you has entitled them to such confidence, and I hope they would not abuse it; but, however, I would not even have it supposed by them that they can be authorized by any contingency to draw their swords in this country except against that foreign enemy they were brought hither to oppose.[21]

A similar tactless proposal was made by Prince Frederick (a future Commander-in-Chief) to arm a corps of Germans and Swiss resident in London, 'and to lead them myself against the seditious'.[22] It was refused.

By the end of 1763 the army had been reduced by the disbanding of all regiments junior to the 70th Foot, and all cavalry junior to the 18th Light Dragoons, to about 45,000 men. Many of these served abroad, and only 17,000 were stationed at home. In his speech in Parliament that year the King said:

... and although the army, maintained in these kingdoms, will be inferior in number to that usually kept up in former times of peace, yet I trust that the force proposed, with the establishment of the national militia, (whose services I have experienced, and cannot too much commend) will prove a sufficient security for the future.[23]

The mention of militia had no bearing on the question of civil disorder, which could not be any concern of theirs in peacetime, at least until they were embodied.

Great increases took place during the American war; twenty-five new regiments (one with two battalions) were formed between 1777 and 1780, but this increase was in respect of foreign campaigns and could have little influence upon riot control in Britain. At least the militia were embodied during the war and performed useful service against mobs, particularly in 1779 and 1780.

War Office documents in 1768 provide interesting information not only of the numbers and distribution of the army in Britain in that year, but also of the use to which it was put. In the middle of the Wilkes cycle of riots in London the Secretary at War was asked for troops by the magistrates of Newcastle.[24] The keelmen of Newcastle rioted constantly in this period and successive Secretaries at War were familiar with requests for help from the authorities there. Lord Barrington provided short-term help[25] and revolved in his mind the idea of a permanent garrison.[26] He asked the Quarter-Master General of the army, Lt.-Col. Morrison, to inquire how far it might be practicable consistently with other services to station an entire regiment in the town.[27] The report of the Quarter-Master General showed that such a regiment would have to be taken away from duties in Scotland or South Britain, whichever the Secretary of State wished, and spoke of the shortage of troops:

> Upon the disposition of the thirteen regiments of foot (exclusive of the invalids) stationed in England and Scotland after the late war: Four regiments were stationed in Scotland, one in the North of England and the remaining eight in the South, as the duties on the coast, and in the barracks required; one of which has annually been sent upon the foreign relief, and the regiment returning not in a condition of taking the above, or other duties, for some time after their return.
>
> The following year upon representation from the Commander in Chief in Scotland, there was one regiment added to that station; which leaves for the South of England seven regiments, and for great part of the summer (during the time of the relief) only six regiments.
>
> There has most frequently been so many applications for detachments from those regiments for the assisting of His Majesty's officers of the Customs in different parts of the coast and for the quelling of riots in several manufacturing towns etc, that it has hitherto been found, that

number has scarcely been sufficient to answer these purposes, and at the same time to give alternately some regiments the necessary opportunities of being assembled for the preservation of their discipline.[28]

The Adjutant-General wrote to one of the officers in Scotland that the cavalry would have to stay at Newcastle indefinitely until a plan could be made to release an infantry regiment; 'I am sorry for it, but we must submit to these inconveniencies, till Government establishes a few more regiments in Britain; they are really much wanted.'[29]

This admission of insufficiency of numbers is common at the time. Considerable peacetime commitments meant that the 1763 reduction caused great difficulties. Minorca, which before the war had four regiments, now had seven, to avoid a repetition of the surprise of 1756; and because of similar fears Gibraltar's garrison was increased from three to five regiments. There were also the new conquests in many parts of the world to garrison. In 1774 the Secretary at War was again complaining of insufficient numbers, with four battalions in America that ought to have been on the British establishment. He expected riots in manufacturing districts because of the high price of bread and the interruption of the American trade.[30]

A large part of this army consisted of cavalry, which was useful in dealing with internal disorder, especially if such disorder was sporadic and spread over a wide area. Cavalry was armed with sabres, pistols with 14-inch barrels and short carbines with 27-inch barrels. New light horse regiments were raised in 1759, the first being Elliott's Light Dragoons (later 15th Hussars). It was felt that the light dragoons were needed for reconaissance and similar work, where the 'handy nag' and absence of heavy accoutrements would be of advantage, although they showed at Minden that they could do more than reconnoitre. They also proved serviceable in dealing with travelling rioters and smugglers in cases where a speedy interception march was called for. But both light and heavy cavalry found itself at a disadvantage in facing a determined and numerous street mob in a city, and became a liability.[31] The slower infantry regiments could often not come up with the mob at all in the case of a rural food riot, but became useful in fighting with dense and dangerous mobs in streets.[32] They were armed with the so-called Brown Bess (a term in fact not used until 1785), a smooth-bore flintlock musket hurling a spherical projectile with a velocity and trajectory of poor efficiency when compared with modern weapons; over a distance of 120 yards the bullet dropped considerably, sometimes up to five feet. Firing at a man-sized target at ranges of more than 80–100 yards was a chancy business. In the circumstances it is not surprising that the gunsmiths did not bother to include sights. A recent writer has gone to much trouble to gauge the efficiency of weapons in the past, and concludes, after stating all the pitfalls involved in such research, that highly trained professional armies of the eighteenth century could hit with some 10 per cent to 20 per cent of the shots ordered to be fired, that is to say, at ranges considered to be effective.[33] Such ranges cannot have been very great, but long-range shooting was not called for when the battlefield was a street. Accuracy in conditions of warfare was thought less important than speed, and rates of discharge improved during the century. The Prussian army claimed to have trained its troops to discharge five rounds a minute, at least in parade practice, but most other armies managed two or three. Wolfe wrote: 'There is no necessity for firing very fast; a cool well levelled fire, with the pieces carefully loaded, is much more destructive and formidable than the quickest fire in confusion.'[34] The destructive effect of such a volley at close ranges is well known and had terrible results in some riots. That it did not do so in many cases was due to the officers ordering the men to load with powder only, or with swan shot (as did Porteous in 1736[35]), or to the soldiers deliberately firing high, which seems to have been fairly frequent.

The marching qualities of these troops were no better or worse than most other infantry forces since the ancient world; some units managed over 20 miles a day on riot duty in England on fair roads in reasonable weather.[36] At times invalids were asked to perform surprisingly arduous marches.[37] The intervention of cavalry from a distance was much more striking in many riots. The rapid march of the Inniskilling dragoons from Northampton to Coventry in 1756 immediately quieted the town.[38] The arrival of two troops of the 15th Dragoons in Birmingham in 1791 was thought to have saved it from destruction. The dragoons received the order at 7 in the morning and marched from Nottingham at 10.30, having hastily collected some of their horses from grass. They travelled the first 40 miles without a halt and arrived after a journey of 53 miles at 7 p.m. on the same day, in time to stop the rioters from destroying the house of Withering, the botanist. The taking up of horses from grass and subjecting them to such a strain was always a risk; the horses were the worse for it the next day and one died.[39]

The fitness of the military force for the task of riot control must now be considered.

It had only a very rudimentary system of inquiry, when its resources are compared with those of a regular permanent police force stationed in an area. In some cases a unit might know the district, but often they marched into one which was strange to them and were entirely reliant on information and guidance from the local civil officers.

There were more serious defects than this, however: the very constitution and mentality of such a force unsuited it for the task. Put simply, the army was not ideal for it, and further, it had no wish to be. The usual performance of the eighteenth-century soldier in action was probably not appropriate for many of the incidents of riot duty. Unfortunately, we are not well informed as to what that usual performance really was. One

modern view would make the soldier into little more than a marionette
with nothing to do but follow orders. The holders of this view point out that
in the training of the time initiative and self-reliance were not called for. It
was thought important to make him into a highly trained automaton
capable above all things of the classical manoeuvre of marching in line
abreast with his fellows with grave unhurried precision towards an enemy.
At the high point of his training, during a great war, the soldier, colourful
but stiff and uncomfortable in his restricting equipment, was well able to
take his part in the elaborate and terrible choreography of the set-piece
battle, provided the other side performed the same evolutions. His very
lack of flexibility accorded well with the slow geometrical manoeuvre
under orders. But these qualities would make him an indifferent operator
in the context of civil disorder. Here the enemy did not obey the rules; he
had more in common with the irregular troops in North America or with
modern urban guerrillas.

The above case needs to be made, but some modern writers have
overstated it; it is in fact only one of a number of over-simplifications that
have arisen in the discussion of eighteenth-century armies and warfare.
Perhaps in their generalisations about eighteenth-century war (and in
particular their strictures on the narrow mould in which tactics were cast)
writers have had in mind the Prussian soldiers – 'des automates roidis' in
the famous phrase of Berenhorst. The system of Prussia was the highest
expression of the military system of the *ancien régime*, seen at its most
successful and in some ways at its most grotesque. Other nations sought to
imitate it, but for various reasons they did not succeed and the system
cannot safely be regarded as typical. In some countries it was not always
thought desirable. Marshal Saxe spoke of the necessity of creating what he
called an 'imbécillité de coeur', but did not believe in making robots of the
men. Tactics in other armies did not reach the Prussian level. Many British
officers were bitter about the way their men threw away their fire
prematurely at Dettingen.[40]

In peacetime a study of the smuggling service and the riot duty also
shows that the crudely mechanistic picture of the operations of the soldier is
exaggerated; he was sometimes capable of acting in very small detachments without officers and even on his own. In smuggling operations on the
coast a mere handful of men were at times disposed in a fifty-mile cordon
watching for smugglers. In 1763 a solitary sergeant tried to persuade a mob
to disperse by fair words (although without effect).[41] The resolution of a
single private soldier saved a building in London in 1768.[42]

The lack of physical flexibility of the soldier may have led historians to
imagine a lack of mental agility as well. But it must surely be unlikely that
the natural independence of mind, as great in a pre-machine age as today,
of the men would vanish on recruitment. In proposing such a model that is
what the protagonists of this point are asking us to believe. In any case not
all infantry was uniformly heavily equipped. Light infantry began to make

its appearance in the middle of the century, at first in the form of light companies to existing regiments. The Highland soldier in his light pumps or brogues was a more agile performer than the infantryman of the line.[43]

It is true that the practice of the fire-fight with the flintlock in a battle involving large numbers had to give rise to a complex linear deployment, which, carried out perhaps under cannon fire, needed much care and practice to habituate the men to it, and that this deployment, with its premium on reflex reactions, shifted the thinking from the men to the officers. This does not mean that the men, even if unlettered, were incapable of original thought: it was merely not required in this particular situation. But there were other situations. It is perhaps useful to remind ourselves that not all campaigns were battles, that the soldier's life was not all war, and that even in peacetime his day was not all drill.

In fact in equipment, tactics and personnel the army was not as incapable of dealing with mobs as at first appears. More deleterious to its effectiveness in riot duty was the attitude of that personnel towards this duty. The army resented the view that it should be used in peacetime for unmilitary tasks, such as the smuggling duty or the road building corvée in Scotland, for the performance of which there existed no other body of men. Their chief distaste was reserved for the riot duty. For differing reasons neither men nor officers relished it. The men quite simply came from the same social group as the mob and often sympathized with it. The guardsman in 1780 who approved of the mob but observed that it ought to pull down rather than burn houses of Catholics lest the fire spread to Protestant property, was not untypical.[44] The attitude continued into the next century. One of the soldiers involved in operations against the Luddites refused to fire 'because I might hit some of my brothers'.[45] Lord Barrington's famous letter to the officers of the Guards in London in 1768 expressing the King's approbation of their action against the mob of 9 May was a bid for the loyalty of the men, who according to his biographer had been the object of attempted subversion by rioters; it was read out at the head of all battalions of the Guards.[46] The letter appeared in the *Gentleman's Magazine*[47] and was taken up by a writer in the *Public Advertiser*, possibly Junius, who made play with the implications of the last paragraph promising help to soldiers responsible for killing or maiming rioters: 'And in case any disagreeable circumstance should happen in the execution of their duty, they shall have every defence and protection that the law can authorise and this office can give.'[48]

The correspondent wrote scornfully:

For the mere benefit of the law the prisoners will hardly thank him. It is a benefit they are entitled to and will certainly have whether he and his office interfere or not. If he means anything more, let him look to his words.[49]

Barrington probably did not mean any more than to reward the loyalty of, and to give moral support to, a soldiery which at that juncture felt itself to be more than usually detested by the public.

The officers as a group varied greatly. Some were casual and insouciant, regarding a few years' service with one of the more prestigious regiments as part of the social round. A few studied their profession seriously. Both categories united in their detestation of the riot duty. They had never been given any guidance as to how they were to act in controlling mobs, and in particular how far they could use force without becoming liable in law to victims, although the War Office always issued cautions about the use of what they vaguely termed excessive force and the need to be conformable with the directions of the civil magistrates:

> Give me leave to add the caution I have always thought necessary on such occasions, that the strictest orders be given to the officer whom you shall think proper to send on this command, to take great care that the forces under his command, do not at all interpose in any of these things but at such times as they shall be required by the civil magistrates, or officers, who best will judge when they stand in need of military assistance.[50]

In the same year the Secretary at War wrote to a magistrate, after reluctantly ordering a detachment to his help: 'Frequent use of soldiers to suppress civil commotions, has an evident tendency to introduce military government, than which there can not be a more horrible Evil in a State.'[51]

Several times in the early part of the century the War Office took the opinion of the Attorney-General. The tenor of these opinions was that there was nothing illegal in the use of soldiers against mobs, in spite of the opinion of many contemporaries, that suppression of disorder was one of the incidents of citizenship, and that the status of citizen was not lost by the man who put on a red coat.[52] This useful advice remained buried in War Office files and no one communicated it to officers. The only result of these opinions was that orders to act against mobs were always drafted to end with the cautionary words 'but not to repel force with force unless in case of absolute necessity or being thereunto required by the civil magistrate'. This order by its wording did not entirely exclude the discretion of the officer present, but he was supposed to bow to the discernment of the magistrate as to what amounted to 'absolute necessity'. In any case it would have been a rash officer who disagreed with a magistrate. Unfortunately the magistrate had little or no idea what his powers were, and no one told him either.[53]

This complete lack of guidance to officers on riot duty is the more surprising when it is remembered how much of their peacetime life was occupied with it. In fact there did exist many manuals of conduct and discipline for the use of officers, usually more or less following the precedent of Bland in their layout.[54] As guides to the eighteenth-century army's view of what its role as an army was they are disappointing, being little more than drill books. Nowhere do they disclose any interest in possible manoeuvres or regulations for riot duty. Their preoccupation is with the movement and alignment of columns in echelon and squadrons on march, and all the complex drill evolutions which help to make eighteenth-century war resemble a branch of plane geometry. It is probable that the average officer was loath to give his mind to such a question. It was not in his opinion part of his job to chase rioters. There was no profit or glory in it, but rather a good chance of being insulted in the press, attacked in Parliament or pursued in a court of law for his actions. In short, it was novel and burdensome and no part of the military task.

General Bland was a high-ranking officer but he could hardly have taken the step of setting forth his ideas on the subject of guidance for officers without a clear statement from above. The Secretary at War also could not risk making such a statement on what was felt to be a high point of constitutional law without some directive from the Secretaries of State, although if encouraged by them he could easily have prepared a summary of the opinions, already referred to, of the Law Officers of the Crown. For their part the Secretaries of State could have caused to be made a digest of the judgments of the Court, in which the principle that violence could be used against crowds had been repeated many times and the argument of unconstitutionality rejected. In 1768 Lord Barrington urged the administration to publish the account of the trial of the magistrate who had ordered the soldiers to fire on the mob in St George's Fields.[55] The summing-up of the judges contained a lucid and unexceptionable statement of the law of the time, and would have given the officers (and magistrates) some useful guidance, but nothing was done.

This lack of guidance bred in the minds of officers a want of confidence which was often inimical to the effective handling of riots. In the sort of probing confrontations set up by mobs in the early stages of a riot the uneasiness and irresolution of an officer uncertain of his powers was soon realised. There would quickly grow up a contempt for both officer and magistrate, and the mob would proceed to excessive acts of violence, needing eventually far more force to quell it than would have been required at an earlier stage. It is true that a proper caution contained in orders can have a humane effect, if it arises from information; this caution was the result of confusion, and the result was often more bloodshed. The case of the Gordon Riots is the best known but is only one of many.

It is to the discredit of government that they never gave guidance, seeming rather to prefer to leave the matter ambiguous. No Act of Parliament made it any clearer, although there was a clear precedent for such an Act in the several statutes of limited scope defining special tasks of the army in the time of Charles II.[56] Guides for officers which faced the issue only began to appear in Victorian times. In modern times the very full statements on the subject contained in the *Manual of Military Law*[57] and *Queen's Regulations*[58] give the officer today exactly the sort of guidance which his counterpart two hundred years ago needed so sorely. Perhaps the failure of the Secretary at War in the eighteenth century to press for a simple manual of conduct for officers arose from his unwillingness to admit that riot control was regularly part of the army's commitment.[59]

Even when a particular emergency had arisen Secretaries of State and Secretaries at War refrained from giving any but the most general instructions. There was no briefing of officers: they were expected to know how to act in any situation. As a result there developed an excessive reliance on the ability and good sense of the man on the spot, who was frequently urged to act with 'firmness and Zeal', but 'with Discretion'. When the sheriffs applied for a Tyburn guard in 1728 the Secretary at War gave orders for three sergeants and a party of 60 private men to attend, adding 'and I make no doubt but you will take care that the Sergeant in chief with this detachment be such a one as will act discreetly upon this occasion'.[60] Lord Barrington wrote to the commander of a cavalry detachment on riot duty: 'I am to signify to you His Majesty's Pleasure that you send a careful and intelligent officer, for whom you will be answerable, to command this party.'[61]

The absence of guidance meant that the officer really could not be sure what he was allowed to do. On the one hand he lacked official information about his role, on the other he could read in newspapers and journals the frequent though highly inaccurate opinions about his lack of standing in riots or any other civil context, opinions which he was half convinced were true. In 1766 Edward Harvey, the Adjutant-General, wrote sympathetically to an officer on riot duty in the West Country:

> These commands are most exceeding disagreeable, as no line has ever been drawn to Act by, by proper authority. It's lucky for the country and military when it's entrusted to prudent and proper hands.[62]

Some officers wrote to seek guidance. In 1757 Lord Barrington wrote to James Wolfe on riot duty in Gloucestershire:

> Though I very much approve of your communicating your doubts in what circumstances it may be lawful, for the soldiery to use their arms for repelling riots, I am not able nor indeed is it possible to resolve them, so well as I could wish to do. The orders in these cases are not to repel force with force unless it shall be found absolutely necessary, or being thereunto required by the civil magistrates. While the magistrates do their duty, it is certainly the business of the troops to be assisting to them, and to act by their directions; but if the troops (as there is too much reason to apprehend from your letter) should be left alone, the

commanding officer must then be the judge of that necessity in which only he is permitted to use force, and in such case, both his prudence and humanity should make him very cautious of proceeding to extremity with an ignorant and miserable multitude, whose grievances are sometimes real and to be pitied, though their misguided attempts to redress them are to be checked and repressed.[63]

Wolfe's orders to his detachments after this were cautious:

Delaune marched into the Forest of Dean this morning, but under such restrictions that his weapons will be useless; for I have forbid them to fire (without express orders from the magistrate) even though the enemy (who have fire arms) should begin; they are to receive the insults of the rabble with a soldier-like contempt.[64]

In the same year the Duke of Marlborough also wrote asking for advice. The War Office merely sent the form of the order

which is always given from this office to the troops upon such services. That part of it which describes the cases in which force may be used, was originally drawn up by the advice of the best lawyers, and is therefore proper to be inserted in all orders which Your Grace may think fit to give upon like occasions.[65]

The problem appeared in its most acute form outside Britain, when the situation in America was changing from riotous to revolutionary. It is clear that the War Office again blamed the government for not giving the guidance so badly needed. In 1774 the Secretary at War wrote to the Secretary for the Colonies, Lord Dartmouth, imploring the administration to give proper directions to the military to fire without waiting for magistrates who were clearly not going to come.[66] Once again the Law Officers of the Crown were asked to advise on the legality of the use of armed force without magistrates, with the difference that the troops in question were stationed in Massachusetts, Connecticut, Rhode Island and New Hampshire.[67] The War Office view was clear: no officer would take a command without asking for directions how to proceed, and General Gage could not be expected to give directions without guidance from London.[68] It was in a cruder and more clear form exactly the same problem as in Britain.

In the absence of a practical guide it is not surprising that one of the few hard facts which impressed itself in the minds of officers was the case of Captain Porteous, the man who appeared to have overreached himself. The Colonel of a regiment on riot duty in Bristol a few years after the Porteous riot wrote:

. . . the Mayor was pleased to desire me to come to consult with the magistrates how best to frustrate any attempts upon the peace of the city. I believe I made them sensible that I could not repel force by force without an order from the Regency, and, after that, having a written order from a proper magistrate. Captain Porteous's unhappy fate was too fresh in my memory not to make me act with the utmost caution and security.[69]

The Porteous case was only the most notorious of several incidents in which soldiers or officers obeying orders were pursued at law. The riots at Leith and Cork in 1717 both gave rise to prosecutions which were stayed by writs of *nolle prosequi* from the Attorney General.[70] A captain of a detachment who fired on a mob during the Glasgow malt tax riot of 1725 was actually tried and found guilty but was pardoned by the Lords Justices.[71] In 1728 a party of soldiers fired on a mob of smugglers who were trying to recover uncustomed goods confiscated by the soldiers. One of the soldiers and a corporal were prosecuted. The Commissioners of Customs wrote:

We think it somewhat extraordinary that the Crown should be put to an expense in carrying on such a prosecution, and the Revenue in defending of it . . .

If soldiers when attacked by a mob and most barbarously beat and abused must upon firing in their own defence be imprisoned and run the risk of being hanged, (and 'tis too well known that the Juries here will very readily contribute all in their power towards it,) it is not to be expected our officers can have any further assistance from them.[72]

Some years later another officer wrote after a riot at Henley:

What would be any of our fates had we the misfortune of killing any of these people even in our own defence? They will not quarter enough of us in one town, for were we more together we might with sticks and other weapons turn out against a mob, and get the better of them, whereas our small numbers with firearms, which they know we dare not use, only makes us appear more despicable, and more liable to have our brains beat out.[73]

The last straw as far as the army was concerned was the witch-hunt after the suppression of the riot outside the King's Bench Prison on 10 May 1768.[74] There were a number of casualities, several of them fatal, an officer and several soldiers were put on trial and narrowly escaped, a full inquiry was pressed for (although unsuccessfully) by Burke, and the newspapers poured vitriol on the military. The effect was to fix in the mind of the officer of the time what he had always suspected, namely that his hands were tied and that he must certainly never take action against a mob unless a magistrate was at his elbow. In fact in 1768 the trial of the soldiers arose out of an incident in which a young man was chased away and eventually shot dead at some distance from the scene of the riot. The firing on the crowd which took place several hours later gave rise to no legal process against soldiers because a magistrate was present and gave the order; instead, the magistrate himself was indicted, but also escaped conviction.[75]

The disagreeable situation of an officer on riot duty unaccompanied by a magistrate was well illustrated by an incident a fortnight later, which provides an interesting tailpiece to the 1768 riots. A guard of 100 men remained at the prison, but by 23 May the Surrey magistrates, believing the affair over, had relaxed their attendance, as appears from an anxious note from the officer commanding at the prison, Colonel Rainsford. He complained that in spite of 'repeated applications', he could persuade no magistrate to be in attendance.

> Your Lordship knows how very ineffectual our force must be without a Justice of the Peace to direct us, and this being a holyday we have a reason to expect a great assembly of the people in the evening. Those gentlemen are in general very unwilling to attend and showed a great dislike to it when they were applied to this morning at their meeting on St. Margaret's Hill. It is now past three o'clock, and none of them have appeared. I could do no less than represent this to your Lordship, who knows the difficulties the military are subject to in cases of riot, when not supported by the civil authority.

> . . . the place of meeting at St. Margaret's Hill is a mile at least from this place and much mischief might be done before a Justice of Peace could arrive if the mob would give him leave.[76]

The foregoing is a very clear statement of the attitude of mind of the average officer placed in this position; it would be wrong to regard Rainsford as unduly jumpy about his position. The situation was serious enough when a magistrate was present – when he was not the position became impossible.

Barrington felt strongly about this incident. He was anxious that in case of inquiry his own conduct should appear correct, and the documents show his care. The War Office in-letter book[77] has at this point (*a*) Rainsford's letter of the 23rd (an original); (*b*) Barrington's letter of the 23rd to Weymouth, asking rather testily if it would not be better to remove the guard altogether if the civil arm could not be persuaded to do its part (a copy letter which in a book of this sort, composed entirely of originals, is quite out of place, showing that special instructions must have been given for its copying and inclusion;) (*c*) Robert Wood's[78] letter of the 23rd assuring Barrington that Weymouth had ordered the J.P.s to remain in attendance at the prison. Barrington then caused to be added an attendance note (which is also unusual) that Rainsford on coming off duty on 24 May had gone straight to the War Office to complain that in spite of his requests no magistrate appeared on the previous day until 10 p.m., when Ponton and another came

> and said they were ready to head the military by day or night as occasion required, but that the other Justices at St. Margaret's Hill shewed a backwardness and unwillingness (as they said) to meet danger.[79]

These incidents go a long way towards explaining the disaster of 1780. On this occasion most magistrates absented themselves from the scene, and it was not uncommon for a file of soldiers to arrive, watch the destruction by fire of houses, and march away again without interfering. Some historians[80] have called this a paralysis of will, but it was really an understandable determination to work to rule.

The army was therefore not an ideally-fashioned instrument for the task of mob control. But it must be admitted that given conditions which were not unreasonable the eighteenth-century crowd could in most cases be controlled by the eighteenth-century army. It is true that vacillating politicians held up its operations, that it often only arrived after a great deal of damage had been done and perhaps the original aims of the rioters had been attained (although at such times it could prevent them from developing and carrying out new ones), and that on occasion it could not avoid a direct clash involving bloodshed. These clashes – Porteous, Wilkes, the Gordon Riots – bulk large in textbooks, but in statistical terms are only part of a wide picture which on close examination shows the army to have been used to an enormous extent, without for the most part any violence. The appearance of soldiers in the riot area and their success in allaying riots which had lasted for days is discussed elsewhere[81]

THE EFFECT ON THE ARMY

This is an interesting but elusive subject. Speculation is easy, but not quantification. There is some information about how the peace-keeping role modified the routine of the army and interfered with its efficiency in military terms, but it does not go to the root of the matter. The War Office documents indicate that in some cases autumn reviews were affected by absence of troops on riot duty.[82] In 1768 they were inconvenienced,[83] and in 1766[84] they could not be held at all. The need to take up horses from grass, to be ready to march to riot areas, has been mentioned.

The nuisance factor is often referred to in correspondence:

It is not without concern that I find myself obliged to comply with such pressing requests from the civil magistrates at this season of the year, when it is least convenient for H. M. Forces to change their Quarters.[85]

A colonel in 1757 complained that his men were only issued with six rounds of ball cartridge each, which might now have to be used in riot duty, thus prejudicing their performance at a forthcoming review.[86]

But these are details: it is the much greater but unseen effect upon the army which it is difficult to estimate. The riot duty must take its place with the smuggling duty[87] and a host of other non-military factors, including billeting and constant movements of troops in and out of quarters as a result of fairs and circuses or the visit of assize judges, which together combined to make a coherent programme of training impossible,[88] and contributed to the poor performance of the army at the commencement of eighteenth-century wars. Also although it is clear that the demands of security against internal disorder kept in Britain forces in wartime which might have been employed abroad[89] no evidence exists as to how large the forces were. In England at any one time during a war there would be forces about to be sent abroad or being regrouped, or still being raised and trained, besides units kept at home in case of a French invasion. Any of these forces might find itself involved in keeping the peace, and it is possible that no specific assignment of them to one task or another was ever thought of. Only the Guards in London were clearly marked for riot duty.[90] Papers on the defence of Britain in case of invasion appear with increasing frequency in the latter part of the eighteenth century, the work of enterprising and professional officers. A common assumption in these papers is that if the French arrive the working-class will rise, and that such risings would stem as much from disaffection as from desperation deriving from the incidents of armed invasion. A force disposed to protect the capital from an enemy marching through Kent would have also to consider the London crowd in its rear. Special care would have to be taken to watch for the first sign of disloyalty:

The detachments [i.e. of cavalry] will be of infinite use likewise to maintain order and tranquillity in the interior of the kingdom, which for various motives many will endeavour to put in confusion.[91]

4 The Mob

There exist two main schools of thought about crowds and protest in modern history. Perhaps it would be more true to say that one of them is in almost total retreat before a newer and more carefully researched view. The old view held by historians of the past, such as Lecky, back through history to link up with the complaints of eighteenth-century observers, was that of the crowd as 'mere mob'. The emergence of any grievance or excuse would be sufficient to bring out the rogues and criminal elements who were always ready to pillage. Perhaps (although even this was doubted) the process began with a genuine grievance, but the primary purpose was soon submerged and the crowd became a mere cruel horde, whose goals and pretensions need not be taken seriously. In many cases the primary purpose itself, such as machine-breaking, was retrograde and pointless.

The more recent view has been propounded with such effect by Rudé, Hobsbawm, E. P. Thompson and others that there can hardly be said to be a debate any more. Drawing extensively on contemporary sources, such as the records of the courts in which rioters were tried, Professor Rudé has examined in detail the 'faces in the crowd'. In so doing he has produced evidence to show that the men who made up the mob were respectable wage-earners or 'sober workmen', and has dismissed the stereotype of what may be called the Hogarthian mob, composed of mere riff-raff. Edward Thompson has written of the 'legitimizing notion' of the crowd, the attempt by force, since all else would fail, to impose a standard, usually in relation to settling corn prices or destroying turnpikes or enclosures, of what was felt to be morally just and right. He comments on the surprising restraint of the leaders in not going outside the avowed objects of the campaign and in preventing their followers from pilfering under cover of riot, and on occasion in rendering the correct money, according to the mob-regulated 'just price', back to bewildered farmers and corn factors. Professor Hobsbawm sees some crowd behaviour, such as machine-breaking, as only a form of collective bargaining in an age before the working class was able to organise the strike of the modern type. More recent theories of riot as, for example, a species of patrician-plebeian ritual, show that we may expect more sophistications and developments of the subject. Certainly we are a long way from the idea of mob as a vain and crazy rabble whose aim is destruction and anarchy, even though there must still have been some riots with frivolous origins and merely destructive purposes.

When we come to consider the question of suppression, however, a good deal of the subtleties of the modern theories become unnecessary. The distinction has to be made between the *motives* of the crowd, which have been of such interest to the modern school of historians, and which now seem to have a much greater content of social protest than used to be realised, and its *behaviour*, which is a matter of the first importance to the suppressors. The government did at times consider the question of motives, but its conclusions were much less sympathetic than those of the modern historian, and inevitably coloured by what it could observe of the crowd's behaviour, which often seemed mere gangsterism and arson. A mob that conducted itself in such a fashion, contemporaries thought, could not have any serious object other than rapine in the short term or the overthrow of the social order in the long term. In short, the government usually considered that its main function was to keep order, not to alleviate the causes of disorder. If we are to understand how eighteenth-century administrators faced this task we have to accept their own crude and practical criteria. Even so, some knowledge of why riots occurred was valuable, as it bore directly on the question of when and where they might occur. An administrator who knew of the approach of widespread industrial unemployment would also be ready for trouble in manufacturing districts. A poor harvest would result in many more riots in the north and west of the country than in the south and east where the main wheat-growing areas were.[1] Such simple strategical matters were for the government and the War Office. It was also useful to know how crowds once collected might behave, and this was a tactical point of concern to the officers on the spot.

Eighteenth-century administrators lived in a riotous age and were well versed in most of the common causes of riot, although the suddenness and intensity of some outbreaks could take them by surprise. We can see now that their worst fears of revolution were exaggerated; even such great risings as the corn riots of 1756, 1757 and 1766, although on a widespread scale, kept largely to their particular programmes and showed little disposition to exceed them in searching for some general political objective. Even in London, where riot-behaviour was more protean and a Wilkes might rally the crowd for a time, a revolution of the French type was no more likely to happen than a rebellion of another Monmouth. This is clear to us with hindsight, but the public men of the time were much agitated by fears of an attempt to develop and extend simple riot into something more sinister. Frequent references were made to the 'levelling spirit' among the masses. Almost as alarming was the idea, not without foundation, that some powerful group or party was using the mob for purposes of its own. Setting aside the young men-about-town, whose response to their own high spirits, drunkenness or jaded *ennui* was to attack the watch and molest sober citizens, and for whom riot was a form of sport, there was no doubt that political gangs to fight at election times were deliberately engaged, such as the mob employed on behalf of Sir William Beauchamp Proctor during the 1768 election. Mobs were organised (sometimes by magistrates) to break up Methodist meetings. But leaders who at least appeared to have larger aims in view constantly alarmed the government. Up to the 1750s it was still possible to point the finger at Jacobites.[2] Such accusations lost credibility in the sixties, and the purpose of the secret leaders became as vague as their identity. The fears remain, however, and signs of intelligence and organisation in the mob, which was considered incapable of such qualities, were thought to be significant. At the time of the 1757 riots a writer in the *Gentleman's Magazine* no doubt voiced the fears of many when he wrote

> I may confidently affirm that some persons of figure and influence are always acting behind the scenes, and that the real mob are only the tools of those who are led by either principle or interest, to wish for a general confusion, in order to overthrow the government.[3]

After the Gordon Riots, George Grenville wrote: 'I dread higher characters than a mob in a rage were at work',[4] and Lord Macclesfield wrote to the Secretary at War:

> I should think that by getting some artful person to insinuate himself with the prisoners, or by getting the surgeons and nurses of the hospitals to converse with the wounded rioters under their care, something might be got out so as to trace the persons employed in convening, paying and directing the efforts of the mob, and many other things which might tend to discover the *primum mobile* of this business.[5]

Certainly there were several reports at the time of well-dressed men directing the rioters, but conspiracy theories were bound to be as popular in June 1780 as in 1666 after the Fire of London. The other extreme, that of disdainful scepticism, can be found in the opinion of the Quaker, Sarah Hoare:

> Many are suggesting suspicions and doubts in their minds respecting the cause of this tumult and one party reflecting on another as being instrumental; but I apprehend one need not go deep for causes. The collection of such a large body together must consequentially bring many evil-minded persons together, and these would be ready enough at so fair an opportunity of doing mischief.[6]

Professor Rudé's discussion on types of leader is useful. He distinguishes the leader-in-chief, often a figurehead, in whose name the crowd riot, the intermediate leader, and the mob captain,[7] a distinction well enough understood by eighteenth-century politicians. However, from the point of view of control, their rather exaggerated fears of the intermediate (and often unknown) leader from outside the crowd, and of other indications of a threat to the social order, led them into policies of massive over-reaction at times. It may also account for their failure to recognise, or rather their determination not to recognise but rather to hold up to ridicule, the genuine causes of riot. Magistrates frequently write to describe disorder rising from a 'pretended' or 'alleged' dearth of corn or other supplies. In government circles there are constant references to rioters as 'misguided', 'deluded wretches', or the 'giddy multitude'. A Coventry magistrate wrote in 1756:

> The riotous and tumultuous behaviour of the populace, in many parts of this kingdom, hath been begun by artful and designing villains, with a view to rob their neighbours [and] carry away their property, that they may support themselves in idleness.[8]

And in 1727 the Mayor of Falmouth commented on the behaviour of the rioters in giving away or selling at a quarter price the plundered corn as clear proof that the scarcity in the area was not genuine.[9]

The idea of social protest, in short, was not a palatable one, and designing men must therefore be manipulating simple people. The authorities found it hard to admit to themselves that the harvest had failed, or that city slums were overcrowded, or that the poor were desperate.

The classification of mobs into categories by historians has so far been based on causes. Thus we have hunger riots, industrial riots and political riots, which in turn are subdivided into corn riots, cheese riots, machine-breaking riots, enclosure and turnpike riots, election riots and so on. But to understand the subject of suppressing riots a quite different classification is needed, according to such factors as predictability, longevity and intensity.

(1) A common type was the riot of an evanescent and wholly unpredictable type, which really qualified for Burke's famous description of 'little lambent meteors that pass away in the evening'.[10] There was no knowing how or when such riots might arise; they could be instantaneous in their inception, short-lived and often very destructive, and usually disappeared before the cumbersome machinery of pursuit and suppression could be put into operation at all. London and many provincial cities were subject to these riots to such an extent as to justify the use of the term endemic. Many of them were light-hearted affairs, and expended themselves in the smashing of windows, the destruction of the stock of the unpopular tradesman or the premises of a bawdy-house. In 1749 the mob attacked the Star Tavern, a well-known London whore-house. The assailants, flushed with their success, made the mistake of repeating the attack on the following night, developing it in the customary manner of the eighteenth-century street-riot, into a plundering of the neighbourhood.

The Guards from the Tower were ready for them and some arrests were made.[11]

A prison riot, which could quickly become terrifying, often arose from a trivial occurrence. Other riots seemed to contemporaries to have no cause at all and they may have been right; it is probably a mistake in the case of many minor riots to look beyond the natural turbulence, desire to destroy or even sense of humour of a depressed urban working class. The environmental approach in the studies of certain modern zoologists are as likely to throw light on this phenomenon as an earnest study of social protest. Georgian town planning at its best was a good combination of elegance and utility, but in many of the poorer sectors of cities there was no planning at all, and brutal violence was familiar.

Sometimes such riots had a more sinister air, such as the occasional lynching mob, or seem to have arisen in connection with crimes. Certain areas of London – Alsatia, Broken Cross, Thieving Lane, Little Sanctuary and many others – had their own lookout system to defeat the watch, and any raids into these dangerous districts needed soldiers to make them effective. From such confusing warrens and courts a fast-moving crowd might speedily collect, bent on no particular objective except the destruction of property, the despair of householders and government.

(2) Another type of urban riot arose from a known event or situation, equally short-lived but at least predictable by the government, which could take counter-measures in advance. Fairs, cockfights and other sporting events, and execution processions were notoriously productive of disorder. It was rarely thought safe for executions at Tyburn to take place unless attended by the Guards. The hanging of the revivalist preacher and forger Dr Dodd in 1777 attracted so much notice that no less than 2000 men were held in readiness in Hyde Park in case of an emergency.[12] Riots at theatres and public ballrooms were common. When the early hydrogen balloons began to form part of public entertainments there were several cases of crowds, impatient at the slowness of the inflating mechanism, rioting and destroying the balloon.[13] The student of urban society in the eighteenth century is tempted to believe that with almost any public event involving the collection of crowds there was a strong likelihood of a riot.

Neither of the first two types of riots in (1) and (2) fit well with the modern view about eighteenth-century crowds, although E. P. Thompson has warned of the need to distinguish the 'great risings of the people' from the mere brawls and squabbles outside bakers' shops.

From the point of view of control both (1) and (2) were very difficult to deal with, the common street mob perhaps more so than the sporting fixture or Tyburn saturnalia. It was very difficult to come up with and make contact with such a crowd; it might rage through the streets at a great rate, gathering strength as it went and perhaps even throwing up temporary leaders, but an hour later the guard, turned out from Somerset House, Savoy, Tiltyard or Tower, would find streets littered with the wreckage of the mob's passing but otherwise deserted. Sometimes a few meagre arrests would be made from the drunken tail of the mob, but it was a poor return when seen as a proportion of the total number involved. The arrests often proved disappointing; it was difficult to get evidence, and such evidence as was forthcoming tended to show that only the least dangerous participants had been discovered. It was partly with such mobs in mind that Henry Fielding instituted the horse-patrol,[14] and the War Office recognised that the faster-moving dragoons, as in the case of the smuggling service, had a better chance of catching a crowd on the move than the slower foot guards. It was however a puzzle to cavalry to know how to act if the pursuit led into the narrow alleys and courts mentioned above. Some successes were recorded in 1780 when mixed groups of horse and foot were sent out, but their quarry was street mobs which showed fight. The chief difficulty with the small objectless mob was that it would not turn and fight, but took refuge in a flight which in view of the physical layout of eighteenth-century London was bound to be successful, whether its pursuers were horse or foot.

(3) On a more dangerous scale, but by virtue of its nature more susceptible of control by the military, were the large mobs, determined to attain some economic or political objective. There is a wide difference between the spontaneous effervescent crowds previously discussed, which often expended themselves in a mere brawl, and the planned, structured mobs, with very clear ideas of their goals. With their stronger element of social protest they were felt to be much more of a threat to the established order than the casual crowd. The word insurrection was often used by contemporaries.[15] Such mobs were often disciplined and aware of the value of drums, music, colours, disguises, passwords and slogans. They marched about rural areas, sometimes covering many miles in pursuit of their aim. Mills and warehouses were besieged and broken open and the contents sold at a fair price or given away. Farmers or factors were forced to promise to bring supplies into market, and contributions of money for the mob's subsistence were exacted, although petty thieving and looting were often checked. Sometimes the fury of the mob reached such a pitch that a good deal of food was purposely destroyed as a mark of contempt.[16]

A leader, or more often a group of leaders, would soon emerge. Sometimes parts of the nucleus floated off like spores to carry out the purposes of the parent body. Martyrs might appear as well, as the case of William Allen in 1768 showed.[17] Newspapers, pamphlets, and even prints[18] at the time ensured that Allen quickly took his place in the popular martyrology.

Often the activities of such mobs continued for several days or even weeks, allowing time for the forces of law and order to be marshalled against them. In many cases they could be predicted in advance; the known result of the last harvest and previous experience of certain trouble-spots assisted the War Office in making plans.

In London and other urban areas these mobs were often to be found directing their activities against forestallers of the market, whether in grain, cheese, bacon or other produce, or in some cases (e.g. the Spitalfields weavers) machine-breaking. The rural mob could often be contained or dispersed by the army, who were able in open areas to conduct their operations in the style of a military manoeuvre. In the town however such mobs were often seen at their most dangerous; operating at night, well led but often in liquor, indulging in spectacular gestures such as the use of missiles and fire. Sometimes dense and slow-moving, they needed a determined soldiery to combat them. A political or religious mob behaved in a similar way. All such mobs, however, showed on occasion that they were capable of keeping within reasonable bounds and became violent only when interfered with. The Gordon riots were an exception, becoming in the end a frenzied uncontrolled horde, and any mob might contain a criminal element accompanying it for purposes of its own. There were however plenty of examples tending to show that the appearance of the army often caused a riot or aggravated an existing one, and a wise Secretary at War often declined to send troops unless absolutely necessary, lest, in the words of Sir John Fielding 'they provoke what it is intended to prevent'.[19] If the army had felt more sure of its role in using force against crowds the position might have been different; as it was, the War Office felt that a half-hearted intervention, with all its dangers, was probably worse than no intervention at all.

If the army and the magistrates had no guide for their conduct, neither had the mob. Naturally nothing resembling the modern manuals of subversion and street-fighting were available to them. Even so we may discern interesting tactics and strategems and even rudimentary strategy. In 1740 during the corn shortage the inhabitants of Kettering arranged a football match to be played after the manner of the time, with five hundred men a side, but this was merely a cloak to the more serious purpose of destroying a nearby mill.[20] Mobs were frequently brought together at short notice by placing placards on doors, signposts and trees over a wide area, or by the blowing of horns. At other times members of a mob moved off to an assembly point, or approached a gaol to rescue their comrades, under cover of disguises, often women's clothes. Sometimes sections of a mob would create diversions to keep soldiers marching aimlessly back and forth, as did the Nottingham corn rioters of 1779.[21] Turnpikes were persistently attacked at night, often by men with blackened faces, in spite of the penalties under the Black Act. And at times crowds were capable of a stand-up fight with soldiers. All the foregoing techniques were already familiar in many parts of Britain to a population frequently engaged in smuggling; and the subject has many similarities. But the parallel must not be too closely made. The corn mob presented the same sort of difficulties to the army as the large smuggling gang, being captained, prepared to operate by day or night with force or cunning, and with a definite object.

Its strength lay in its determination to carry out its purpose and to resent interference. But a good many street riots of the types discussed above were difficult to suppress for other reasons. Their strength lay in their spontaneity and unpredictability. Faced with crowds of either type, therefore, any peace-keeping force faced formidable difficulties.

PART II
Strategy

5 Strategy and the Mob

INTRODUCTION

Tactics – the conduct of troops in the presence of an adversary (in this context a mob) – are considered in a later chapter. Here it is proposed to examine the problem from the point of view of the government, and the use of the term strategy becomes appropriate. It is true that in many cases strategy amounted to no more than merely getting the nearest troops to the scene of the riot. The ordinary procedures[1] in the office of the Secretary of State and the War Office were sufficient to accomplish this, but even in quite simple cases there were departures from the ordinary course of the two offices, sometimes in response to the particular situation, and at other times because of the personal and eccentric practice of the office-holder for the time being. Furthermore there were occasions when riots were of such a dangerous or widespread nature that genuine strategical difficulties arose. The corn riots of 1756 and 1766, and the militia riots of 1757, were widespread, long-lasting and exceedingly bitter, and in all three there were instances in War Office documents of avowed shortages of men to deal with the problem. The threat to London of what appeared to be organised insurrection in 1765, 1768 and (worst of all), 1780 caused enormous concentrations of men in the area of the capital, and the tale told by the documents resembles that of a wartime operation in an unfriendly theatre.

Briefly, for reasons that are discussed below,[2] the usual course of conduct when a riot occurred was for the householders to complain to the local J.P., who would report the matter to the Secretary of State in London. The Secretary of State would forward the letter to the War Office with his covering note endorsing its sentiments and requesting a military intervention. The Secretary at War would then send to the officer commanding the nearest detachment of troops ordering him to march to the riot area and co-operate with the civil magistrates.

The emergency might continue, and there are constant references in the documents to requests back to London for advice on plans for pacifying the neighbourhood or for further reinforcements. In some cases (e.g. Bute, Holdernesse, and Stormont) the Secretary of State might take a leading part; at other times it would be left to the War Office. There was, as usual, no hard and fast rule, although a timid or newly-appointed Secretary of State would often prefer that the matter should be left to the War Office, with its greater expertise in such matters, and would therefore intervene only *pro forma*. At a later stage he might come forward to perform tasks outside the scope of the War Office, e.g. to issue proclamations against rioting, to pursue at law apprehended rioters, to dispatch informers to the area through the Treasury Solicitor, and on the basis of their reports, to brief the Law Officers of the Crown, to arrange special assizes and, where advisable, to arrange reprieves for the convicted.

When we come to consider the part of central government in combating civil disorder, the work of each office will be described in turn according to its normal procedure, before the exceptions are examined. Firstly, certain continuing strategical problems that they both faced must be examined. The procedure outlined above for obtaining sanction for military intervention was correct but slow; although by the standards of the mid-eighteenth century it was performed as promptly as possible this was often not prompt enough. Both the topography of eighteenth-century England and the political problems created by contemporary constitutional ideas were responsible for this.

(1) Slowness of Communications.

The poor state of eighteenth-century roads is well known. Defoe, Postlethwayt, Arthur Young, Parson Woodforde and many other writers of the time refer to the difficulties of travel. Defoe was eloquent on the Great North Road, the standard of which dropped as soon as it entered the many belts of clay encountered between Biggleswade and the Trent.[3] Clay also helped to make Sussex an almost impassable county in wet seasons, thus rendering pursuit by the dragoons on smuggling service more difficult. Clearly, before the days of planned surfacing the state of English roads was intimately connected with the type of bedrock of the area, and a study of the geological map of the country indicates the difficulties facing the War Office, not only of strategy but also of simple communication. Even if we do not believe, for example, all the well-known strictures of Arthur Young on English roads,[4] the reality must have been sufficiently bad. Some improvement was being effected by the turnpike trusts, but these only covered part of the road network in many areas of England, and it would be a simplification to imagine a steady upward curve of improvement throughout the century. Besides, not all turnpikes seem to have been uniformly good. In his Northern Tour Young found that out of 940 miles of turnpiked roads 490 were good, 210 middling and 240 bad.[5] But it does appear that he expected a turnpike to be better than a parish road. What is not so clear to the modern reader is what is meant by the terms 'good' and 'bad'. Certain general statements can be made: that the roads in the South were often better than those of the North, that roads over clay and chalk were more likely to become waterlogged in winter than those over gravel, that some areas were better served than others because of turnpikes. But contemporary opinion about the excellence or otherwise of roads in the eighteenth century is hard to assess. By what standards were they judging? One recent writer, after discussing the development and administration of the turnpike system, is cautious about the effectiveness of its engineering techniques.[6] The period of greatest activity in turnpike history, sometimes called the Turnpike Mania, was from 1751 to 1770, in which 389 new trusts were formed.[7] Even before this period, the thirteen main roads serving London were turnpiked and many provincial areas were similarly provided for.[8] But these trusts were under no single controlling authority, and in the absence of any new road technology merely adopted the existing methods of the time. McAdam many years later was to comment savagely on the poor construction techniques of these trusts, but did concede that a turnpike road was better than a parish road. At least it seems likely that the former were repaired, even if the repairs were not of a high standard. But a new principle was needed before real progress could be made. McAdam's account of the manner in which many of the roads of England during the winter of 1820 'broke up in a very alarming manner' and became impassable, particularly where chalk or clay was included in their composition, reads like one of Defoe's diatribes a century earlier.[9] But the work of McAdam and Telford in roadmaking and of John Palmer of the Post Office in introducing the mail coach fall outside the period of this study.

Many areas of England remained economically backward simply because of poor contact with the rest of the country. It seems likely that bad communications were almost as such to blame as poor harvests for times of dearth. The shortage, however caused, was the most common cause of the rural riot, although the real famine years in the strict sense of the word had become a thing of the past. Gilbert White, commenting on the ten or eleven wet seasons which occurred between 1760 and 1773, said there had not

> been known a greater scarcity of all sorts of grain, considering the great improvements of modern husbandry. Such a run of wet seasons a century or two ago would, I am persuaded, have occasioned a famine.[10]

There was some truth in the accusations of the mob that there was a glut of corn in some areas and a dearth in others, and that racketeers were holding on to supplies for their own purposes; it was less true that the transport of corn from one area to another would have been a simple matter.

From the point of view of this chapter the poor state of the roads was an important strategical matter to government and in particular to the War Office, upon whom the task of control chiefly fell. The rains that washed away harvests and brought riots also spoilt roads and made the sending of messages to and from London, not to speak of the approach of infantry or cavalry to the riot area, doubly slow. These factors were appreciated by the

War Office and some attempt was made to guard against them, particularly by Lord Barrington, who was very conscious of the difficulties of riot control, and whose long tenure of the War Office gave him good opportunities to develop ideas in this direction.

A summer riot in the middle of the eighteenth century in normal weather conditions in an area remote from London, for example, St Austell, might follow this pattern:

(a) *Day One*. After some hours of rioting during which the local counter-measures had been in vain, a message would be sent by the magistrates to the office of the Secretary of State, probably not until late afternoon. In mid-century conditions of transport this could not arrive at the Cockpit or Cleveland Row until

(b) *Day Four* in the evening, or early on Day Five. On the same day a message would be sent across to the War Office and after a quick consultation with the secretaries the usual order authorizing the intervention of the nearest troops (perhaps at Falmouth) would be sent.

(c) *Day Nine or Ten* would see the arrival of the order to act in the hands of the officer; a force of cavalry might be able to intervene in aid of the St Austell magistrates later the same day, but a company of infantry, even if a careful officer who knew of the disturbances had been holding them in the first degree of readiness, could hardly do so until at some stage half-way through the next day.

Such a system could only exist in the absence of any substitute. Cornwall, it is true, was an extreme case. The condition of its approach roads accentuated its frontier-province status. In an essay in the *Gentleman's Magazine* an anonymous writer described the roads from London to Land's End:

After the first 47 miles from London you never set eyes on a turnpike for 220 miles. The respective parishes either can or will do nothing; nor have the inhabitants abilities to make or mend a road, though one gave them all the revenues of the Exchequer.[11]

But other towns were nearly as badly off, and many eighteenth-century riots took place in areas remote from the capital. Apart from Cornwall, which with its population of turbulent miners was a constant scene of riot, disturbances took place in Devon and South Wales, Manchester, Leeds, Newcastle, Berwick-on-Tweed, and a number of towns north of Birmingham. Nearer districts, such as Essex and Sussex, were almost equally difficult of access. Lincoln at 130 miles distance was two days from London, Bristol at 110 was a day and a half to two days. The Bath coach, travelling on one of the better roads of the kingdom, had by 1765 cut the journey to 29 hours,[12] and by 1782 to seventeen hours.[13] The post boys' contract time was five miles in an hour, but urgent expresses were often included on board stage coaches, a policy which although illegal, was often quicker. The War Office commonly used the express form of endorsement on orders to commanders to march on riot duty.

All the above times could in times of snow and heavy rain be multiplied by a factor of two or more. The middle years of the eighteenth century seem to have suffered from unlucky extremes of weather.[14] In 1766 a hard winter was followed by a wet spring and the wettest summer in human memory, ruining the harvest, causing riots and converting the roads into quagmires. Sarah Osborn wrote in July:

> . . . the weather . . . has been continually weeping for ten weeks past. The thundering and lightning we have lately had has made me hope it would clear the clouds, and let us once more see the sun; however, these hopes are vain, and weeping still continues, to the sorrow of those who have large crops of hay all spoiling.[15]

The same correspondent wrote in 1768, another year of ruined harvests and widespread floods,

> My kitchen and offices below were three or four feet deep in water. People who keep exact accounts of the weather say more rain fell that day than in the usual course falls in a month. All the land springs have risen to a degree not remembered by anyone.[16]

The Chatsworth rain gauge registered 39.919 inches for that year (most of which evidently fell in summer): the average for the period 1761 – 1810 was 28.411[17]. In 1770 the floods drowned 200,000 acres of the fens.[18] It was in such seasons that the roads were difficult even to identify and travellers needed guides.

All these difficulties were known to the War Office. Given a free hand for a plan for riot control it might have advised on the design of a proper road system. This is not so far-fetched as it appears; the placing of military units and later the building of barracks was arranged with internal security in mind. The building of many miles of roads by Wade in the Highlands had a simple strategic purpose to answer, and a military road was constructed in the 1750s from Newcastle to Carlisle. But such a plan could never seriously be suggested for England in general, and the Secretary at War had to accept the situation as he found it. His attempts to anticipate trouble after wet seasons and bad harvests, and to short-circuit the laborious process of dealing from London with riots will be considered below.[19] This latter point however needs further explanation.

(2) The Constitutional Procedure.

The peculiar unpopularity of the army has already been alluded to. Its achievements were praised in newspaper and ballad in time of war, but no one had any doubt in the eighteenth century that it was a scourge to society. The vicious system of billeting the troops upon the country, with its resulting endless bickering with innkeepers, magistrates and inhabitants generally, ensured that this attitude remained unchanged. On another level the very existence of a standing army was (or was affected to be) regarded with great suspicion by the public. Its attitude derived from the view of the Lockeian Whigs, who strongly opposed any tendency (as they saw it) to increase the power of the executive, while choosing to forget another tenet of Locke, that the most important function of civil government was the protection of private property, which in practice required the vigorous intervention of that executive. Any attempt on the part of the magistrate to take what might logically appear to be the most efficient course and apply directly without reference to London to the nearest troops – who might be near enough to be actual spectators of the riot – would be regarded as a procedural impropriety; any attempt on the part of those troops to intervene without the invitation of the magistrate would be met with charges of major-generalism or praetorianism.

Action by troops at the request of the magistrate without the sanction of the War Office during the period under review was not unknown, but it was nearly always frowned upon, and in any case was usually confined to movement of troops into the area, not direct action against a mob; for that the careful officer waited for orders from London to cover him. Some officers thought that merely moving troops nearer to the scene might itself be exceeding their powers. In 1773 a local commander refused to march to the scene of a riot on a requisition from the Mayor and Deputy Recorder of a town without instructions from London.[20] Again initiative by the War Office without the sanction of the Secretary of State in any but the most routine context was uncommon, until the era of Barrington, and in acting so the Secretary at War ran a real risk. The Secretary at War explained the policy of his office, carefully developed over many years, to an agitated correspondent during the riotous period of 1773:

> . . . In a matter of so much importance as the question stated by you, I have always thought it my duty to follow the constant practice of my predecessors in office. Whenever disturbances have happened, and the magistrates have found military aid absolutely necessary, it has been usual to state this to the Secretary at War, applying for the assistance of a military force, which is generally complied with. When orders are issued for any part of the troops to be aiding upon requisition made by the civil magistrates, it has been thought proper to remind magistrates of not calling upon H. M. Forces for their aid till every effort of the civil

authority has been exerted, and found ineffectual. The military on their part have seldom judged themselves authorised, without orders from hence, to march out of their quarters upon the requisition of a magistrate. Your opinion may probably be well founded as to the right the magistrate has to call upon every individual for his assistance in preserving the peace, but I am rather inclined to think that the mode now in use tends as much to the secure guidance of the magistrate as of the military, who must at all times be under strict government, so essential to the being of an army in this country.[21]

Action of troops without the concurrence of magistrates at all was out of the question. Only once in the century were troops permitted to act unilaterally, during the Gordon Riots of 1780, an emergency of such magnitude that any political criticism about counter measures was silenced. In other words the short-circuiting of any of the essential parts of the quadrilateral process previously described in order to save a day or so was uncommon, at least in the first part of the century.

The result was a procedure which was constitutionally correct but very slow. This cautious policy, to which Barrington's predecessors at the War Office had adhered, was designed to give no one in or out of Parliament any justification for complaining that the army was acting *ultra vires* or eroding the liberties of the state. Policy was supposed to be formed by the Secretary of State (at the instance of the local agents), and put into effect by the Secretary at War; both of these were answerable to Parliament for what they did. In 1764 Sir Philip Francis, then First Clerk at the War Office, wrote of the constitutional dangers of constant interventions on the part of soldiers to help magistrates especially if such interventions were to become too familiar to the public, and urged his opinion that the Secretary at War ought to resist all but the most pressing requests. He added meaningly that, even in the most dangerous cases, 'I think he should not take any step whatever without a written order from the Secretary of State.'[22]

On balance it seems clear that the strategy of the War Office was more successful than the tactics of the troops. There were occasional mistakes, but allowing for the difficulties discussed above, movements of troops into the areas was as efficient and speedy as was possible. What was not so clear – and this dilemma is discussed in Chapter 13 – is what the troops were to do with the mob once they had made contact with it.

6 The Role of the War Office

As discussed above, internal order was one of the recognised responsibilities of the Secretary of State. As far as possible he tried to discharge that responsibility through the local civil agents. But however much he might berate them for their failures (and he always did), no minister ever doubted that in most cases he would have to use the army. He would then turn to the Secretary at War.

THE SECRETARY AT WAR

This curious and anomalous office has been occasionally noticed by historians,[1] but more work on it needs to be done, and one of the best accounts, that of M. A. Thomson,[2] is vague on many important points of detail, using terms of probability and speculation about the areas of responsibility of, and duties discharged by the War Office.

Definition is far from easy. Internal service procedures and external political and constitutional pressures shaped the office, and its activities were affected by many other overlapping empires, such as the Treasury, the Ordnance and the Paymaster's office. In theory questions of policy were for the Secretary of State, and the Secretary at War carried out the policy. His functions were not supposed to begin until a measure and the manner of carrying it out had been decided in cabinet. This subordinate status accorded well enough with the idea that the Crown and its close servants should have the government of the army, subject to reasonable check by Parliament by means of the Mutiny Act and by the army's liability to account for its expenditure. In fact of the two controls the annual presentation of accounts by the Secretary at War was probably the more important. Apart from his financial role, which was crucial, the Secretary at War dealt with many burdensome and minute details of the internal economy of the army. It is not surprising that the most successful holders of the office were those who were hard-working, painstaking and not afraid of long hours.

The bald and simple view of masters who planned on the one hand and on the other of an industrious departmental official who did what he was told, however constitutionally correct it may be, has a number of exceptions. Throughout the eighteenth century, it is true, the Secretary at War appeared to be acting on the instructions of other people, sometimes the Monarch or the Commander-in-Chief (when there was one) and sometimes the Secretaries of State, leaving the impression that his role was an entirely subordinate one, even if at times it was not clear to whom he was subordinate. On closer examination however a good many of his actions in peace and war prove to have arisen from his personal initiative, and they were not necessarily insignificant actions. Naturally, any holder of an office who has developed expertise in a vital area of public administration is bound to be able to develop freedom of action at times.

This aspect has not received much attention by historians, who seem to have accepted the statement of one of the most famous incumbents of the office that 'he was no minister, and therefore could not be supposed to have a competent knowledge of the destination of the army, and how the war was to be carried on.'[3] And in many other ways and on many occasions[4] the Secretary at War reiterated that he was a mere executive officer who carried out the instructions of others. In fact his relation with the House of Commons was marked by an intermittent campaign on their part to rivet the role of minister on him so that they might make him the target of their attacks, and by the attempts of that target to move out of range. Some Secretaries at War, particularly Barrington, would have preferred to be regarded as a civil servant with responsibility for a junior department, who happened also to have a seat in the Commons. It is true that not all holders of the office shared this view: for some ambitious young politicians it was a stepping-stone to preferment. Others were mediocre and incompetent. The men of Barrington's stamp were at least competent, but unambitious and content to be efficient within a narrow compass. In all three cases the War Office was likely to remain politically undeveloped and secondary in importance. The long tenure of William Blathwayt,[5] an industrious man with whom Barrington had some points in common, did much to establish the later structure and limits of the office. One author considers that Blathwayt had virtually become a 'junior assistant Secretary of State' and did much to raise the office from that of a mere secretary to the Commander-in-Chief.[6] It is true that during William III's wars the increase of business in Blathwayt's department caused a change in the status of the office, but his own rise derived from his other important roles, and there were several of them.[7] The vital factor, which Blathwayt shared with other Secretaries at War, was that although the office carried with it no seat in the Cabinet[8] there were constant opportunities for access to the Closet. In Anne's reign other factors became important. The War of the Spanish Succession made enormous demands upon War Office organisation, and the government was content to allow the Secretary at War to take a considerable part in organising overseas expeditions. The presentation of army estimates 'by order' jointly with the Paymaster-General from 1702 onwards was also significant. This was regarded in Parliament as the best opportunity for making attacks on government military policy, and not merely on financial grounds, and the Secretary at War took the brunt of this. The tenure of St John from 1704 to 1708 was probably more crucial to the development of the office than that of Blathwayt.[9] He was a forceful and efficient Secretary at War who took a leading part in ordering expeditions and reinforcements. His successor, Walpole, was prepared to use all the considerable power that St John had acquired, but apparently had no interest in the War Office save as a stage in his own rising career. During his time the potential of the office ceased to expand. Towards the end of Anne's reign, at the high point of its power, it occupied a strong position at a meeting point between Cabinet, Commander-in-Chief and Queen. For several reasons it did not decline after 1714. The annual presentation of estimates was still important. The enthusiasm for the army of the first two members of the new dynasty, with whom the Secretary at War continued to work closely, kept military matters to the fore, as did Jacobite and Spanish scares, even in a period of peace. From the political point of view the office was one of profit under the crown, with a seat in Parliament, and therefore unlikely to be relinquished by any government anxious about support. And the ever-increasing role of the army as a keeper of the peace at home, a function which it fell to the Secretary at War to organise because of his part in issuing marching orders to units in Britain, meant that for some purposes he was indispensable.

But all these factors did not make it one of the great offices of State. The position after 1714 remained confused, and it was often not clear what orders the Secretary at War could give, or to whom. Commissioners concerned with army supplies for example, would accept his orders sometimes, at others demand the signature of a Secretary of State. And successive Secretaries at War seemed not concerned to make any more bids for power, but were content to work hard in their office. If they were politically important it was, as before, because of their relations, usually unofficial, within the circle of government. They seem to have preferred to be thought of as subservient, and certainly much of their power was exercised in contexts removed from public scrutiny. In spite of this, whether or not the Secretary at War was a 'civil servant' – and the term needs to be used with care at this date – membership of the House of Commons came to be regarded as essential.[10]

There were many cases of independent action taken by Secretaries at War, without authority, and sometimes without the knowledge of their masters. One of the best examples of this was Barrington himself, usually reckoned to be the model of the faultless and proper civil service approach. Taken together his actions do not make him into the sort of minister-in-secret of the opposition suspicions, but they are enough to erode the image of himself he tried to project then and which is accepted now.[11] His desire was however for efficiency rather than power.

In the field of riot-control this independent line is clearly seen. It is easy to see why. Nominally the task of the Secretary of State, it fell nearly always to the War Office to carry it out. The effect of constant calls for help over the years was to make the Secretary at War into a sort of police chief or minister of the interior. In the official documents, in addition to the development of a special expertise and a formula, signs of long-term strategic movements and plans can be observed, some of which were kept secret even from the Secretary of State.[12] The Secretary of State, even if ignorant of the details, was usually prepared to tolerate this tendency. It was true that peacetime riot strategy was theoretically his job, just as was grand strategy in time of war, and the original involvement of the Secretary at War was only due to the fact that he had acquired the functions mentioned above connected with the billeting and marching of troops around the kingdom. But the Secretaries must have realised that the War Office knew more about riot duty than they did, and left the task almost entirely to it with gratitude. Consequently by the middle of the century it often had the strategic as well as the merely departmental handling of a riot.

The Secretary at War for most of this period was William Wildman, Viscount Barrington (1717–93).[13] He has been called 'probably the most conscientious man to hold the office during this period'[14] but is allowed to be no more than 'a competent executive, and self-confident within a comparatively narrow range, but also acutely conscious of his own limitations'.[15] Newcastle was warmer in his praise: 'Lord Barrington is undoubtedly in all respects the best secretary at war that ever was, and a most steady and useful friend of mine in that office, and of great service to my friends',[16] was his verdict, although the last part of it should put us on our guard. Although an admirer of Pitt, Barrington remained on intimate terms with Newcastle, whom he often visited; War Office letters over the signatures of his deputies often begin: 'In the absence of my Lord Barrington, who is gone to Claremont . . .'

He held several other offices,[17] but seems to have been content with the War Office, to whose familiar routine he was relieved to return in 1765. In an age of preferment-scrambling he asked for little and was content with what he received; he never asked for an English peerage. 'My invariable rule therefore is to ask nothing, to refuse nothing, to let others place me, and to do my best wherever I am placed.'[18] His speeches, although their subject matter was not commonly more than departmental, read well today. Horace Walpole puts him among the twenty-eight best speakers of the House.[19] In the Commons he always vigorously defended the interests of army personnel, and his care for them is one of his more endearing qualities. In a letter to the Advocate-General he wrote: 'The poor, though deserving officer, should always find at the War Office, a constant asserter of his rights, and a faithful guardian of his interests.'[20] He was on the other hand generally against the granting of nepotic favours,[21] and was relieved to be able to give up the patronage of the army to Lord Granby when the latter was made Commander-in-Chief in 1766.[22] Four years later however, the irksome responsibility returned with Granby's resignation,

> a fatal event to me. It restored to the War Office an invidious patronage,
> which has cost me some old and valuable friendships not to be replaced
> at my time of life; and I have not suffered it to produce so much
> advantage to me, as to the ministers.[23]

He was ready with reproof when it was merited, but unlike many in his
position his praise could be called forth as well. After the pacification of the
clothing areas in the West he wrote to Wolfe: 'To a proper disposition of
that regiment and the prudence and spirit shown in executing their orders,
the peace of three large counties (much disposed to riot) is owing.'[24]

His evident humanity even extended to the mob which gave him so
much anxiety. In another letter, during the same disturbance, to Wolfe,
who had asked for guidance about the use of force in the absence of a
magistrate, he wrote:

> But if the troops (as there is much reason to apprehend from your letter)
> should be left alone, the commanding officer must then be the judge of
> that necessity in which only he is permitted to use force, and in such case
> both his prudence and humanity should make him very cautious of
> proceeding to extremity with an ignorant and miserable multitude,
> whose grievances are sometimes real and to be pitied, though their
> misguided attempts to redress them are to be checked and repressed.[25]

This and other examples of a humane approach contrast curiously with
that of some fire-eating officers of the army, who would have welcomed
(and did welcome in 1780) an unfettered opportunity to try accounts with
a despised class.[26] Only in the autumn of 1766 do we find him losing
patience and recommending salutary punishment of mobs active in many
parts of Britain.

Barrington treated magistrates with polite distaste; they created endless
problems for him over the (admittedly difficult) question of billeting, and
he suspected them of fostering local contempt for the army and even of
raising their own mobs at times, but they never failed to send in their
supplications for aid if a riotous situation developed. At such times he sent
help but could not resist reminding them of their own shortcomings.

Although contemporaries and historians praise his care and industry he
made rather a fumbling beginning and took time to grow into the job. It
was he who was the author of the famous trio of letters to Governor Fowke
of Gibraltar in 1756, with which the defence made so much play at the
subsequent trial; in his attempt to extricate himself on the score of
inexperience Barrington concluded lamely by saying: 'I had been but
about four months in my office.'[27] The disturbances of 1756 and 1757,
which he handled at first rather diffidently, gave him his baptism in this

sphere. By the autumn of 1757 he had learned a technique which he was to apply with confidence henceforward. He retained his interest in the problems of the office, especially those connected with public order, after his supersession. Horace Walpole, although saying rather unkindly of him 'Lord Barrington had a lisp and a tedious precision that prejudiced one against him', did concede that he 'made civility and attention a duty'.[28] This attitude, which foreshadows the civil service approach of politicians at the end of the century, can be contrasted with the amateurishness in many administrative matters of the Secretary of State's office at the time. Unlike the later Secretaryship of State for War, his was an office with little power – in the early part of his career he appears as little more than Cumberland's military Secretary, as if the previous 70 years had produced no change – but considerable usefulness if properly discharged, or potential for great embarrassment to an administration if misused.

The personnel of his office was small. In 1757 it consisted of a Deputy Secretary, Thomas Tyrwhitt, and a First Clerk, William Bowles, and eleven other clerks. There was also a Paymaster of the Widows' Pensions, a messenger and an office keeper.[29] In 1766 the Deputy Secretary was Christopher D'Oyly, and the First Clerk Philip Francis,[30] who, it has been hinted, was not scrupulous about keeping his master's secrets. The clerks had risen to twelve in number and six 'extra clerks' are mentioned, presumably part-timers; five of these were still being used in 1768.[31]

In 1773 the Deputy Secretary was Anthony Chamier, and the First Clerk Matthew Lewis. There were still twelve other clerks.[32] By 1777 Lewis was Deputy Secretary and was also described as First Clerk. Twelve other clerks continued to be employed, and other personnel have appeared – an Examiner of Army Accounts to help with the increasing complexities of military finance, and a Necessary Woman.[33] M. A. Thomson has noticed the presence of persons of distinction – Hume, Rowe the dramatist, Prior the poet, and others – as employees in similarly subordinate situations in the office of the Secretary of State,[34] no doubt for personal financial reasons in many cases. In the War Office Thomas Tyrwhitt, Deputy Secretary at War from 1756 to 1762 was a well-known and respected writer of commentaries on classics and English literature: Charles Burney thought him one of the great critics of the century.[35] Anthony Chamier, who succeeded Philip Francis in 1772, was an intimate of Dr Johnson;[36] Matthew Lewis, later a holder of substantial property in Jamaica, no doubt the fruits of judicious investment of the considerable War Office fees, was the father of Monk Lewis, the Gothic novelist.[37] The mysterious Francis, brought into the War Office by Welbore Ellis in 1762, remains one of the favourites in the long list of possible candidates in the controversy over the authorship of the Junius letters. It may well have been Francis who leaked to the press Barrington's letter praising the soldiery for their part in the Wilkes riots of 1768.[38] At all events he appears to have disapproved of some of Barrington's methods, particularly the practice mentioned above of dealing directly with magistrates without reference to the office of the Secretary of State. His friend Christopher D'Oyly was M.P. for Wareham from 1774 to 1784.[39] It seems probable that neither he nor Francis found Barrington a congenial master. On giving up his post at the War Office D'Oyly wrote to Francis:

> This morning, my dear Francis, I desired Lord Barrington's permission to retire from the War Office. My request was readily and, which is mortifying, without one civil speech, granted. I am persuaded whenever you please you may have the same permission on easy terms.[40]

In fact Francis did not long survive his friend, but resigned in March 1772. A correspondent in a newspaper signing himself 'Veteran', in fact one of the Junius pseudonyms, asserted that Barrington had driven Francis and D'Oyly out of the War Office.[41] But we know little of this far-off little office revolution, and the three actors in it remain shadowy figures: it is not possible to ascribe blame without more facts.

It is clear that the War Office was never over-staffed, and the employment of extra clerks at intervals may be an indication of the load of work. This extra load would be easy to understand in time of war; the retention of the services of supernumeraries after 1763 might well be due to the work of troop deployment for riot control, for the rest of the decade was fraught with bitter rioting, notably 1766 when disturbances took place in over 60 districts of England and Wales, and with the frequent demands of the smuggling service.

The Deputy Secretary was an important figure, often guiding his master by producing the correct precedents, and running the office in his absence. These absences, at least in the case of Barrington, were not frequent, but when they did occur were of fairly long duration, and often unluckily coincided with emergencies. Tyrwhitt was not happy about taking responsibility at such times, but his successors D'Oyly and Lewis were bolder, and many War Office directives, containing the words 'it is His Majesty's pleasure' in circumstances when this meant nothing more than the use of a customary form of words, appear in the letter books over their signatures, often addressed to officers of considerable seniority.

The clerks, although kept late at the office during emergencies, were reasonably treated, and under normal pressure of business only worked a five-hour day for six days a week.[42] Barrington appears to have been a kindly although at times a slightly testy master.

He paid many of the clerks no more than £50 a year:

> I have not ventured to give them more, because if old establishments are once increased it is very difficult to know where a stop can be made. The poor soldier still serves on the pay of the last century, though he has a

better right to assistance than any of us who do not wear red coats.[43]

In 1759 the Deputy Secretary was receiving £225 a year and the First Clerk £121. Barrington's own salary was £2002 11/6.[44]

It is tantalising not to know more of the ordinary programme and equipment of his office, although occasional glimpses appear. What road-books were kept? That they were used seems clear from the unhesitating and close knowledge of even remote areas revealed by the detailed routes sent out with the marching orders. Many eighteenth-century road-books merely brought the famous survey of John Ogilby[45] up to date; William Morgan's manual[46] included 500 market towns and a table for finding any road, city, or market town and the distance thereof from London. It ran into eleven editions up to 1752. Bowen's famous manual,[47] of which at least twelve editions appeared between 1720 and 1764, also included all towns and mileages. Any one of these works would be a likely candidate for use in the War Office.

WAR OFFICE PROCEDURE

The out-letter books (the series known as W.O.4) and the marching orders (W.O.5), which are the chief sources for War Office policy, show that most of Barrington's time was spent in moving detachments of the army around the country, in what at first appears to be an endless and aimless pattern. Gibbon wrote of 'the arbitrary, and often capricious orders of the War Office', but in fact almost none of these movements was performed without a reason. The burden of billeting troops upon innkeepers at a rate *per diem* which was justifiably held by them to be insufficient led to many petitions and complaints to magistrates, and rather than risk difficulties Barrington nearly always gave way, withdrawing the troops and quartering them elsewhere. Soldiers were also removed from towns during assizes and elections.[48] And out of regard for the off-duty conduct of the contemporary private soldier, common prudence reinforced the urgings of the magistrates that he be removed from towns where fairs, circuses or horse-races were to take place. Other marching orders show that the War Office was careful not to let a town stand host to regular soldiers and militia simultaneously if it could be avoided. Finally the troops at appropriate times are found marching to summer camps or autumn reviews. In peacetime these latter were the only movements performed by the army in pursuance of what it regarded as its relevant role; almost all the other troop movements were dictated by non-military factors.

The arrangement of this pattern was well organised by the War Office, but the result did not make for military efficiency. Also many detachments were charged with the task of helping the revenue officers in the endless war against smuggling, as well as being on riot duty for long periods of time. In these conditions any form of training was difficult. One colonel complained that he could only assemble his men on Sundays; at other times they were dispersed over a large area and.he seldom saw them.[49]

All these matters engrossed Barrington's attention. He had to ingratiate himself with touchy local satraps for whom he had a secret contempt, look after the army and see that its unpopularity at least did not increase, and perform a difficult role for which he was not well equipped, in which he received little or no guidance, and for which he would get no praise in the case of success, although he could count on censure in case of failure.

The more particular problems of War Office policy in case of riots remain to be considered.

The worst defect in the discharge of the strategic role, apart from the conditions of eighteenth-century transport, was the delay which always occurred through applying to London for troops. The four-point channel of communication has already been discussed.[50] The time-lag of days was often enough to make the intervention too late. Many riots however were of several days' or even weeks' duration; food riots were particularly long-lived. On arrival the army would in such cases still find something to do, although this was a poor consolation to humiliated magistrates marooned in a sea of lawlessness until rescued, or to owners of property already ruined. And yet it was hard to see how the delay could be avoided. It was true that once the Secretary of State had been applied to and the emergency registered with him he could pass on the case to the War Office, and the subsequent dealings of the magistrates could then be directly with the Secretary at War, at least during that particular disorder. But what was really wanted was a forewarned and forearmed system of security, which would enable the local military as well as the local civil forces to anticipate trouble in advance, and to intervene immediately as if they had authority from London. This ideal was of course impossible to achieve, but there were many interesting exceptions to the usual procedures which show that Barrington was trying to work towards it.

FORECASTING OF RIOTS

Some riotous situations were impossible to forecast. Beyond saying that it could happen at any time, the common street riot could not be predicted, unless it arose from some certain event, such as an execution procession or a fair. But a bad harvest put all J.P.s and property owners on their guard. The terrible riot year of 1766 saw Barrington making his preparation as early as January.[51] J.P.s were asked for their views about the peace of their areas. Sometimes if they were conscientious, or alarmed, or merely alarmist, they volunteered the information themselves.[52] There were other ways in which preparations might be made. Officers could be ordered to have their men ready to turn out at a moment's notice. An early contingency plan appears on the letter books during the silk-weavers' riots of 1765. It was only a short-range one and concerned, not an expected riot, but one which had already arisen and threatened to get worse. All the Guards (Foot and Horse) in London, and four cavalry regiments in or around London were ordered to be in readiness to march without delay.[53] The expertise of the War Office was becoming well developed by this date, and it seems likely that the permanent officials suggested this plan to Welbore Ellis, the Secretary at War.

On several occasions during the Wilkite riots of 1768 Barrington ordered troops in London barracks to be ready to march at a moment's notice.[54] It is difficult to estimate the time it might take in the mid-eighteenth century to turn out a company of infantry (or a troop of cavalry, which would take longer) where no previous alert had been given. Keeping them in the first degree of readiness probably saved up to an hour, which was a great saving in the destructive days of 1768.

An hour however would be of little consequence when the riot was remote from London. There was a wide difference between planning for tomorrow or next week, as in the above examples, and planning in the long term. There were bad years and bad areas, and no officer stationed in, for example, Newcastle or the West Country in 1756 or 1766 would have riot problems far from his mind. There were degrees of alertness, and troops could not be kept ready for action-for weeks on end. Other ways of saving time needed to be explored.

At least matters could be arranged so that the detachment, if not actually ready to march at once, was kept in a state of tolerable readiness to intervene in a day or so, particularly in respect of its constitution and equipment. This was particularly true of cavalry, which was always useful in combating the country food riot. As a general rule during the summer the horses of the cavalry were put out to grass in areas leased by the army, and watched over by a 'grass-guard'. These areas were often at some distance from the quarters of the regiment. As the putting out of horses to grass was almost universal in the home forces, a large part of the peace-keeping force of the country was rendered ineffective for half the year. In the first place it would take a long time to collect horses and remount the regiment, with all that this implied in terms of equipment; cavalry was notoriously the most complex arm of the service until the advent of modern war. Further, horses were not of much service for some time after being taken up from grass. Barrington wrote in 1758:

> I am convinced that if these regiments of dragoons embark next week, the horses just come from grass, and before there is time to put a little corn in their bellies, they will not afford the assistance wished or expected. This is the opinion of some very knowing officers, and though I

have never told them so, I cannot help thinking as they do, when I consider the sad condition the dragoons were in last year after an encampment without fatigue of six weeks near Salisbury.[55]

In 1766 the Adjutant-General directed the commanders of thirteen Cavalry regiments not to ruin the horses by violent manœuvres after they had been taken up from grass.[56] Cavalry horses required to do hard service always need corn, but in the eighteenth century army the need for economy forced the regiments to put them to grass. The Secretary at War's correspondence shows his concern at the awkward possibilities of the situation should riots happen unexpectedly and the cavalry become needed. Both Sir William Yonge[57] and Barrington ordered horses to be brought back to their regiments in a potentially riotous summer season, in spite of the 'inconvenience to the service' so often complained of in their letters.

In 1766, as the long-expected riots began in late summer and autumn, the War Office ordered a dragoon regiment at Worcester to take up horses from grass and march to aid the magistrates of Gloucester.[58] This was a discretionary order ('in case it shall appear to you necessary for the better execution of this service') from Barrington's secretary. From the letter book it appears that Barrington was away from the office from 12 to 23 September, and the Deputy Secretary had to handle the beginning of the crisis. Christopher D'Oyly was quite capable of dealing with ordinary business on his own, but he must have secured the approval of the Secretary of State before taking the drastic step of collecting in horses. At one stage even D'Oyly was away, and no order was possible until he had been discovered at Twickenham and brought back.[59]

Three days later Barrington ordered all dragoon regiments south of the Border to take up their horses from grass, although the usual time had not expired.[60] This may have been at the request of the Secretary of State, although there is no note of it;[61] Seymour Conway, with his army experience, had more conception of military realities than most other holders of that office.

Again in 1768 the cavalry were not even permitted to put all horses out. The Wilkite riots began before the appearance of the late spring grass, and, anticipating a difficult summer, Barrington ordered seven cavalry regiments, when the time came for turning out to grass, to keep in hand ready for instant call the horses of two troops per regiment, or a detachment equal to two troops.[62] They remained in readiness throughout the summer and must have materially added to the army's fodder bill.

BY-PASSING THE OFFICIAL PROCEDURE

Useful as the above devices might be for saving time, there existed more radical possibilities. If one of the middle-men in the J.P. – London – army channel could be cut out, a much more profitable saving might be achieved. Policies involving keeping troops ready and provided were all legitimate within the correct procedure governing the use of the military as a police force. But to go outside that procedure, designed as it was to give no offence to those who refused even to admit that the standing army had become engrafted onto the constitution, was to court severe political censure. Even so Barrington was determined to try, and his efforts fall into two distinct stages:

  1. his habit of by-passing the office of the Secretary of State, and
  2. his attempts to have the nearest local troops under general orders to intervene without sanction from London at all.

1. Communication between the Secretary of State's office and the War Office was the shortest link in the chain, and to cut it out would not achieve a great deal. It seems that the first example of this in Barrington's time was due to his lack of experience of procedure rather than for any desire for speed. The summer riots of 1756 were his first experience on any scale of the problem. Part of Cholmondeley's regiment (the Inniskilling Dragoons) was ordered by Barrington to Northampton and Nottingham to aid the magistrates;[63] his own instructions in this case came from Holdernesse, Secretary of State,[64] who was able to exercise some control from London because of the long duration of the riot.[65] Meanwhile further riots broke out in Sheffield, and were reported this time not to the Secretary of State, but to the War Office, by Rockingham, the Lord Lieutenant. Barrington acted quickly but on his own authority, and wrote to the officer commanding Chomondeley's at Nottingham that any assistance required at Sheffield or its neighbourhood was to be provided at once by him.[66] When Holdernesse found out he was not slow to convey his resentment to Rockingham:

> Give me leave, my dear Lord, to hint to you that I ought regularly to have been your correspondent upon a point of this nature, the Secretaries of State being the proper channel whenever the interposition of the Crown is found necessary to preserve the public peace.[67]

Rockingham's reply, expressing his genuine surprise, is interesting:

> I was quite ignorant, till your Lordship's Information, of the regular way of requesting the assistance of troops, or otherwise should certainly have applied through your Lordship, but indeed it seemed to me the most direct way to apply to the Secretary at War as the shortest and most speedy manner of attaining them.[68]

In the event the riots died away; a government inquiry into the price of corn in different market towns, obviously aimed at forestallers, 'frightened the badgers, and made them bring out their hoards very expeditiously',[69] and the fine weather appeared to promise a good harvest.[70] Thus no application ever had to be made to the troops at Nottingham; the possibility that such application might be made without the order or at least the knowledge and permission of the Secretary of State was sufficient to arouse his irritation. In 1756 it was thought improper, even though the development of the procedure was still recent enough for prominent persons such as Rockingham to be unaware of it. Holdernesse also wrote to Newcastle, on the occasion of the Warwickshire riots of the same month:

> I have also sent to the War Office to know particularly what troops have been sent to those parts, where they are ordered to march, under whose command etc. and I hope [you] will not think I do too much if I show my Lord Barrington the propriety and necessity that his Majesty's *civil* ministers should have immediate information of this kind.[71]

Barrington accepted the reproof,[72] but not the procedure implied by it. There were several ways in which it might be avoided. In the first place it was always possible, once the Secretary of State had passed to him the task of suppressing a particular riot, to deal with it himself without referring back to his master, so long as the disturbance was confined to that area. No Secretary of State would object to that, and he would receive reports on progress from the War Office from time to time as a matter of form and courtesy. But it was always a short step from this to the next stage, that of direct dealings between magistrate and War Office from the beginning of the riot, and although Barrington had undertaken not to offend Holdernesse again he seems to have been unable to accept the principle (or at best to have treated it lightly) that the Secretary of State was to be the guide. From there it was only another short step to becoming careless even about giving him information.

The spring riots of 1757 were handled by Barrington without any direction from the Secretaries.[73] This was a dividing line in the development of the procedure, and it remains a mystery; the disappearance of many war Office in-letters at this time adds to it. Barrington's opportunities for access to the Closet may have assisted the process,[74] also the fact that from 6 April to 9 June Holdernesse alone held the seals. Also, while some magistrates adhered to the proper procedure, many of them seemed not clear who initiated action from London and, wishing to save time, wrote directly to the Secretary at War from the first. Rockingham was not the only politician who wrote directly to the War Office; others who from their public position might be supposed to have been familiar with the correct course did so and thereby helped to undermine it. Lord Hardwicke in the midst of the 1757 militia riots wrote directly for help to Barrington.[75] In the same year the Duke of Bedford wrote to the Secretary at War enclosing a letter from 'the local gentlemen' describing the riots at Biggleswade. He wrote also but in much less detail to Holdernesse telling him that if he wanted more information he should apply to Barrington.[76] The proper procedure, as viewed by Holdernesse and his predecessors, was thereby reversed, but Holdernesse seems to have become tired of arguing and no reproof came from him, indeed I find no sign of any Secretary after 1756 trying to check this development; they all seemed to recognise that the War Office could be left to discharge the task, although they liked to be told what was happening. By 1765 Welbore Ellis was stating to a magistrate that his request for troops must not go to the local commander but must come to London *to the War Office*,[77] an example of the way in which procedures are adopted and quickly achieve the status of long tradition; Ellis stated what he regarded as an established procedure.

This is not to say that after 1756 the Secretary disappears from the scene so that the War Office becomes a sort of autonomous Home Office for riots. The 1761 Hexham militia riot, in which 21 people were killed, was reported to Holdernesse.[78] He wrote to Lord Ligonier, the Commander-in-Chief, saying that after discussing with the King the next day he would give him orders.[79] So eventually Barrington got his orders from Ligonier and reported back to Holdernesse.[80] As usual there is no consistency, and at times after 1756 the Secretary of State controlled simply because the case happened to have been sent to him in the first place.

In 1763 Saunders Welch, a London magistrate of many years' experience, who was well aware of the dangers of losing time, wrote directly to the Secretary at War, Welbore Ellis, to inform him of an armed riot.[81] In 1764 information of an expected riot came directly to him from the magistrates of Manchester.[82]

The serious riots on the part of the Spitalfields weavers in 1765 were dealt with at first by the War Office, but the Secretary intruded once the initial surprise was over. On 16 May Ellis moved a detachment of Guards from the Tower into the public houses in Spitalfields,[83] and the next day alerted the rest of the Guards in London[84] and a dragoon regiment at Lambeth.[85] On 17 May it was quieter; a mob estimated at 8000 collected in Palace Yard but molested no one, and by this time the Secretaries of State came in to control the operation, and are found instructing the Secretary at War as to the next orders he should give. Ellis felt sufficiently uneasy at his independent use of the formula 'It is His Majesty's Pleasure' to write to the king for retrospective approval of it:

I most humbly ask your Majesty's pardon for this presumption but having been obliged to issue so many orders in your Majesty's name yesterday and this day to your Guards and to Ancram's Horse,[86] and being called upon for more I find myself under the necessity to report to your Majesty what I have done and to know for my own justification whether I have your Majesty's approbation.[87]

Ellis was much more worried about the limits of his office than Barrington ever was, and the next day when the Secretaries instructed him to move in two more detachments of cavalry[88] he asked for the request in writing.

> This letter was drawn in consequence of my letting them know that I could not venture to issue such an order without your Majesty's express commands or a letter from their Lordships for my justification.[89]

The riots of 1766, beginning in August, became by early autumn so serious as to engross the attention of the King and the Privy Council as well as the Secretaries of State, but during the first few weeks J.P.s wrote to the War Office, not the Secretaries, and Barrington issued such orders as he saw fit. The first appearance of the Secretaries of State was not until the latter part of September, when Shelburne caused four companies of the 13th regiment at Salisbury to march to Devizes, and Seymour Conway ordered a squadron of dragoons to Gloucester, Stroud, Hampton and Painswick.[90] This was due not to any sudden desire of the Secretaries to assert themselves, but because Barrington was out of London and the Deputy Secretary, Christopher D'Oyly, was unwilling to overreach himself in the absence of his master.[91] Once again Barrington had been able, at least until the third week in September, to use a confused administrative situation to achieve speed and efficiency and to operate unhampered by the Secretary of State's office.

The forces of riot scored so many successes in London in 1768 that it is fair to ask if in fact anything had been learned about mob-breaking. It is true that tactically the troops made little impact until 10 May when their drastic action did at least secure the peace. But their failures were largely due to the doubts about the legality of the use of force which have been discussed elsewhere. From the point of view of strategy there were failures also; many mobs were never confronted at all by troops and raged quite unchecked through the streets in the night time. And this was in London, where the excuse of remoteness from the centre of control could not apply. But even in London the convention applied that the military should wait, if not for the Secretary of State at least for the magistrate before intervening. The reluctance of the magistrates to call for military help and the determination of the Secretary of State, Lord Weymouth, to be controller of events hampered the War Office. The record shows that Barrington was better prepared than Weymouth.[92]

The events of 1780 are in a class by themselves, for the disaster was of such magnitude that the entire operation passed into the hands of the Commander-in-Chief, Lord Amherst, and the role of the Secretary at War immediately declined to that of a department concerned with time tables and troop movements.

GENERAL ORDERS

At times Barrington toyed with more drastic courses to save time. The best course from the point of view of pure efficiency would have been to place all troops on general orders all the time to assist the local civil officers when requested. No one could seriously have suggested this in the eighteenth century, but something very like it was at times adopted as a temporary measure. There were plenty of precedents for this in the form of 'general orders for special purposes', some of them dating from a generation before. There was the never-ending smuggling duty, a service which would have been impossible for troops if they had been told to requisition a fresh authority to deal with each new liquor-running. Another example was the Haymarket Theatre guard, dating from 1727 when Henry Pelham was Secretary at War: whenever the Foot Guards were notified by the proprietor of a ball to be held there a detachment of 100 men was to be provided to keep order, without such notification passing through the usual channels. In other words not even the War Office would be involved.[93] In the same year a similar general directive was given to the detachment of guards stationed at the Tiltyard barracks to assist whenever called upon by the keeper of the Fleet Prison.[94] Pelham also ordered troops stationed at Northampton to give assistance when it was asked by the ranger and keepers of Salcey Forest to prevent the inhabitants from cutting firewood and destroying the deer;[95] similar orders were given for troops stationed near Whittlewood Forest.[96] No one objected to the setting of these precedents on constitutional grounds, if indeed they noticed them, and they provided a basis for a possible next step.

At other times Pelham showed that he was a friend to efficiency, and casual about possible political difficulties. The numerous disturbances in many areas in 1727 lasted for weeks, enabling some direction to be exercised from London in the usual way. A sudden outbreak in Newark however showed how some officers were still prepared to short-circuit the system. Part of a regiment quartered at Nottingham was marched to Newark in response to a direct appeal from a local magistrate, and it was several days before Pelham heard of it. The officer cannot have been easy about it for he wrote to the War Office for retrospective approval. Instead of a rebuke he received a reassuring reply and a cavalry reinforcement.[97] This curious episode seems to show that the convention of control from London was still imperfectly formed; a generation later an officer would not have been so ready to march without authority, even though a Secretary at War such as Barrington might have been willing to countenance it afterwards. It was precisely this formality, which developed in the thirties and forties, that was later to make life so difficult for Barrington. Magistrates were less cautious; the Leeds magistrates in 1753 wrote directly to the commanders of troops at York and Manchester for protection of a turnpike, and only then wrote to London excusing their request, 'as it would be dangerous to be without troops till orders could be dispatched to Manchester from the War Office'.[98] There were other exceptions to the procedure, more apparent than real. Once orders had gone out to a local commander from London he might act in aid several times in the course of a few weeks without writing to London for authority, as mentioned above. Officers were not always sure about it, especially if the original riot died down altogether before breaking out again, or if it began in one town and proceeded to another. At such times they always wrote nervously for approval.[99]

In general by 1755 the convention of application to London had been established and it had become irregular to disturb it. But all Barrington's experience tended to show how dangerous delays were, and he began to cast around for methods of anticipating and preparing for trouble. The most remarkable instance of this was the secret order drawn in January 1766. In view of the economic situation 1766 was obviously going to be a trying year, but the dangers of the course he was taking were considerable, and he went about the task cautiously. The order went out to seven cavalry units and three detachments of foot in well-known trouble-spots in South Britain to assist magistrates of the area in which they were quartered when invited to do so by them; the wording of the order does not differ from the usual form[100] except in its preamble, which includes the novel words 'in case of any riots or disturbances that may happen at or in the neighbourhood of your quarters', and the only difference was that there had not as yet been any riot. A covering letter accompanied the orders:

> The present state of things makes it apprehended that many manufac-
> turers must soon be discharged in many parts of the kingdom. Poor men
> out of employment especially when they are in large numbers, generally
> grow riotous, and too often are above the management of the civil
> magistrate, unassisted by military force. The safe and usual method of the
> War Office has been to defer any order till application should be made to
> it in form, but there are occasions when men in public employment
> should venture for the public good, and prevent delays when delays
> might be dangerous.
> I have therefore unasked, but not uninformed of the present state of
> your neighbourhood, sent you an order herewith enclosed, which I
> desire you will keep entirely to yourself, till the civil magistrate shall
> apply to you for assistance. If that never happens, the order had better
> never be known and therefore it is not yet entered in my books, or
> communicated to more than one or two in my office. I trust safely to your
> good sense and discretion.[101]

The long-expected storm of riots did not break until August, and the weakness of Barrington's scheme becomes at once apparent. He had told the officers but not the magistrates. He had even avoided telling the

Secretary of State's office. He had in fact been too discreet. So accustomed were magistrates by this date to the order and form of things that in most cases they did not ask the nearest troops directly, anticipating the usual stiff reply, but wrote very properly to London. The usual delays ensued. Only one officer received a direct application from a magistrate to which he was able to respond in the spirit of the secret instructions. Lt.-Col. Warde sent a detachment of the 4th Dragoons from Worcester to Gloucester, and Barrington later supplied an additional authority for making detachments as needed.[102] By the last week in September riots had become widespread in England, and Barrington issued the same order as before, but told commanders to inform magistrates of it. The result was more successful. As the riots had already begun it was safe for this latter order to be entered on the letter-books.[103]

Although they were hardly successful, the orders of January represent Barrington's boldest bid to escape from the impasse in which he found himself. The orders were never copied into the letter-books, and now exist as several sewn pages in a parcel at the Public Record Office. There may have been others of a similar nature which a public inquiry would never have uncovered. Two years later, during the controversy after the St George's Fields Riots, Barrington was pressed in the Commons by Colonel Barré to open the War Office books, and declared himself ready to do so: 'I am not in the least flurried. My sleep will not be discomposed. I have done nothing but what I am justified in.'[104] More accurately he had done nothing that was going to be found out.

TEMPORARY COMMANDERS IN RIOT AREAS

The placing of several regiments or parts of regiments over a large area under the most senior commander present was another step which would seem an obvious one towards efficiency, but which evolved gradually and with misgivings on the part of the War Office. In 1756 Lt.-Col. Harvey of the Inniskilling Dragoons had detachments of two other regiments put under his command.[105] Later in the same year Wolfe received three companies from another regiment to help cope with the West Country riots. Neither of these expedients worked well, as the commanders of the subordinate units continued to receive orders from London as well as from their local commander.

Barrington learned a good deal from 1756; his handling of the 1766 riots in this respect as in many others, was much more decisive. By the end of September riots had appeared in many parts of England, and Lt.-Col. Bonham was ordered from Blandford with two troops of his dragoons (Albemarle's) to the West Country. Six companies of infantry (the 13th) were in the area, four at Devizes and two at Trowbridge. These were added to his command. 'You will agree that so many troops of different sorts require a field officer's presence.'[106] As the riots grew and more troops were moved into the West, two of the Devizes companies were removed to Chippenham and Calne.[107] The regiment's commander happened to be with this detachment at the time, and wrote to the War Office objecting to being subordinated to Bonham; Barrington, who was usually careful of the feelings of prickly officers, rescinded his order:

> As I judged it necessary that a field officer should be stationed at the Devizes, I had given directions to Colonel Bonham to repair to that place, but without knowing that the detachment from your regiment was under your command. As I am perfectly satisfied with your attention to the service, I have signified to Colonel Bonham, that his presence will not be necessary at the Devizes, and shall for the future as long as it may be necessary direct all orders to your care.[108]

The companies at Bradford and Trowbridge were told to tear up their orders of the 19th and follow the instructions of Major Hill. In spite of this false beginning Barrington was determined not to let his design founder because of the objections of one touchy officer, and two days later appointed Lt.-Col. Warde to command the detachments in the West. 'It is thought highly expedient that they should all be under the command of one officer of judgement and experience.'[109] Warde's command consisted of detachments of two cavalry regiments and two of infantry, in districts as far apart as Ottery St Mary in the west and Winchester in the east, and a detailed plan of deployment with copies of all orders were sent to him. Barrington also found time to write to the commander of the 13th Foot in soothing terms: 'This step is thought necessary on account of the large detachments of horse who properly require the command of a horse officer, and not from any doubt of your care and judgement.'[110]

After this Warde was left to dispose of his area as he might,[111] and Barrington was able to turn to other towns who were pressing him for help. Within a fortnight the West was quiet, but the cautious Secretary at War did not start to move some of the troops from the area until early in November, by which time he could report to the Secretary of State that the disturbances were 'tolerably well settled'.[112]

The London riots of 1765 also raised the question of unity of command in and around London. The Dukes of Cumberland and Richmond, Lord Granby, and the Adjutant-General were suggested for the command[113] but the weavers suddenly subsided and no appointment was ever made. None of these suggestions however came from the War Office. Neither was it concerned with the appointments in respect of certain areas in 1780, as the conduct of the operation quickly passed to the Commander in Chief.

To sum up, the odious task of aid to the civil power was performed by the Secretaries at War in the period with prudence and care. Barrington, the

Secretary with the best record, showed that the War Office under determined direction could rise above the merely formal or procedural function and assume one that can properly be called strategic. In his desire not to offend local susceptibilities or to exacerbate an existing situation he acted with tact in troop deployment. He knew well that the sight of a red coat was at times as likely to cause as to allay a riot. In the harassing days of 1768 he refused the magistrates' request for light horse to be quartered in the inns on the Surrey side; assistance would be sent across the river 'if you should judge that Horse are absolutely necessary'.[114] The attitude of the populace of the Borough of Southwark if it was learned that horse were quartered in their midst was too readily predictable, and Barrington preferred to delay. At other times he refused to march troops into areas where magistrates expected riots, preferring to give orders for them to be ready to march at short notice, or even moving them unobtrusively into areas nearby. This was in contrast to the policy of earlier Secretaries at War (e.g. Yonge, Strickland, Henry Fox), who obligingly sent troops on mere rumour. By the nineteenth century this cautious technique of Barrington had become an accepted axiom of conduct in cases of disorder. The plan drawn up by the Duke of Wellington just before the great Chartist rally of 1848 involved the placing of troops in concealment but ready for instant march to threatened points if the civil power was overwhelmed: the memorandum concluded 'but if not required it would be better not to shew them'.[115]

When Barrington was not in office it is clear from the continuity of policy that the residual expertise of the office (which he very largely helped to develop) was available to other Secretaries at War – Townshend, Ellis, Jenkinson – in the form of written precedents, and at times, for those who were willing to listen, the discreet word of advice.[116] A year after he had quitted office he went to much trouble to organise an association of propertied men in Berkshire, where his country house was situated, in response to another wave of public disorder. His plan owed much to views formed in his years at the War Office. In order to avoid constant calls for military help, the civil power must be strengthened by being more prepared than hitherto, instead of trying to deal with each outbreak in isolation as it occurred. Every magistrate and man of property, including farmers – those, in his words, 'who have something to lose' – should sign and subscribe to the association, and a handlist of members should be circulated, so that any threatened proprietor would know at once whence he could expect support. Volunteer companies were to be armed and taught the musket exercise.[117] This was precisely the sort of system of self-help that Barrington had wished to see in the provinces when he was at the War Office: a forewarned network of dependable magistrates and gentlemen as mutually-supporting strongpoints in a hostile countryside, grimly determined not to call for soldiers except as a last resort. The obvious drawback to the scheme was that it must have appeared as an unfortunate and objectionable sharpening of class-alignments, but Barrington was not the man, either by training or temperament, to pay much attention to this. William Blackstone and Barrington's brother, the Bishop of Landaff, gave support, and several magnates including the Duke of Marlborough subscribed sums of up to £500. Drilling and training of recruits went on until the end of the year, although a combination of local apathy and opposition on detailed points caused it to be dropped.

7 The Rural Riots of 1756

For the guardians of public order 1756 was at first a peaceable year. The aftermath of riots at Carmarthen of the previous December hung over for a space,[1] but the Secretary of State's office and the War Office were not agitated by riots or rumours of riots throughout the spring and early summer, a longer period of domestic quiet than eighteenth-century government could usually expect. London itself, always a plague spot for riots, was quiet, and remained so throughout the year, a circumstance referred to by Sir John Fielding in a letter to the Secretary of State, to reinforce his claim for moneys owed to him and his colleagues:

> And we flatter ourselves that the great tranquillity, and freedom from outrages, that this Metropolis has, for this last twelvemonth, enjoyed, will be an ample testimony to your Grace of our care, diligence and activity in the execution of our respective offices.[2]

In fact apart from the Carmarthen riot, which was over by January, and an isolated riot at the Haslar Hospital, no calls were made at all upon the army for controlling riots until the end of August. The early part of the year was taken up with the ordinary routine of the army at home. Smugglers were chased, detachments were moved away from areas where there were by-elections, race-meetings and fairs, or simply where they had become so unpopular as to be intolerable, the cavalry put out its horses to grass, and nothing more notable appears on the letter-books than the escorting with many precautions of the unhappy Admiral Byng to London.

The beginning of the war however was followed shortly by a widespread breakdown in public order, due to the high price of provisions,[3] and eventually 1756 became almost as bad a year for riots as any in the century. Government was always sensitive about riots in wartime; considerable forces had to be retained at home which might usefully have been employed in theatres of war overseas, or sent to areas of disturbance when they should have been on home defence duties in coastal areas, but in the absence of any other peace-keeping force there was no choice, as the events were to show.

The forces available for these operations appeared on paper to be adequate. The 1748 reductions aimed at an establishment of about 30,000 men, of which about 19,000 were stationed at home. After Christmas 1755 work was begun on the construction of ten new regiments (50–59th), and a light troop was added to each of the eleven regiments of dragoons. In the last few months of peace the army at home south of the Scottish border totalled nine cavalry regiments, and the Horse Grenadier Guards and Blues in London,[4] and 22 regiments of foot, and the three regiments of Foot Guards in London.[5] Two cavalry regiments and seven regiments of foot were stationed north of the border but could not intervene in riots in England without being formally taken off the Scottish establishment, as was in fact done in 1768.[6] There were also 49 companies of invalids scattered among 18 different forts.[7]

As war approached some acute observers considered these numbers perilously small. An Admiralty memorandum presented in September, but referring to the strategic situation in March, showed a wide appreciation of army matters:

> At this time great bodies of troops were assembling along the French coast particularly in Normandy and Brittany: and the army in England was between 2 and 3,000 men short of its number; deducting from that army the Horse Guards and four battalions of Foot Guards which could not stir from London; also between 3 and 4,000 invalids employed in garrison; and the new regiments which were then raising, were incompleat and without the least training; there remained no more than about 13,000 foot and 4,000 dragoons to take the field on any emergency.
>
> The Hessians were but just required, the Dutch were not expected, the Hanoverians were not moved for, and the earliest that any of the foreign troops could be here was in May.[8]

On 23 March it was resolved to retain in garrison 6988 men, and to cause 15,370 to be 'fit and ready to take the field'. In fact they did not do so, partly because of the widespread rioting in England, and partly because of the fears of a French invasion, fears which were expressed before war was declared. As early as February it was reported from The Hague that Marshal Belleisle, seconded by d'Argenson, had proposed a descent on the South Coast, in conjunction with naval movements to draw off the British Fleet.[9] The French expected help from the smugglers of Kent, Sussex, and Hampshire.[10]

These factors, added to the slowness of recruitment and the poor state into which the army had been allowed to lapse, account for the fact that little was achieved in the war during this year or in 1757. That was the year of Klosterseven and other reverses; it was also a year of riots on an even bigger scale than 1756, absorbing greater numbers of men. Makers of grand strategy in these years, however ambitious their plans for distant theatres of war, had to consider the demands of civil security, however irksome.

About the middle of August riots broke out in a number of parts of Staffordshire and Warwickshire. On the 17th the newspapers reported that mobs were active at Walsall, Wednesbury, Nuneaton (where one man was shot, presumably by a mill-owner), Atherstone, Polesworth, Tamworth, Baddesley Ensor, and Hartshill.[11] A mob, which had assembled at Werrybridge near Walsall, pulled down a large corn mill, 'alleging that the owner is a great engrosser of corn'.[12] The Atherstone riot was near enough to Leicester (fifteen miles) to alarm its Recorder, who wrote to the Secretary of State, Fox – 'not doubting but your wisdom will find means to nip this plant of sedition in the bud, before it has taken too deep root. I fear there is too great a propensity in the populace to follow the example of these rioters' – but made no suggestion as to the means of suppression,[13] a contrast to most magistrates, who bluntly asked for soldiers at such times. Enclosed with his letter was a long account of an eye-witness. The mob had pulled down a meeting house, two Quakers having bought up all the corn of the district, and had destroyed large quantities of grain, bacon and other foodstuffs. At Nuneaton they had extorted contributions from property owners, at Polesworth mills had been partially or wholly destroyed, at Hartshill they had robbed and were marching to Tamworth and Burton-on-Trent, where the magistrates expected them to be joined by mobs from Birmingham, Walsall and other large populous places. They promised a visit to Leicester the following Saturday.[14]

A fair impression of the progress of a rural food riot appears in this and many other valuable even if colourful accounts of the time; the news of the rising spreads quickly through the area and crystallises the half-formed resentments and intentions of a deprived group, the mob itself appears, marching from place to place, coalescing with other mobs, gathering food and money for its sustenance and arms for its protection, and operating against the objects of its hatred with a violence and efficiency that at first disarms the forces of law and order.

Another account from an anonymous source, this time to Lord Holdernesse, the Secretary for the Northern Department, described the same mob 'that paid not the least regard to the reading of the proclamation', and forecast, quite correctly, further difficulties:

> I am credibly informed that corn is dearer farther north, and I fear every post we shall hear of disturbances in other parts of the kingdom, and if the future part of this summer should prove as rainy as of late, corn must be inevitably very dear.[15]

These letters, dated 19 and 21 August, took some time to reach London; the hundred miles of road were no doubt rendered more difficult than usual by the same continuous downpour which ruined the 1756 harvest, and the War Office did not issue orders until 24 August.

Meanwhile the local J.P.s were to show that the theory, often advanced by the central government, that the local civil power should be equal to these emergencies, had some substance. Sir John Willes, the Lord Chief Justice, who was on assize at Warwick, rallied the civil magistrates, told them he was against sending for soldiers on general principles and also because news of it might get to France and encourage her to invade. When rioters were brought before him, he sentenced four to death, two of whom were respited for a week, when they would be pardoned if the insurrection was over.[16] Willes' scheme, as notable for its velocity as for its novelty, resembles the irregular expedients of a general striving to keep order during a retreat, but it was effective; the execution of the first two rioters was carried out on 25 August after all the county constables had been brought in to assist, and the rioting gave way to an uneasy quiet, although the magistrates did not doubt that troops were still needed to preserve it.

However the War Office had already ordered the commander of Cholmondeley's regiment[17] to Leicester,

> or to any other place or places as you shall be informed the rioters may be at, or should the said rioters disperse themselves into parties, you make such detachments as you shall think proper and be aiding and assisting to the civil magistrates in suppressing any riots and disturbances that may happen, and in apprehending the said rioters, for which purpose it is H.M's further pleasure that the said troops shall be quartered in such place or places as you shall think convenient from time to time for the more effectually answering the purposes aforesaid.[18]

A detachment of invalids already in Leicester were also ordered to assist if required by the civil power.[19]

Holdernesse, the Secretary for the North, was informed of the riot, but as mentioned above Fox acted first. When he heard of it Holdernesse seems to have been unaware that Barrington's troop movements had been sanctioned by his brother Secretary. He wrote to the War Office to enquire what units had been sent to the area, and to remind Barrington that the Secretary of State's office ought to have immediate information of the marching orders.[20]

Holdernesse evidently thought that he had discovered an instance of the War Office dealing directly with magistrates, a point on which some Secretaries of State were more sensitive than others, but it was merely an instance of insufficient liaison between the two Secretaries of State. This was only one example of many contradictory policies and misunderstandings in the Departments until the reorganisation of the offices in 1782.

Although Fox had taken the initiative it soon passed to Holdernesse, – it is not clear from the extant documents how this happened – and he handled the 1756 riots himself. He began by writing to the *custodes rotulorum* of the counties affected for more authentic accounts, with affidavits and statements from the J.P.s concerned.[21] He also wrote to the Post Master

General to ask him to make enquiry of post masters in all the principal market towns of the country as to the current prices of corn.[22]

Meanwhile Barrington's order, with its wide discretionary powers, had hardly been issued before the disturbance abruptly shifted to Nottingham, 25 miles north of Leicester. The first news came on this occasion to Holdernesse, and its tone throws light on the doubtful quality of the magistrates of Nottingham. A procession of colliers had appeared in the morning, armed with hatchets and pickaxes. At first the magistrates felt strong enough to read the Riot Act proclamation and seize three ringleaders, but this spurt of courage evaporated and they began to weaken under pressure from the mob that their fellows should be released to them. Eventually they capitulated to this pressure; their letter to the Secretary of State is filled with quaint self-justifications on this head[23] and their conduct provides a striking contrast with that of the local civil forces in Warwickshire a few days before, which had rallied and become effective, at least in the short term, under the inspiration of a determined if unorthodox circuit-judge.

It was clear that the Nottingham riot was the more serious, and the accounts later received in London seemed to confirm the impression gathered from Willes' letters that the Staffordshire disturbance was almost over.[24] Holdernesse therefore wrote to the War Office enclosing the timid letter from the Nottingham magistrates, with the King's order to march a sufficient number of troops from the nearest area and aid the civil power,[25] and sent a reassuring message to Nottingham.[26] The Duke of Cumberland, the Commander-in-Chief, was not in London:

> as the Duke is out of town and there seems to be no time to be lost I propose to write immediately to Lord Barrington (unless your Grace disapproves it) directing him in the usual office form to send some troops to Nottingham without loss of time.[27]

Barrington thereupon moved the three troops of the Inniskilling Dragoons away from the area now presumed to be quiet and towards Nottingham.[28] He had not been long at the War Office, but there are indications at this date of early attempts on his part to develop the effectiveness of his department's role, and instructions of a type not found before are found in the letter accompanying the marching orders to Lt.-Col. Edward Harvey:

> I desire you would send me frequent accounts of your proceedings in the Service upon which you are sent, and also such intelligence as you may receive concerning any riots in the country, and the knowledge of which you may think expedient for his Majesty's service; if anything extraordinary occurs you will send it by express.[29]

Barrington's widely-drafted instructions to Harvey with discretion to go in pursuit of rioters, 'who are of a very ambulatory nature', shows that he had already grasped one of the essentials of the rural riot. He regarded Willes' presence in the area as a happy accident of which he could take advantage, and wrote to tell him that Harvey 'who is very much a man of sense' would come to or stay away from any place at a hint from the Lord Chief Justice.[30]

Only one of Harvey's reports has survived; perhaps there was only one. He appears as a not entirely unsympathetic observer of the distresses of the colliers but would have liked to see some exemplary punishments to save bloodshed. He reported that they could raise 300 rioters in two hours, that corn was very dear, and that the local gentlemen were of no use to him, three more classic factors of the rural riot. His account of a parley with the mob is in the same terms as that of the Mayor of Nottingham included in Chapter 13.[31] As a measure of safety the remainder of the Inniskilling Dragoons (except the 7th or light troop) was moved from their quarters at Egham to Northampton to watch the Leicester-Warwick border.[32] This precautionary reserve was fortunately placed, for the quiescence of the area was only apparent and temporary, and Coventry was the next area to be affected.

At Nottingham the appearance of troops helped to allay the unrest. The Lord Chief Justice, still at his lodgings near Warwick, and well informed of events to the north, disapproved of this move, but with qualifications:

> . . . [I] am satisfied that if the civil magistrates would have done their duty with the courage and resolution that they ought, they might easily have quelled it without the assistance of a military force. But since I find that they were so intimidated, as to desire it, to be sure, it could not be refused them and I hope that it will soon have its desired effect, and without bloodshed.[33]

Harvey's troops marched into Nottingham on the morning of 30 August, and found that no riot had taken place since the first alarm of the 25th. The J.P.s were pleased to see him, however, and began the task of making arrests, which they had not cared to venture upon before. He wrote back to London:

> I shall acquaint the magistrates of Derby and all other places adjacent where there is a probability of disturbance that I have troops here ready to be detached at a moments warning if required. . . .
> I shall make it my particular business to enquire in the different parts of the country where the troops may be most useful, and if required by the civil magistrates immediately march[34]

The view that the real danger was around Nottingham seemed to be reinforced by a further letter from its magistrates, written before the arrival of the dragoons, with more accounts of mill-breaking, in which, so it was alleged, property belonging to friends of King and Government particularly suffered. At that stage the property-owners still did not feel strong enough in the absence of military force to do more than apply palliatives; some mills escaped by giving bribes, and an advertisement was circulated calling upon all setters-up of corn to bring in their supplies to market.[35]

Hard on the heels of the Nottingham riot came news from the area first affected. An express from the Mayor of Coventry to Holdernesse[36] described a riot of 300 colliers of the area. The magistrates had persuaded them to go home with assurances about prices, but it was rumoured that they intended coming in next market day. As before, the magistrates detected, or thought they detected, Jacobite sympathisers all about them:

> . . . I am informed by credible witness at some of the late riots in the county that the ringleaders being asked where such proceedings would end they answered they knew not till the Pretender came to stop them.[37]

Jacobite scares were common, and the Secretaries' papers were full of such alarms, which engrossed a disproportionate amount of their time. Newcastle had already considered the point, and its possible wider implications. The riots, he wrote

> are bad symptoms, and though perhaps not immediate proofs of disaffection or Jacobitism, will be interpreted as such abroad, and will particularly favour the King of Prussia's opinion that Marshal Belleisle had some secret correspondence and encouragement from hence.[38]

The War Office instructions went out to the dragoons at Northampton to intervene in aid of the magistrates when asked to do so,[39] and the light troop previously left behind on smuggling duty was ordered to join the regiment there.[40] Once again the question of a reserve was uppermost in Barrington's mind. Holdernesse wrote to the Mayor of Coventry on the same day to tell them of the availability of troops but recommended that he first endeavour 'to preserve peace, and good order, by the usual and common methods of justice',[41] a common enough wilderness-cry of mid-eighteenth-century Secretaries of State, and not entirely a fanciful idea – as the events in Warwickshire a few days before had shown.

As these disturbances spread the scope of the strategical problem for the War Office also developed, and the orders begin to contain contingent precautions; Major Hepburne must inform the War Office and Lt.-Col. Harvey if he moves into Coventry or elsewhere and leaves Northampton uncovered; the light troop must not move from quarters until relieved; every action provokes another reaction, delayed in each case by 24 or 48 hours, in an army too small for the task and widely scattered over the kingdom. When the Derby disturbances began in the first week in

September Barrington would not allow Hepburne to leave Coventry, which he was convinced would need further protection, until relieved by fresh troops. Thus a second cavalry regiment now became involved, the Third or King's Own Dragoons (Albemarle's), three troops of which were ordered from Henley and Reading.[42] Barrington's instinct was correct, for Holdernesse's correspondence was again puncutated by another Cassandra brief from the watchful but anonymous writer in the Warwickshire area describing fresh riots. The Bedworth colliers were up again; many of them were out of work because the coal could not be moved from the area on account of the condition of the roads, another testimony to the part played by the weather in these events.[43] But by the same post came news from Nottingham that upon Harvey's appearance rioting had ceased.[44] With the help of small detachments from his regiment the arrest of a few rioters was effected, including one of the men rescued by the mob on 25 August. The magistrate was in no doubt about the efficacy of military intervention:

> The country justice who indorsed my warrant is fled for fear of the colliers: there's scarce a constable that durst execute a warrant; it is only the troops that keep the colliers in awe. We see here by experience that there's a prevailing effeminacy among our county gentlemen: they would make bad captains over a militia: and then their men, however well regulated, would be of no service.[45]

Two days later the colliers came to a confrontation with the army and retired without force being used on either side; the incident is quoted at length in the chapter on Tactics.[46] Seven arrests were made, and the disturbances at Nottingham died down, the subsequent correspondence being confined to legal discussion between the Secretary of State, with the help of the Attorney-General, and the magistrates, as to whether or not the men were admissible to bail, and with what offence they should be charged. Although outside the scope of this chapter these letters provide another noteworthy example of the confusion produced by the Riot Act in the minds of magistrates as to whether acts done within the statutory period of one hour after proclamation could be felonies 'within the Act' when in fact these acts (destruction of mills, etc.) were obviously felonies, Act or no Act.[47]

At Coventry the Mayor, John Hewitt, had taken every step he could think of to give the rioters a 'warm reception' without military force, which he had resolved not to requisition; he got together 240 constables and assistants, sent out scouts to collieries to distribute printed abstracts of acts against forestalling, and in general showed what an energetic justice of peace might achieve. His brother magistrates were not so confident, and the gentlemen of the corporation, upon opening Barrington's express letter offering help (without Hewitt's knowledge) immediately sent for soldiers, 'who made such haste that they was at Coventry by 12 o'clock or sooner on Friday. All hath been quiet since and most of the colliers gone to work.'[48] The troops mentioned were the detachment of Major Hepburne placed at Northampton with orders to go to Coventry if called for. So far the War Office plans had been successful.

The Mayor seems to have been indignant at the action of his colleagues; he had gone away to meet the gentlemen of the county at Warwick races and remained there on Friday night for the ball. He came into Coventry at dawn the next morning to be in time for an early meeting of constables and was surprised to find that a quartermaster had arrived from Northampton to arrange for the billeting of the approaching cavalry.

> I then repented my permitting the opening my express, and blamed in myself the trusting my proceedings with any one, and which taught me a lesson I never after forgot, on matters which required secrecy, as well as resolution in the execution and direction.[49]

The same anonymous correspondent observed the events of the same day with satisfaction. From his letter the Mayor's original plan becomes clearer. The magistrates hoped to meet the invading colliers at the end of the town and settle the dispute before the townspeople joined them, but the cavalry appeared before the expected time of arrival of the colliers, after which

> . . . fear was vanished from every well disposed person, and hope from everyone that was ill disposed, and though some warm fools among the Tories objected to military force coming, yet I myself heard some of the most moderate of them approve of it. The middle price of wheat was five shillings and sixpence a bushel, and we have had warm dry weather since Wednesday August 25th.[50]

It is not clear from extant documents how the news of the Derby disturbances came to London. The order to cover Derby with Major Hepburne's detachment proceeded from the Duke of Cumberland by way of Barrington, and the information may well have by-passed the Secretary of State and come straight to the War Office.[51] As the situation in the Midlands worsened more troops were moved in; the remainder of Albemarle's and part of Cholmondeley's were ordered away from Basingstoke, and in anticipation of a long stay the quartermasters of the former regiment were ordered up with the baggage.[52]

It was fortunate for the army that there was rarely any concerted plan among rioters during this century; the miseries of the people over a wide area would often bring about the appearance of a general rising of the sort that the government feared, but it was not part of any system among rioters. At this stage, as the more southerly area subsided, the dragoons there were told to give help to Harvey if he needed it.[53] He had been roughly handled in Derby, and two of his soldiers fired, without (it seems) being ordered to do so.[54]

A lull in the disorders ensued after the second week in September. The area from Derby in the north to Northampton in the south, and as far west as Wednesbury, had been pacified after a fashion, at least so as to prevent open breach of the peace, and detachments of troops remained at points within that area. No further instructions came from the Secretary of State to the War Office, nor were any needed from the War Office to the troops, who had the orders they needed already. When the disturbances broke out again it is noteworthy that the Secretaries only gave directions very intermittently and at times left the strategic direction in the hands of the Secretary at War, preferring to confine themselves to correspondence with the Law Officers of the Crown about prosecutions. It seems that the Secretaries had begun to realize that there was little political danger or constitutional impropriety in permitting a civilian official such as Barrington to act in suppressing domestic riots, that he was competent to do so, and that they disliked the task in any case.

About the middle of October riots began in the clothing districts of Gloucestershire. It would be more accurate to say that a period of unrest and strikes arising from wages-disputes between masters and men lasting for several weeks had culminated by that date in riots.[55] The Lord Lieutenant, Lord Ducie, sent to Fox, who asked Barrington to send troops.[56] It was not thought safe yet to strip the midland area of troops, and instead orders went for the march of three companies of Howard's (3rd Foot or Buffs) and three of Kingsley's (20th Foot) with James Wolfe to be quartered at Stroud, Painswick, Dursley, Wotton-under-Edge and Tetbury or anywhere else that the magistrates might require.[57] The War Office expected the disturbances to spread throughout the clothing areas of the West, but Somerset was only mildly affected some weeks later, and Wiltshire remained quiet.[58]

Wolfe was relieved to move, his camp at Blandford having become unhealthy during the autumn rains that were so much a feature of this unhappy year.[59] Several of his letters survive in the Holdernesse bundle of the Duke of Leeds papers in the Egerton Series, and provide a much-needed account of strategy at the local level. They came to Barrington in the first instance and he sent them to Fox, but Fox was more preoccupied with his own political destiny at that date and 'sent them back without taking any notice of the contents'.[60] Feeling that they ought to be noted by a Secretary of State Barrington sent them to Holdernesse. From these letters it appears that Wolfe arrived on Monday 25 October[61] after a march of five days, and immediately consulted with the magistrates for the best distribution of troops to secure arrests. The situation was confused and Wolfe's task was a difficult one; he also had a certain sympathy with the wretched situation of the weavers.[62] Many of the clothiers had left the district on pretence of business, and the J.P.s were not uniformly helpful, 'having, perhaps, different interests to pursue'.[63] Some clothiers had schemes for settling the disputes but were unwilling to take the first step 'because they will not submit to their own servants'.[64] Weaving was the key industry of the area, and he forecast a complete standstill in a week or two, with upwards of 25,000 people in want. But although he observed all this accurately enough, Wolfe could do little but stand by and hope that the two sides would negotiate, and make his own preparations on a pessimistic view of the outcome. This task at least he was determined to perform with care, and the (perhaps not disinterested) advice of magistrates was not always taken. One of them proposed quartering a company at Tetbury, but he brushed aside the advice. There were few weavers and no disturbances there; Hampton, he suggested, was a meeting place of rioters and a better place to quarter a company.

> I have told the justices that it would be a wiser step, to prevent mischief, by the presence of a larger body of troops for a short time, than to use the weapons of a few to disperse the rioters, and that when these disorders were at an end, the quarters might be extended for the ease of the people.[65]

Barrington was usually prepared to allow the officer in the field to know best, and Wolfe was told to take up whatever quarters he thought right.[66] He reported that he had done so with a view to combining the comfort of the populace with the requirements of security.[67] As an experienced commander he knew that he had a narrow path to tread: the loathing of the householder for the troops billeted on him would only very grudgingly be suspended, even in dire need, if those troops gave as little offence as possible. Altogether he was not happy about the posture of events in the area. Although the wages had at last been raised at a meeting some were not in agreement, and others doubted if the magistrates could make the new arrangement work. He did not relax his precautions, although he remained sympathetic towards the weavers, whose claim he thought a just one: 'I am afraid they will proceed to some extravagancies, and force the magistrates to use our weapons against them, which would give me a great deal of concern.'[68]

As before, the target would not remain stationary, and Wolfe had hardly garrisoned the area assigned to him when he was told by Barrington to be prepared to send help into Shropshire if it was asked for by the civil authorities.[69] The complaint in this case came from a magistrate to the Secretary of State's office.[70] Again Barrington was aware that Wolfe's force might become inadequate for its task, and moved seven more companies of Kingsley's from Plymouth to join those already in the area, with the result that two companies were at Cirencester, two at Tetbury, one at Sodbury, one at Wotton-under-Edge, one at Dursley, one at Hampton, one at Stroud, and one at Painswick.[71]

In spite of this firm beginning, what followed can hardly be called a success story. Barrington was still learning his job, and the episode shows the consequences of even an apparently minor oversight in communication. The first order to Wolfe (13 November) was rightly understood by him to be discretionary, and he undertook to help if the magistrates of Shropshire sent for him, either to go himself with 200 men, or to send a captain with 120 or 130 as occasion seemed to require.[72] Unfortunately no information went to the magistrates that orders of this kind were out, and they were unaware that it was now up to them to send for Wolfe. Consequently they waited anxiously for several more days and wrote again on 24 November to Holdernesse in even greater distress, complaining that no soldiers had arrived,

> though in consequence of Lord Barrington's letter to Your Lordship, the gentlemen depended upon having a party of them to support their endeavours for the public service. . . . The disappointment which has followed it, has given great uneasiness; the whole country being still under no inconsiderable alarm.[73]

In fact help was already on the way, for Barrington himself had received direct news from the sheriff of the turn of events in Shropshire, and had sent positive orders on 19 November to march to the area,[74] but the usual delays, made worse no doubt by the rains, meant that by the 24th they had not appeared. Arguably it was Holdernesse's part as Secretary of State to keep his magistrates informed, but he blamed Barrington. His letter of complaint has not survived; Barrington's reply exculpating himself and hinting at Holdernesse's responsibilities explained that definite orders to intervene had gone out on 19 November,

> and if detachments were not sent before into Shropshire it is the fault of the civil magistrates, who knew by my letter to your Lordship that the commanding officers both in Gloucestershire and at Coventry were ordered to furnish them with troops on their requisition.[75]

Meanwhile the soldiers arrived and put down the riots many days after they had started and after the usual damage to property had resulted. The impression of failure was not mitigated by the inability of the magistrates to mount a prosecution because of insufficient evidence.[76]

In Gloucestershire Wolfe reported that the new wage rates had not 'been productive of that tranquillity which some people expected', and that the soldiers were assisting constables in making arrests, although the ringleaders had in many cases disappeared.[77] His occupation of the area was fairly uneventful, with none of the ugly confrontations between mob and soldiery so common in mid-century riots, and provided a good example of the successful strategy of tactfully controlling an area by the presence of troops.

The midland area was still not thought to be safe, and a considerable reserve was dispatched in the second half of November from Southampton. The existing garrison of the area would have found itself overborne if the riots, widespread so far but still sporadic, had begun again more or less at the same time. The troops employed (part of the repatriated Minorca garrison) were disembarking at Southampton when the orders reached them, and cannot have been in good condition for route-marching. One regiment (the 23rd Foot) was sent to Leicester, another (the 24th Foot) was divided so that five companies could be sent to Derby and five to Nottingham, and another regiment (the 34th Foot) was sent to Norwich.[78] There had not yet been any riots in this latter quarter, and the sources indicate no fears of riots, but it was a well-known spot for disorder and could not be left out of the War Office calculations.

At the same time reports of riots came from the Somerset part of the clothing area, and four companies of Wolfe's (8th Foot) were moved from Wells to Taunton and Shepton Mallet and ordered to help magistrates if required.[79] As Gloucester appeared quieter Kingsley's was moved to the area of greater danger around Shrewsbury. All this amounts to a considerable movement of troops in a domestic context for a country at war. By the end of November two cavalry regiments and a number of regiments or parts of regiments of foot, amounting to between 70 and 80 companies, sufficient for some major activity of war, were patrolling the riotous areas and diminishing by so much the military strength of the country. In the absence of entirely accurate information about the size of a company in 1756, estimates of numbers is difficult, but between five and six thousand troops were probably involved.

December posed as many problems for the War Office as the previous month, and more troops were involved. One regiment, the Inniskilling Dragoons, was ordered off the scene at the end of the month, but only when relieved by Cornwallis' regiment from Plymouth.[80] Keeping out cavalry in winter was expensive and might be ruinous to the efficiency of the regiment. However the sporadic unconcerted nature of the riots again operated to the advantage of those whose task it was to contain them. Once more Barrington discovered that troops could be moved from one area to another as disorder receded in the former and arose in the latter. The emergency was such that the War Office could only live from day to day, and the idea of pairing these adjacent areas was an obvious one. As a result during this month troops from Coventry could be sent to Warwick,[81] and later to Bridgnorth,[82] from Cirencester to Monmouth,[83] and from Newcastle to Berwick-on-Tweed.[84] Riots also occurred before the end of the year in Tiverton,[85] Penryn[86] and Padstow, and troops were sent from

Exeter and Falmouth, both of which remained quiet at the time, to the first two towns. In the case of Padstow, in spite of a petition from the merchants of the town, Barrington had to tell them that the service would not admit of sending a party at that stage; if their situation became desperate they would find that the officer commanding Anstruther's regiment (26th Foot) at Falmouth had orders to assist.[87] This hint of overstrained resources is common in times of widespread rioting throughout the period; in fact until the militia as newly constituted later in the war by Pitt became embodied there could never be enough troops for internal policing, especially in time of war. In general the strategy had been successful from the War Office standpoint and many potentially dangerous and destructive situations had been rescued by the prompt appearance of troops. A critic might point to the vast numbers of troops involved, fourteen troops of cavalry and seventy-eight companies of infantry, but this does not denote inefficiency, rather does it demonstrate the size of the problem for government. He would be on safer ground if he mentioned the Shropshire operation.

TABLE 7.1

Summary of Troop Movements and Interventions: 1756

Extracted from W.O. 4/52, W.O. 5/43 and 44. This summary only includes actual orders to march, or if the troops are on the spot, actual orders to intervene. Also included are movements of troops from place to place within affected areas, and withdrawals later, but not orders for enlargement of quarters within the same area for billeting reasons, or for movements out of election towns for a few days. Tiverton and Warwick both had elections in early December.

	Date	Unit	From	To	Remarks
	August				
1.	24	*6 Dragoons* 3 Troops (Lt.-Col. Harvey)	?	Leicester	3 Troops left behind at?
2.	25	*Invalids* 1 Company	(Leicester	Leicester)	Already at Leicester; ordered to act with magistrates.
3.	26	*6 Dragoons* 3 Troops (Lt.-Col. Harvey)	Leicester	Northampton	Unless Leicester magistrates wish cavalry to remain.

	Date	Unit	From	To	Remarks
	August				
4.	27	*6 Dragoons* 3 Troops (Lt.-Col. Harvey)	Leicester	Nottingham	Countermands order of 26 August.
5.	29	*6 Dragoons* 3 Troops (Major Hepburne)	Egham	Northampton	Light troop left behind at Newhaven. Discretion to go to Coventry if magistrates wish.
6.	31	*6 Dragoons* 1 Troop (N.C.O.s)	Newhaven	Northampton	Seventh or Light troop.
	September				
7.	4	*3 Dragoons* 3 Troops	Henley	Coventry	If rioters dispersed quarter in parties accordingly.
8.	4	*3 Dragoons* 3 Troops	Reading	Coventry	As above
9.	4	*6 Dragoons* 3 Troops (Major Hepburne)	Coventry	Derby	At Coventry at magistrates' wish. March when 3 Dragoons arrive.
10.	7	*3 Dragoons* 6 Troops	(en route to Coventry)	Northampton	
	October				
11.	16	*33 Foot* (*2nd Battn*) 10 Companies	?	Leeds	
12.	16	*19 Foot* (*2nd Battn*) 10 Companies	?	Morpeth	

	Date	Unit	From	To	Remarks
	October				
13.	18	*3 Foot* 3 Companies	Blandford	Stroud, Painswick,	Or anywhere else desired by
14.	18	*20 Foot* 3 Companies		Dursley, Wotton-under- Edge, Tetbury.	magistrates.
15.	23	*Independent Company* ½ company	Sunderland	South Shields.	From W.O.4/ 52: no mention in marching orders W.O.5/43.
	November				
16.	11	*3 Dragoons* 1 Troop	Brighton	Northampton	The Light Troop.
17.	16	*20 Foot* 7 Companies	Plymouth	Cirencester, Tetbury, Wotton-under- Edge, Dursley, Hampton, Stroud, Painswick.	On arrival of this detachment Wolfe ordered (20/ 11) to send back three companies of 3 Foot to Plymouth.
18.	18	*24 Foot* 10 Companies	Southampton	Derby (5 Companies) Nottingham (5 Companies)	'On disembarking' (ex Minorca)
19.	18	*23 Foot* 10 Companies	Southampton	Leicester	'On disembarking' (ex Minorca)
20.	18	*34 Foot* 10 Companies	Southampton	Norwich	'On disembarking' (ex Minorca)
21.	19	*20 Foot* 3 Companies	Gloucestershire	Shrewsbury	
22.	20	*8 Foot* 4 Companies	Wells	Taunton	

	Date	*Unit*	*From*	*To*	*Remarks*
	November				
23.	30	*6 Dragoons* 7 Troops	Nottingham	Maidenhead and Orkney Arms (1 Troop) Windsor (2 Troops) Egham (1 Troop) Slough (1 Troop) Colnbrook, Slough and Salthill (2 Troops)	March when 24 Foot arrives
24.	30	*24 Foot* 10 Companies	Plymouth	Derby (5 Companies) Nottingham (5 Companies)	'On disembarking' The 24th had been expected at Southampton.
	December				
25.	2	*37 Foot* 5 Companies	Coventry	Warwick	
26.	2	*4 Foot* 1 Company	Exeter	Tiverton	
27.	13	*20 Foot* 1 Company	Cirencester	Monmouth	A retrospective endorsement: Wolfe had already sent troops and applied for approval.
28.	16	*3 Dragoons* 'A party'	London	Northampton	Probably a recruiting party joining the regt.

	Date	Unit	From	To	Remarks
	December				
29.	18	*37 Foot*			
		1 Company	Coventry	Bridgenorth	
30.	30	*26 Foot*			
		50 men	Falmouth	Penryn	
31.	31	*36 Foot*			
		2 Companies	Newcastle	Tweedmouth, Spittle and Ord	

TABLE 7.2

1. By 31 December 1756 the following units or detachments of units had been employed on riot duty:

> 2 cavalry regiments
> 12 marching regiments of foot
> 1½ independent companies of invalids

as in 2. below.

2.

			Troops
(*a*)	*Cavalry*:	Cholmondeley's 6 Dragoons or Inniskillings	7
		Albemarle's 3 Dragoons or King's Own	7
			14
			Companies
(*b*)	*Infantry*:	Howard's 3 Foot or Buffs	3
		Duroure's 4 Foot	1
		Wolfe's 8 Foot or King's Regt.	4
		Beauclerk's 19 Foot (2nd Battn.)	10
		Kingsley's 20 Foot	10
		Huske's 23 Foot or R. W. Fuziliers	10
		Cornwallis' 24 Foot	10
		Anstruther's 26 Foot	2
		Hay's 33 Foot (2nd Battn.)	10
		Effingham's 34 Foot	10
		Manners' 36 Foot	2
		Stuart's 37 Foot	5
		Invalids	1½

	Total	78½ Companies and 14 Troops

8 The Rural Riots of 1757

Rioting continued to be widespread in 1757, again chiefly on account of the shortage of provisions, but with the added complication of opposition to the Militia Act. During the year over fifty towns in thirty-one different counties were affected, and in some cases, notably the bitter militia riots of the East Riding, they persisted for weeks. The scale of these riots gave rise to some subsequent developments in the strategical handling of riots in general. The Secretary at War was increasingly a free agent and acquired more confidence in the role, although a Secretary of State would still take control at times after this date. The handling of the East Riding riots showed that this could be a hindrance.

The formal and proper course whereby magistrate, sheriff or deputy lieutenant made application first to the Secretary of State has been discussed above.[1] Breakdowns under stress of circumstance in this cumbersome procedure had not been unknown in the previous half-century, when riots were particularly savage. But they were regarded as emergencies, and by some Secretaries of State, notably Holdernesse, whose fear of being backgrounded is well known, as extremely improper emergencies. The events of 1757 placed a great strain on the formal procedure, not only because of the intensity of the riots, but also because of the demands of war and diplomacy which occupied most of the time of the distracted Secretaries of State and disinclined them to deal with secondary matters. The correspondence about the Convention of Klosterseven alone fills many pages of their letter-books. Consequently they permitted many encroachments which they would not have tolerated in 1756.

During the year Barrington (and even his own secretary Thomas Tyrwhitt) issued many orders and made on his own initiative many plans of the sort which would not have been tolerated by Holdernesse a year earlier. Much more direct correspondence took place between local magistrates and the War Office, and in many cases the former applied to the latter in the first instance instead of to the Secretary of State, in the interests of speed.[2] It is true that this was not entirely unknown. Craggs, Pelham and William Yonge had all corresponded directly with magistrates, but only on infrequent occasions. It now began to be more common as the scope of the peace-keeping role of the War Office widened. Also it may be that the long association between the War Office and H. M. Commissioners of Customs over the use of soldiers in the smuggling duty, an association entirely carried on without the interposition of the

Secretary of State, helped to establish a precedent.

At times during 1757 the War Office not only received the first report from the riot area, it received it from an officer commanding a detachment whose help had been requisitioned by a magistrate.[3] The Secretary of State's office retained the right to be informed of War Office action even though they had not ordered it, but even this requirement was rather sketchily complied with. Perhaps the fate of Wolfe's letters sent by the War Office to Fox, then offered to Holdernesse, who filed them without comment, discouraged Barrington and gave him the impression that he was on his own. At least it enabled him to form his own systems and methods without interference.

This is not to say that the War Office solely directed operations in 1757: complete consistency cannot be expected. The handling of the Bedfordshire and Yorkshire militia riots show that the Secretaries and even the Duke of Newcastle might be involved for special reasons. In the first case Lord Hardwicke complained of the riot to Newcastle. In the case of Yorkshire Lord Rockingham (who had been reminded of the formal procedure by Holdernesse in 1756), Lord Irwin, Conyers Darcy and other magnates made their first reports to the Secretary of State. But most of the disturbances were handled by the soldiers acting with the magistrates, but directed in their overall strategy by Barrington without reference to the Secretaries. Until the end of August he enjoyed an almost unfettered control of events. In September the Secretaries again exercised some control, partly for the reasons mentioned above, but also because, unlike the sporadic rioting earlier in the year, the September militia outbreaks were of a more serious nature and contained an avowed object of great importance which enforced the attention of the alarmed Secretaries. In applying to the Secretaries of State rather than the War Office the local magnates seem to have recognized this.

Forces available. The recruitment during the year increased the establishment of the army considerably; existing regiments of foot were building up numbers (with difficulty) from around 815 to 1034 men, many gave birth to a second battalion, and new numbered regiments were formed. However a great increase in commitments overseas meant that the War Office could not rely on any increase of numbers to deal with riots, at least until the new militia was embodied and trained.

On July 27 the War Office presented a paper to the Duke of Newcastle showing that the establishment in South Britain was 39,066 men.[4] But of this apparently respectable total only a small number could be available for inland policing; much of the army was necessarily immobilized and various inescapable deductions had to be made. See Table 8.1.

Thus there remained to march on any service in England a total of 16,271. The object of the paper was to show the number available for forming the nucleus of a warlike operation. Only the foot guards were directly assigned

TABLE 8.1

1. Horse Guards and Royal Regiment of Horse Guards, who were in attendance on the Royal Family	1133
2. Regular regiments on garrison duty	4890
3. Invalids on garrison duty (in areas threatened by possible French invasion)	4008
4. 12 battalions on eve of departure for active service	9780
5. 'Four out of seven battalions of Foot Guards which are necessary to preserve the peace in London etc.'[5]	2984
Total	22795

a police role in a special area.

By early 1758 another return[6] shows that after similar deductions had been made the force remaining for operations was only 8530, of which 2000 were cavalry; the army had increased in numbers, but so had its commitment in Germany and other foreign stations. The return added with emphasis:

> . . . out of which number of 8530 must be furnished guards for prisoners in various parts all over the kingdom, troops to suppress riots, wherever they may be, or apprehended; patroles on the coast; and various other duties, the amount of which altogether is very great.

At the beginning of the year many detachments were still doing riot duty on orders from the previous year. Cornwall daily expected a rising of tinners on account of corn prices.[7] There were already 100 men at Truro and 50 at Penryn, 'which is all that the service can at present spare in Cornwall',[8] and the magistrates of Padstow[9] (for the second time) and Helston were told that they could not have a force of their own, but that they could apply to Truro for troops if an actual rising occurred.[10] The policy of refusing to give help on mere anticipation of a riot was adhered to throughout the year, in fact it was forced upon the War Office by the shortage of troops. The sheriff and magistrates of Cornwall tried again in March, but Barrington put them off, saying that the Duke of Cumberland could not spare more troops, and that the detachment of Anstruther's regiment (i.e. 26th Foot) left in the country 'with inconvenience' last year would soon have to be recalled.

> I will watch every opportunity which shall furnish the means of sending troops into Cornwall, since they are so earnestly desired there: but you will permit me through you to remind the gentlemen how important it is for the honour of this Government, for the public peace, and the preservation of our constitution; that civil riots should be

suppressed by civil magistrates without the intervention of a military force. . . . at least the experience of this year has shewn that wherever the civil power has been exerted with a proper spirit, the most formidable riots have been suppressed with the greatest ease.

I know that some riots are of such a nature as to overpower the utmost efforts of the civil magistrates: I hope none such will happen in your county.[11]

A discretionary order was sent to the troops at Plymouth to help if riots occurred and were beyond the civil power.[12] The unhappy magistrates at Padstow made yet another application in April directly to Barrington, and at last secured the promise of an officer and 30 men.[13] Cornwall continued to be disorderly throughout the year and to make appeals for help at intervals. A report that Launceston Gaol, where several mob leaders were imprisoned, was to be broken open by a mob of tinners, brought another detachment from Plymouth.[14] Barrington received an account in May of a battle between tinners, two of whom were wounded, and the troops,[15] which made him realize that Cornwall needed a more substantial garrison, in spite of the billeting problems in that county. The presence of large numbers of French prisoners in the area reinforced this impression.[16] Three days later the scattered troops in the Duchy were relieved by five companies of the 4th or Duroure's regiment of foot, a force which remained there for the rest of the year.[17]

In January Bristol petitioned for more force in the Forest of Dean; the magistrates believed that the city would starve because provision barges were being stopped by mobs on the Severn. Barrington was at this date so short of troops that he felt he could do no more than arrange for an escort of invalids from Bristol when supplies were next fetched.[18] The dissatisfied magistrates applied with more success to Wolfe, who was still on duty in the West Country. He sent a force over the Severn into the Forest of Dean, fully expecting that its crossing by boats would be contested, and advising its captain to have recourse to 'stratagems and surprises'. The rest of his force was disposed with his usual care: 'The Marquis of Blandford is our only captain on this side the Severn; he does *the whole duty* for 5 companies; and is stationed in the centre and in readiness to support any of the detached posts that may require his assistance'.[19]

Wolfe continued to correspond directly with the War Office as in 1756. Towards the end of February he was given sanction to use his own plan as needed. Barrington wrote: 'You will see by the latitude given you in these orders, and by the dates being left in blank, that I trust much to your discretion.'[20] The order ran:

It is His Majesty's Pleasure that you cause such a detachment as you shall think proper to be made from the 20th Regiment of Foot under your command at Cirencester and march from thence by such route as you shall think most convenient to Gloucester, where they are to remain and be quartered until further order. Given at the War Office this day of   1757.

The Gloucester clothing area gave no further trouble for some months, so much so that' the area was uncovered, but fresh alarms in November caused it to be regarrisoned with five companies of the 30th Regiment.[21] Even so Gloucester was quieter than in 1756.

In Somerset the troops stationed at Wells from the previous year proved sufficient, and no further strategic decisions from London were called for, although several clashes with the mob occurred during the year.[22] One of these illustrates a common problem of local commanders. The officer made use of a discretionary marching order given him some months before but not used on that occasion.

. . . I earnestly entreat your Lordship to give me orders how to act in case I should have any application made on the like occasion from other neighbouring places particularly Bristol or Bath, before I can receive His Majesty's orders, for if I had not had the said routes I could not have complied with their request I believe regularly.[23]

The unwillingness of most officers to intervene, and of many officers even to march at all, unless covered by orders from London, has been referred to above; it certainly complicated the task of control for the War Office, and in the years that followed Barrington increasingly draughted orders to local commanders in as wide terms as possible.

So far nothing out of the ordinary had occurred to strain the resources of the army. A number of other troop interventions took place as a result of rioting in the spring and summer; occurring at widely spaced intervals, they were not part of a single operation, and were dealt with on a day-to-day basis. In such circumstances strategy would mean no more than sending in the nearest troops, and would not need more than a glance from Barrington. A letter from Lord Montfort describing the Cambridge riots of June was passed to a secretary with his scribbled endorsement on the back 'Acquaint My Lord that there are troops at Norwich which may be had in case of necessity if sent for', and 'Order the commanding officer at Norwich to send assistance if required'.[24] Barrington was becoming accustomed to alarmist letters about riots.

Such movements involved no great problems of resources or strategy, but the overall effect upon a force which should have been training for warfare abroad must have been adverse, although its extent is not possible to estimate. These movements are summarised in Table 8.2. There is no sign whatever of any attempt to refer the handling of them to either Secretary of State; Barrington gained in confidence in the task and began to develop techniques of his own in handling multiple emergencies of the sort that had already been so common in the previous year. His attempts to save the loss of time arising from officers applying to him for orders have been considered in Chapter 6. The summer of 1757 saw the first use of 'general orders', the proleptic authority to an officer to act in an emergency without further reference to the War Office before that emergency occurs; their report would be expected afterwards. Commanders of four of the summer camps received this novel order towards the end of June:

> Whenever you are requested by the civil magistrates you do immediately send a sufficient detachment from the forces under your command . . . to be assisting them in the preservation of the public peace.[25]

By July riots requiring military assistance to suppress them had occurred at 25 places and the price of corn remained high. Nevertheless Barrrington thought it safe to issue orders for the marching of many regiments into summer camps at Chatham, Barham Downs, Amersham, Salisbury and Dorchester.[26] This was a yearly saving of billeting expense, just as the putting out of horses to grass saved fodder bills, but both courses of action were liable to have serious drawbacks in a riotous season. Particular danger areas in July 1757 were garrisoned by invalids as the regiments moved out. Invalid detachments came in from Carlisle to Manchester,[27] Bristol to Ross,[28] Ashby de la Zouch to Leicester,[29] and Berwick to Carlisle,[30] and orders were issued well in advance so that the changeover should not leave towns uncovered.[31]

Barrington's gamble proved correct, at least until the end of August, when the hurricane of militia riots burst.

THE BEDFORDSHIRE MILITIA RIOTS

The gentlemen of the counties began to try to put the Militia Act into force at the end of August, and at once encountered savage opposition in many places. The first alarm came from Biggleswade. Sir Roger Burgoyne's letter to the Duke of Bedford describing the riot was taken in by a servant at Woburn, who went out and found his master on the road late in the afternoon. Bedford stopped his journey to deal with it and the letter with his covering note reached Barrington at the War Office that evening.[32] The distance was not great, the weather probably fair, but this must be admitted to have been a very rapid communication at this date. Burgoyne's letter described the morning's riot; he admitted quitting the area on hearing that the mob had marked him down, but prudently left the militia lists at the Sun public house. The mob of several hundred arrived, and got the lists from the landlord. They then exacted the usual contributions of money and liquor from the district. Bedford thought that his area was safe but advised that troops be sent to Biggleswade at once as being the point of most danger. Barrington's express went out immediately to two troops of cavalry at Uxbridge and Hillingdon. The orders, widely drafted, were to march to and be quartered in Biggleswade 'or in other places as you shall think expedient'.[33] If the War Office messenger found the commander before midnight the detachment could hardly have arrived, tired and footsore, at Biggleswade, 45 miles along the road to the North, before the afternoon of 1 September. In any case the detachment was to prove insufficient to contain a disturbance of such force.

Bedford attempted to restore regularity by writing to Holdernesse the following day explaining what he had done to combat the riot in the short run. He thought further measures should be taken to quieten the county, referring to the dangerous consequences of 'the bad example the suffering a giddy and riotous populace to stand in opposition to an Act of Parliament unnoticed, may have upon the rest of the kingdom'.[34] He wrote again to the War Office a week later giving his opinion that 59 men 'are not sufficient to defend this whole county from the insolence of a riotous rabble, who flushed with the success they have met with, cannot be quieted without a more considerable force, than we have at present'. He added meaningly that he had received no instructions from the Secretary of State, to whom he had sent a full account, and had therefore called the deputy lieutenants and magistrates to meet him to work out a plan, 'and I fear I shall find very few of them at Bedford, unless under the protection of a strong military force'.[35] He enclosed the letter of a magistrate of Sharnbrook who had been visited by the mob and deprived of the militia lists in spite of attempting to reason with them; the mob, he reported, had been heard to say that they intended visiting Woburn with a mob of five or six thousand.[36]

Barrington had other reports which emphasised the seriousness of the Bedford risings. Lord Royston wrote that the county was still in an uproar, and recommended Luton, Amptill and Clophill as proper quarters for troops.[37] The news had reached Pitt. His instructions to Barrington after reciting the disturbances were to order Ligonier's regiment at Hounslow, Richmond and Kingston to send two troops to Northampton, one to Newport Pagnell and two to Royston.[38] An order of this sort, needing inside knowledge of the whereabouts of units, must have originated with the Secretary at War, who advised Pitt what orders to give him. It seems probable that Barrington went to Pitt for orders, knowing of the serious nature of the riots and wishing on this occasion to involve a Secretary of State. War Office orders to Ligonier's went out early on 7 September,[39] and two troops of another cavalry regiment at Romford were ordered to march into Bedford[40] so as to arrive on 9 September in the morning, to be in time for the Duke of Bedford's meeting with the country gentlemen. Bedford, Royston and Hardwicke were told of these meetings,[41] and the

Duke of Marlborough received a late apology for being by-passed:

> As the above troops were under your Grace's command, the order
> should properly have been sent to your Grace, but from the nature of the
> service, being pressed in time, I was obliged to direct it to the
> commanding officer at Rumford.[42]

Nine troops of cavalry were now strung out in a zigzag cordon, each place
less than twenty miles from the next, across the area affected.[43]

It cannot have escaped the notice of others besides Bedford that
Barrington, not Holdernesse, was the person to inform for the efficient
handling of such emergencies. It is in such ways that precedents are
established. Only a few years before when Bedford was Secretary of State
for the South all riot orders proceeded from his office.[44] When Holdernesse
inherited the Southern department from him he followed the same policy
of a tight control over the War Office for some years until 1756.[45]

The appearance of more troops helped to settle the area a little, as
Hardwicke, no friend to the Militia Act or to Pitt, had to admit. His letter
to Newcastle on 11 September described the riots of the previous week in
many towns before the reinforcements tightened their hold on the county.
Meanwhile Hardwicke was beginning to arrange the defence of his own
house at Wimpole against an approaching column of rioters when the
Royal Regiment of Horse Guards appeared and drove them off.[46] Another
party marching to pull down Sir Humphrey Manoux's house was also
headed back.[47] The presence of troops also enabled the proposed meeting
to be held at Bedford on 9 September.[48]

The area, although held quiet by the military, was still in a dangerous
mood. Hardwicke reported: 'By the terror of the Blues at Royston, we are
at present pretty quiet; but still there are rumours of menaces to rise.'[49] He
was perturbed at the news that the cavalry would soon be called away on
another service, and wrote directly to the War Office (without mentioning
it to a Secretary of State) asking for two or three more troops to be
quartered at Royston to replace them. Barrington assured him by express
that the Blues would not be removed until an equal number of men from
another regiment was available.[50] He moved another troop of the same
regiment to Newport Pagnell[51] and the remaining troop to Northampton,[52] making eleven troops of cavalry involved in the duty. Soon
afterwards the relief of the troops of the Horse Guards began. It is not clear
why it was necessary for them to be withdrawn, but the movement clearly
created a problem for the War Office. Fortunately Rich's dragoons had on
6 September been ordered to move from Salisbury so as to arrive at Ware,
Hoddesden, Hertford, and Enfield[53] on or after 15 September. This was
merely a routine movement and no part of a riot duty plan, but it was now
fortunately placed to be used, and was moved to Biggleswade (two
troops)[54] and Royston (two troops).[55] Five troops of Hawley's dragoons on

duty in Essex, where a riot had taken place at the beginning of September, were next moved to Biggleswade and Royston,[56] and one troop of Howard's regiment (from Maldon) was now considered enough to keep watch on Essex from Braintree.[57] Another regiment, Mordaunt's dragoons, sent three troops to watch Bedfordshire,[58] but the riots had died down a good deal and the orders were to take up quarters at Northampton. It was always Barrington's policy to keep soldiers away from a district unless their presence was absolutely necessary, to avoid provocation. Another four troops of the same regiment were sent for in early October, and were quartered at the adjacent towns of Daventry and Wellingborough to ease the billeting problem for Northampton.[59]

SURREY MILITIA RIOTS

Riots in opposition to the Militia Act were also taking place in Surrey, and Mr Speaker Onslow made his application directly to the War Office; two troops of the Blues, now back in their former quarters were moved to Ripley and Cobham.[60] Three deputy lieutenants asked for a company of foot because of militia riots in Croydon, which they thought, if added to the troop of Cholmondeley's dragoons already there, would be enough. Barrington told them that the whole of Cholmondeley's would come into Croydon directly for a review.[61] The speed of these movements into an area near at hand to London caused the riots to subside.

YORKSHIRE MILITIA RIOTS

By this date some of the troops concerned in the Bedford riots had been called to Yorkshire. A good deal of information on these riots is to be found in the Holdernesse papers. The gentlemen would naturally complain to him as being one of the great magnates of the Ridings, indeed many of them were relatives or otherwise part of the Darcy connection. Many of them also reported the riots and their misgivings to Newcastle. The response of Newcastle and Holdernesse was sluggish and in marked contrast to the effective measures of Barrington and (when he was consulted) Pitt, and for many days the magistrates of Yorkshire struggled on without assistance. The news was sent to London on 14 September, and the War Office was not permitted to send troops until 28 September, although by that date the Mayor of York had applied on his own account to the garrison of invalids at Newcastle and received a detachment from a commander willing to take the risk of marching without orders. Barrington wrote approving of his action.[62]

The first alarms spoke of mobs of several hundreds 'Armed with clubs, and arms', and led by local constables,[63] an alarming but quite common feature, and levying contributions and taking militia lists. In the East Riding one mob was reported to be over 3000 in number.[64] The Sheriff advised Conyers Darcy not to hold the forthcoming militia meeting at Thirsk:

> My authority as Sheriff is gone, and I therefore write this to you in hopes you will take some speedy measures before the meeting at Thirsk to preserve the peace in the manner you think proper which I should imagine might be done by preventing the meeting, and thoroughly satisfying the people in time that there will be no meeting as Lord Irwin has thought proper to do.[65]

Lord Irwin expressed the feelings of many local gentlemen reluctant to support the Act when by a printed notice to the High Sheriff he postponed all meetings until the government's intentions were known.[66] The lack of enthusiasm for the Act shown by the gentlemen of Yorkshire and elsewhere no doubt encouraged the mob; but although Newcastle himself was lukewarm, as were many members of his government, he could only feel outrage at a flouting of a new Act of Parliament. Holdernesse wrote irritably that the Thirsk meeting should go on, and printed handbills explaining the Act might serve 'to open the eyes of the giddy multitude who are opposing what they do not understand', and reassure those who were afraid of having to serve abroad.[67] In any case there was no power in the Crown to suspend the law 'and the magistrates must judge in their own prudence what is fittest for them to do'.[68] There was no mention of military assistance amidst these unhelpful observations, and the magistrates and gentlemen, who expected that troops would then have been marching to their help, began to mention it themselves.[69]

Newcastle wrote in similarly uncomforting terms to Lord Irwin:[70] the local gentlemen must do what they could with the Act. To the Duke of Ancaster, who described similar mobs in Lincolnshire, who had threatened 'they would lay a town (which principally belongs to me) in ashes', he merely wrote that the King's servants would consider the riot at a forthcoming meeting, and expressed sympathy.[71] Sir Rowland Wynn in Yorkshire was more insistent; the mob, he said, having got most of the militia returns, had grown bolder and begun to pull down mills, 'in short, My Lord Duke unless the government send us down some dragoons *and that soon* we must expect to see all things in confusion.'[72] He reported that 100 soldiers had arrived the day before. These were the invalids from Newcastle sent for by the Mayor of York, and in the absence of transport must have been at least four days on the road. Four hundred citizens of York, fearing an attack on the gaol, where two rioters were confined, had offered to help and were making cartridges.[73]

Infantry might defend York, or a part of it, but cavalry was obviously needed to deal with riots throughout an entire county. The mayor of York, tired of hinting to Holdernesse, asked outright for troops.[74] But still no instructions from the government were received by the War Office, and the reports of the disasters continued to come in. Lord Dupplin described further attacks on mills and the widening scope of the mob's grievances: 'enclosures, game associations, broad wheels, and many others have been mentioned.'[75] Lord Rockingham armed his tenants and prepared to defend Wentworth.[76] The rioters were observed to be well versed in the contents of the Militia Act, which gave rise to the usual suspicions about powerful persons in the background, and Jacobites were mentioned.[77]

The meeting of the cabinet took place on Monday 26 September, chiefly to consider the Convention of Klosterseven. It decided to send a regiment of dragoons to Yorkshire '*to restore power, and respect to the civil authority*'.[78] The investing of a decision, which could long before this date have been informally made by direct application from Yorkshire to the War Office, with such portentous solemnity merely underlines the ineffectiveness of the government in the matter. The discussion at the meeting even served to confuse the issue, for it was suggested that the nobility be armed with a special commission to resist riot. Lord Mansfield, the Lord Chief Justice, considered it rash and wrote to Newcastle the next day pointing out the dangers of a proposal to give men a commission to do what they were in law entitled to do anyway.[79]

As a result of the meeting the War Office was at last authorized, some two weeks late, to send help, and the entire regiment of Rich's dragoons moved off from duty in the Bedfordshire area to Yorkshire,[80] their places being taken by the Royal Regiment of Dragoons from Chelmsford.[81] The former were not to move until relieved by the latter, which probably lost them another day. By this date the mob were searching for weapons and the magistrates of Scarborough began to impound arms in their jurisdiction. No real confrontations took place, although mobs continued to range widely over the county. The presence of troops and the firmness and tact of the local magistrates caused the rioting to die away. Very few arrests were made. Subsequent correspondence on the matter was confined to prosecutions, encouragement of the *posse comitatus*, and measures to enforce the Militia Act. Magistrates who had acted with firm resolve were congratulated.[82]

Rockingham thought that a regiment of foot ought to be at hand and asked the Duke of Cumberland, whom he met at Newmarket, if he would send Brudenell's regiment (51st). Cumberland moved them to Derby and Nottingham, with power to move into Yorkshire if necessary, a transaction which does not appear on the War Office books at all.[83] It must have been one of Cumberland's last acts in office, for Newcastle wrote to Hardwicke about the Duke's fate in the same week:

Yesterday His Majesty told me, what he had said the day before to the Duke of Devonshire, 'That the Duke might retire to Windsor, have nothing to do with the army, which might go on with the Secretary at War, but that His Majesty wished H.R.H. would not give up his regiment of Guards.'[84]

No other troop movements into Yorkshire took place until 26 November, when two companies of Home's foot were transferred from Nottingham to Wakefield as a result of a reminder from a J.P. that as many of the gentlemen of Yorkshire must soon come up to attend to their duties in London, leaving only their servants to act for them in emergencies, more troops were needed. The mob at Manchester had promised to come and visit Pontefract, where there was only one troop of horse.[85] Holdernesse on receiving this news went to Ligonier, the new commander in chief, instead of Barrington, but the order went out through Barrington's books and no confusion resulted. The men of Home's regiment marched from Nottingham on orders sent on 26 November, arriving on the 30th. In the opinion of the magistrate, this arrival alone prevented a rising that day in Huddersfield.[86]

BOSTON ENCLOSURE RIOTS

Enclosure riots were common in the fen district. The letter of the mayor of Boston to William Pitt described in detail the progress of a crowd who had assembled with drums and colours and cut the dykes. The mayor ascribed this uprising to the success of the militia mobs elsewhere.[87] Barrington's instructions came from Pitt, and orders went out for a light troop of cavalry and two companies of foot.[88] The mayor was appreciative, then embarrassed. His letter illustrates the perennial problem of all magistrates; there was not enough accommodation for so many soldiers.[89] In a remote sparsely populated district billeting could become a strategic problem. Pitt told Barrington to move one company away.[90]

The mayor had other worries. Most of the rioters lived in the Lindsey division, and proceedings against them would have to be carried on before other magistrates. He doubted whether he was even empowered to send troops into villages outside his jurisdiction. Local matters of this sort were however not problems for the War Office; their strategical part had been performed without trouble.

GLOUCESTERSHIRE

The clothing area which had been so turbulent in 1756 rose again, and huge mobs ranged about the county confiscating the militia lists. The few arrested ringleaders were at once rescued.[91] Pitt and Barrington again acted with a promptitude not found in the transactions of Holdernesse and

Newcastle, and five companies of foot were sent from Reading, Newbury and Speenhamland to Cirencester and Lechlade.[92] No dragoons were near enough to intervene, but the arrival of the infantry was enough and a quiet fell upon the county.

MANCHESTER

Riots had already taken place in June as a result of the shortage of corn and potatoes,[93] when three troops of Albemarle's dragoons had arrived to support the High Sheriff.[94] They were not able to stay for long, and a company of invalids from Carlisle were sent in to relieve them.[95] After a quiet period the unrest elsewhere in the latter part of the year spread to Manchester. The invalids under Lieutenant Read were still in the town, but were insufficient to contain the riot. The inevitable violent confrontation between soldiers and mob (in which several lives were lost), notorious in Manchester annals as Shudehill Fight, does not belong in a strategical account.[96] It is noteworthy that the troop movements came after the fighting, which entirely fell upon the invalids. In the next few days a troop of Rich's dragoons came in,[97] and two companies of Home's.[98] A further company was placed at Stockport to be at hand.[99] Manchester subsided again under the threat of this military concentration, and no further clashes occurred,[100] although its mayor was reporting a month later that 'there is still a very bad spirit amongst the common people'.[101]

LIVERPOOL

The riots here occurred at the same time as the foregoing and underlined the shortage of troops in the north midlands. The first report shows this to have been a corn riot.[102] Lancashire, with its growing population, was a poor producer of essential supplies, and the opinion of the mob that the importers were guilty of hoarding was perhaps not uninformed. This mob was armed, probably from the stands of muskets on shipboard at the docks. No cavalry was available for a quick dash into Liverpool. Barrington could only send two companies of Home's regiment into Manchester,[103] and move the invalids (when relieved) from there to Liverpool. Two more companies of the same regiment at Derby and one of invalids at Ashby de la Zouch were ordered into Liverpool,[104] but the invalids would clearly get there first and would have to hold on until reinforced. The town became quieter and the mayor was so far eased in his mind as to ask one of the companies to stay at Warrington, which was in some danger, although it is clear from his letter that the billeting problem was uppermost in his mind.[105]

To sum up, the handling of troop movements by the Secretary at War had been generally successful. Requests for troops had been quickly complied with, and units moved off rapidly into affected areas, led by officers armed with widely-drawn orders, to meet magistrates who were authorized and encouraged to place soldiers in the most useful posts. The number of violent fights which took place, having regard to the widespread nature of rioting, was not great; just as in conditions of real warfare, the speedy arrival of force frequently settled the matter without ugly incidents. The disastrous exception of the Yorkshire riots indicated that it was better to treat such emergencies rather as police than political matters and leave them to the Secretary at War.

The effect on the army itself can only be guessed at, and there is little recorded information. The inspection returns for the year show that General Mostyn's attempts to review the 4th Foot at Plymouth on 3 October and the 10th Dragoons at Northampton on 27 October were largely frustrated because in each case the regiment was scattered over a large area on riot duty.[106] Naturally any sort of training in this year, when Pitt was amongst other matters planning his raids on the French coast, must have been very difficult. But although the effect cannot be quantified in the absence of any data collected at the time it must be recognised to have been considerable. Table 8.3 roughly shows the amount of military

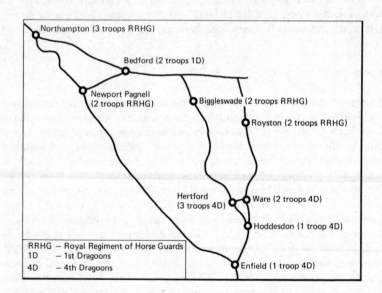

MAP 1 Movements of Cavalry into area of Bedfordshire militia riots, 31 August – 17 September 1757: subsequent reliefs not included

involvement in the riot duty during the year, from which it is clear that compared with the operations of 1756 there was a great increase in the use of cavalry, which had obvious advantage in speedy arrival and intervention in case of riots, and a corresponding decrease in the use of infantry. The operation had involved at one time or another about half the total amount of cavalry in Britain south of the Border, to the number of perhaps 1200 men. The infantry employed may be estimated, having regard to the increased size of companies in 1757, at over 4000.

TABLE 8.2

Summary of Troop Movements: 1757

Extracted from W.O.4/53, 4/54 and 4/55, and W.O. 5/44 and 5/45. The figures are more approximate than those for Table 7.1. Some units were sent on riot duty, relieved and sent elsewhere. In some cases it is not clear from documents if the same or different companies were used in riots separated by several months. Estimates of numbers have erred on the side of caution. Also the practice of sending discretionary orders to commanders to send 'a proper party' or 'a sufficient detachment' increased in 1757, and complicates a statistical exercise. The former has been taken to mean half a company or troop, the latter a company or troop.

	Date	Unit	From	To	Remarks
	January				
1.	25	*50 Foot* 3 companies	Sudbury	Huntingdon, Godmanchester and St Ives	
2.	25	*6 Dragoons* 1 Troop	Kettering	Huntingdon and Godmanchester	At request of Lord Sandwich
	February				
3.	8	? *10 Dragoons* (see remarks) ½ Troop	Arundel	Any area (on requisition)	'The regiment of Dragoons in the duty of patrolling'
4.	14	*36 Foot* 1 company	Gateshead and Newcastle	Anywhere in Northumberland and Durham	
5.	21	*20 Foot* 1 company	Cirencester	Gloucester	

	Date	Unit	From	To	Remarks
	February				
6.	21	*20 Foot*			
		1 company	Gloucester	Cirencester and Tetbury	Presumably a relief for the above
	March				
7.	15	*? 3 Foot*			
		1 company	Plymouth	Cornwall	'the forces at Plymouth'
	April				
8.	8	*3 Foot*			
		30 men	Plymouth	Padstow	
9.	11	*8 Foot*			
		1 company	Wells	Places nearby as suggested by magistrates	
10.	26	*11 Foot* 2nd Battn			
		1 company	Newcastle	Places nearby as suggested by magistrates	
11.	30	*Invalids*			
		1 company	Berwick	Places nearby as suggested by magistrates	
	May				
12.	6	*37 Foot*			
		1 company	Worcester	Worcester and district	A retrospective confirmation
13.	7	*3 Foot*			
		½ company	Plymouth	Launceston	
14.	10	*20 Foot*			
		5 companies	Exeter	Cornwall	To relieve various parties of 3 Foot
15.	12	*2 Dragoons*			
		7 Troops	Romford	Norwich and district	
16.	14	*1 Dragoon Guards*			
		1 Troop	?	Dorset	'frequent risings'
17.	28	*37 Foot*			
		1 company	Coventry	Coventry and district	A corn and cheese riot

	Date	Unit	From	To	Remarks
	June				
18.	8	*12 Foot*			
		1 company	Havant	Petworth	
19.	9	*6 Dragoons*			
		3 Troops	Northampton	Manchester	
20.	17	*12 Foot*			
		2 companies	Winchester	Alton and district	
21.	18	*2 Dragoons*			
		1 Troop	Warwick	Cambridge	At request of Mayor and Vice-Chancellor
22.	21	*Invalids*			
		1 company	Carlisle	Manchester	
	July				
23.	6	*12 Foot*			
		10 companies	Gospoit	Alton and district	Only if requisitioned by magistrates.
24.	6	*10 Dragoons*			
		7 Troops	Petersfield	Alton and district	Only if requisitioned by magistrates.
	August				
25.	31	*Royal Regt of Horse Guards*			
		2 Troops	Uxbridge and Hillingdon	Biggleswade	'and other places as you shall think expedient.'
	September				
26.	3	*1 Dragoons*			
		1 Troop	Romford		Barking and Braintree
27.	6	*4 Dragoons*			
		7 Troops	Salisbury	Ware (2 Troops) Hoddesdon (1 Troop) Hertford (3 Troops) Enfield (1 Troop)	Not clear if this was a routine movement or a plan to move forces nearer the danger area.

	Date	Unit	From	To	Remarks
	September				
28.	7	*R.R.H.G.*			
		5 Troops	Kingston	Northampton (2 Troops) Newport Pagnell (1 Troop) Royston (2 Troops)	
29.	7	*1 Dragoons*			
		2 Troops	Romford	Bedford	
30.	17	*R.R.H.G.*			
		1 Troop	Richmond	Newport Pagnell	
31.	17	*R.R.H.G.*			
		1 Troop	Twickenham	Northampton	
32.	22	*4 Dragoons*			
		2 Troops	Ware	Royston	
33.	22	*R.R.H.G.*			
		2 Troops	Royston	Kingston	When relieved
34.	22	*4 Dragoons*			
		2 Troops	Hertford	Biggleswade	
35.	22	*R.R.H.G.*			
		2 Troops	Biggleswade	Newport Pagnell (1 Troop) Uxbridge and Hillingdon	When relieved by 4 Dragoons
36	23	*10 Dragoons*			
		1 Troop	Petworth	Northampton	
37.	23	*10 Dragoons*			
		1 Troop	Lewes	Northampton	
38.	23	*10 Dragoons*			
		Light Troop	Barham Downs and Canterbury	Northampton	
39.	28	*4 Dragoons*			
		7 Troops	Royston	York	or wherever riots occur in the neighbourhood

	Date	Unit	From	To	Remarks
	September				
40.	28	*1 Dragoons* 5 Troops	Chelmsford	Biggleswade (2 Troops) Royston (2 Troops) Edgeware and Harrow (1 Troop)	
41.	29	*3 Dragoon Guards* 1 Troop	Malden	Braintree	
	October				
42.	4	*R.R.H.G.* 3 Troops	Northampton	former quarters	when relieved by remainder of 10 Dragoons
43.	4	*10 Dragoons* 1 Troop	Petworth	Northampton	
44.	4	*10 Dragoons* 2 Troops	Canterbury	Northampton	
45.	6	*10 Dragoons* Light Troop	Canterbury	Northamtpon	
46.	6	*6 Dragoons* 1 Troop	Croydon	Croydon and district	
47.	6	*R.R.H.G.* 2 Troops	Kingston, Richmond and Hounslow	Ripley and Cobham	
48.	18	*10 Dragoons* 7 Troops	Northampton	Northampton (4 Troops) Wellingborough (1 Troop) Daventry (1 Troop) Newport Pagnell (1 Troop)	
49.	25	*R.R.H.G.* 1 Troop	Royston	Welwyn and Stevenage	
50.	25	*R.R.H.G.* 1 Troop	Bedford	St Neots	

	Date	Unit	From	To	Remarks
	October				
51.	26	*10 Dragoons* 1 Troop	Northampton	Towcester	
	November				
52.	4	*5 Foot* 2 companies	Leicester	Boston	An enclosure riot
53.	4	*10 Dragoons* Light Troop	Northampton	Boston	If magistrates requisition them
54.	8	*30 Foot* 5 companies	Reading and Speenhamland	Cirencester and Lechlade	
55.	17	*4 Dragoons* 1 Troop	York	Manchester	
56.	18	*25 Foot* 1 company	Derby	Liverpool	
57.	18	*Invalids* 1 company	Manchester	Liverpool	when relieved by 25 Foot
58.	19	*25 Foot* 1 company	Derby	Stockport	
59.	19	*Invalids* 1 company	Ashby	Liverpool	
60.	19	*25 Foot* 2 companies	Derby	Manchester	
61.	26	*25 Foot* 2 companies	Nottingham	Wakefield	
	December				
62.	1	*Invalids* 1 company	Warrington	Warrington and district	
63.	10	*25 Foot* 1 company	Derby	Derby and district	

TABLE 8.3

1. By 31 December 1757 the following units had contributed detachments for riot duty:

> 8 cavalry regiments
> 12 marching regiments of foot
> 3 independent companies of invalids (Berwick, Carlisle and Ashby)

as in 2. below

2.

		Troops
(a) *Cavalry*:	Royal Regiment of Horse Guards	7
	1 Dragoon Guards	1
	3 Dragoon Guards	1
	1 Dragoons	5
	2 Dragoons	7
	4 Dragoons	7
	6 Dragoons	4
	10 Dragoons	7
		39

		Companies
(b) *Infantry*:	3 Foot	1
	5 Foot	2
	8 Foot	1
	11 Foot	1
	12 Foot	3
	20 Foot	8
	25 Foot	6
	30 Foot	5
	36 Foot	1
	37 Foot	2
	50 Foot	3

Total	33 Companies and 39 Troops

9 The Rural Riots of 1766

The year 1766 was an anxious one alike for the poor and for the authorities.[1] The opinion of modern economists is that the standard of life rose somewhat for the poor in the late fifties and early sixties. The harvest of 1764 was a good one and that of 1765 adequate. As a result of the government's bounty for corn export, land which formerly produced little was being made by new techniques of husbandry to yield heavily. The corn lands of Norfolk were an example. The bounty seems to have been encouraged originally by the Whigs as a counter to the land tax, but it was unlucky for the consumer, and could become a tactless form of discrimination in bad times. The events of 1766 were to show that the poor were as vulnerable as ever in years of low yield, and as apt as they had been in 1740, 1753, 1756 and 1757 to resent factors which made their position worse.[2] Some of these, such as bad communications, they could not influence. But they were quick to show their anger towards forestalling and other forms of racketeering, as well as towards the exportation of corn. Nearly all the riots of this year arose out of these two factors.

The price of bread was high and the winter was an exceptionally hard one in a century which appears to have experienced many more extremes of climate than modern times. It was followed by a wet spring with heavy flooding, making the sowing difficult in many areas. There was also a good deal of unemployment. At the War Office Barrington was aware that difficult times lay ahead. His issue of a general order in January to troops to act without authority from London upon the requisition of magistrates, and the fate of that order, has already been discussed. The critical period was not reached until the summer, when there was a prolonged period of wet weather and it was clear that the harvest would fail. There was a long waiting period, during which the authorities watched with anxiety for the inevitable public reactions. Some wrote to ask for troops in case a riot might occur, but this was contrary to Barrington's principle. To one alarmist he wrote pointing out that troops were a last extremity, only to be used when the civil power had exhausted all its resource:

> Your Lordship will easily perceive how inconsistent it would be with this principle, for me to order the march of troops upon the bare apprehension of danger, which may never exist, and that too upon information which, I confess, appears to me to be very uncertain.[3]

But in most places the populace remained quiet, although a riot in Suffolk among inhabitants indignant at the building of a workhouse occupied the War Office for several days.[4] In May Barrington issued the usual orders to the cavalry to turn out the horses to grass.[5]

The riots began slowly, the first alarm coming from Devon in the last days of July. The mayor of Lyme, who had quelled a riot in January with military help and whose fears of another rising had been expressed as early as February,[6] wrote to the War Office to describe the destruction of two flour mills at Ottery St Mary by a mob of 500. Barrington's express to Albemarle's dragoons at Dorchester combined the usual caution with latitude to the officer commanding. The cavalry was not ordered to march to the area but to wait for an actual riot at Ottery, Sidbury, Lyme or any place adjacent, and for a requisition from the magistrate, before making 'necessary detachments'.[7]

This was the first of a vast complex of riots which was to affect 68 places in 20 counties. Further riots took place in August at Bradninch and Cullompton (Devon) but no other appeals for help were made to the War Office during the month, except from Newbury, where several mealmen had their property plundered. Barrington moved two troops of Burgoyne's light dragoons from Epsom and Ewell to Newbury.[8] A lull in the rioting followed, probably because a period of drier weather gave rise to hope that the harvest might be saved after all.[9] But on 26 August the embargo on grain exports, imposed the previous February to last for six months, expired. There is no record of Barrington's views or plans at such a provocative event, but in any case the effect upon the people was not long delayed.

The second wave of riots was much more severe, and gave rise to problems of planning and deployment for the War Office. It began in Devonshire again. The magistrates applied to the dragoons at Dorchester and to London, and Barrington's letter to their commander (sent to await his arrival at Cullompton and Ottery) recited the disturbances, of which the War Office had also received a report: bolting mills for twenty miles around had been destroyed.[10] The choice of troops to be sent was left to the commander, except that any troops sent to Lyme in consequence of the order of 1 August were not to be moved.[11] Further riots took place at Tiverton two weeks later. The War Office reported that

> . . . the combers, weavers, and labourers have lately assembled at their clubhouses, and . . . threatening and incendiary letters have been sent to the members of the said corporation.[12]

Two companies of the 43rd regiment already billeted there were ordered to help in case of a riot and a requisition from magistrates.[13] Reports of riots in Gloucestershire[14] and at Devizes[15] came in within the next day or so; these as well as the Devon riots were all dealt with by Christopher D'Oyly, Barrington's capable secretary, in the absence of Barrington himself, who was out of London.

Although signs of military assistance in the first fortnight of September had been few, the numerous reports of corn shortages from all quarters had already alarmed members of the government sufficiently to raise in their minds the question of prohibiting export. This had been necessary in 1757 and the two following years.[16] The King agreed,[17] but Parliament had been prorogued and did not sit at all during the worst of the disorders. It returned on 11 November. Meanwhile there was a good deal of discussion about the best method of achieving the prohibition in its absence. A full committee of the Privy Council was called on 24 September,[18] where many letters from all parts of the country were read as evidence of the shortage. Two City merchants reported on the dearth of grain in other parts of Europe,[19] which had resulted in numerous orders being placed in Britain. They believed that the shortage was so great that an embargo could not be expected to bring down the price, but they believed it might prevent a great rise.[20] The prohibition was passed unanimously, and embodied in an Order in Council two days later.[21]

Although the need had been great, serious discussion followed in governing circles about the monarch's right to perform such an act. The Lord Chancellor believed that it was outside the ordinary prerogatives of the Crown, but that all constitutions had the power, in case of necessity, to provide for the *salus populi*; in his view there was clearly such a necessity. This doctrine displeased some, who observed that ship money had been defended on similar grounds,[22] but good sense prevailed, and although there continued to be real hardship, in the words of one of the City merchants who reported to the Council, 'the chief use of a prohibition will be to quiet the minds of the people'.[23] In the event it probably had no other use, fair and morally right though it undoubtedly was. Such measures took time to achieve their effect. Seymour Conway wrote to the Lords Lieutenant of Oxfordshire and Gloucestershire, where rioting was severe, that after the Order in Council mobs seemed to have increased and become more numerous and insolent,

> and His Majesty's troops . . . [are] in consequence of the many applications, from a great variety of places now almost entirely disposed in, or as near as possible in the neighbourhood of the places chiefly infested with those disorders.[24]

Professor Shelton believes that the proclamation, with its implication that the dearth had been created artificially, encouraged the poor to further rioting against profiteering farmers and middlemen.[25] Further, he has discovered that in many places the riots, initially at least, received encouragement from the gentry.[26]

In the last days of September calls for help increased, as rioting occurred at Devizes, Salisbury, Bradford, Trowbridge, Derby, Coventry, Norwich,

Chippenham and Calne.²⁷ Troops were ordered to march at once to the districts affected, instead of being told to wait for magistrates, in fact after the order in council troops were almost never told to await such a requisition before marching, a notable contrast from the cautious procedure usually followed by the War Office in what may be termed in the context of that time ordinary circumstances, that is to say, when riots were occasional and unconnected. In this the hand of Barrington is clear. He returned to London on 23 September and began to organise the military interventions on the lines of a campaign of interrelated operations. On arrival at the office he sent orders to the commanders of eleven cavalry regiments to take up their horses from grass, some time before the usual date, so as to be ready for a quick intervention in riots.²⁸ On the following day general orders were issued to the same regiments (with the addition of the 2nd Light Dragoons, the Blues at York and the 1st Light Dragoons, who had been attending on the royal family and whose horses had therefore not been at grass), to assist magistrates on their requisition without waiting for authority from London.²⁹ This order was in the same form as Barrington's order of January, but the covering letter told officers to wait on magistrates in their neighbourhood and inform them of the order, thus avoiding the weakness of the system aimed at in January.

The same order went to the colonels of seven regiments of foot,³⁰ and to a number of invalid garrisons throughout the country.³¹ The calls for help subsequently became fewer as troops moved into the affected areas and began to co-operate with the magistrates, although some of the latter, uninformed of the order, continued to apply to London after the manner which they had over the years been encouraged to regard as the most correct.

By the end of the month so many units were in the West Country that Barrington appointed Lt.-Col. Warde as temporary commander there to simplify local planning.³² His headquarters were to be at Devizes 'which is the most centrical place, with respect to the different quarters of the troops, as you will see by the disposition which I send you inclosed'.³³

The existence in the archives of numerous orders and (which is exceptional) several drafts of Barrington's own plans and thoughts shows that he regarded this as the crisis-time, and the West Country as the crisis-area, of the 1766 riots. It would be too much to say that Barrington was rattled, but certainly the cool and sympathetic approach of 1756 and 1757 had been replaced by an anxious and retributive spirit.³⁴ He wrote that the mob were now increasing every day and that in a short time they may join and become 'more mad and dangerous'. Troops could not now be be redistributed except into very small bodies indeed.

This might be of fatal consequence, as a few soldiers commanded by a weak, ignorant subaltern might be defeated by a very large mob, full of men lately used to arms in the army and militia . . .

> If the mob take part with the delinquents [i.e. arrested ringleaders]
> and attempt to succour them, the justices should order the mob to be
> chastised by the troops, and the more roughly it is done the better. . . .
> Some bloody heads would be a real kindness to humanity.[35]

He called for and received on 2 October a list of all troops in quarters in
England and Scotland, together with a memo on the nearest supports upon
which the West Country could depend.[36] The latter showed that five
companies of foot at Windsor, Hampton Court and Winchester could be
moved to Taunton and Exeter if desired, and two troops of cavalry from
Dorchester to Yeovil and Crewkerne. This represented the last reserves
near at hand; many units were at a considerable distance from the West
Country, and five regiments of foot and a cavalry regiment were north of
the Scottish border. Even so Warde could dispose of what amounted to a
small army by the end of the first week in October, composed of nine troops
of cavalry near at hand, and a further two in Devonshire, and 16
companies of foot.[37] Even so the concentration of them in large units, thus
leaving wide tracts of countryside at the mercy of the mob, was the weak
point of the scheme. In his anxiety about small parties of troops being
overborne by weight of numbers, a disaster which had happened several
times during his period of office, Barrington was prepared to pay this price.
Giving a wide latitude to the local commander at least ensured that
wandering mobs, once discovered, could be pursued and dispersed. But
requests for protection on mere anticipation of riots were as usual met
unsympathetically at the War Office; the Earl of Suffolk was told that the
plan could not admit of any change so as to give protection to his country
house without endangering some other place.[38]

Subsequent appeals for help from this area occasionally came to London
before magistrates became used to such a radical departure from the usual
form, and were referred to Lt.-Col. Warde by Barrington.[39] Warde co-
operated with the local magistrates; at a meeting with them at Gloucester
he agreed a plan for the control of the area, the details of which have not
survived.[40] By the time he submitted it to London for approval he was able
to report that Wiltshire at least was quiet.[41] The plan was approved on 21
October and Warde was authorised to move his quarters into Gloucestershire, which was still disturbed.[42] By November the riots there were over,
and an order was sent to march the companies of the 43rd regiment back to
Winchester if it was thought safe to do so: Barrington added 'I hope you
will not send any troops away; if the Lords Lieutenants or Sheriffs of
Glostershire or Wiltshire desire they may stay where they are.'[43] One of the
sheriffs wrote in alarm at this withdrawal of troops, and was reassured by
Barrington that they would remain if they were needed.[44] Pressure from
the same sheriff ensured that Warde's cavalry remained in Gloucestershire
until the end of the year.

The occupation was uneventful and less striking than the strategy that went towards the arranging of it. Dangerous clashes with mobs were avoided as far as possible, but a number of arrests were made. As the assizes approached the magistrates became nervous at the idea of the customary removal of troops; Warde was told to retain troops in the towns concerned if the assize judges so wished.[45]

By the end of October the greater part of the units elsewhere which had been issued with general orders were involved in riot duty. No dragoons could be spared for the smuggling service in Devon at the beginning of October, and not until the riots died down could a sergeant and twelve men be released to help the revenue officers at Seaton and elsewhere.[46] It was not often that the War Office had to confess itself unable to provide such a party.

The issue of general orders and the creation of a command in the West Country was not enough to take certain forms of overall direction out of Barrington's hands. The Marlborough corn riots at the beginning of October needed instant attention from him: troops further west were too heavily involved already. The foot at Newbury, less than twenty miles away, were best placed to intervene quickly. Seventeen miles further away at Reading were two troops of cavalry and a further company of foot. But this area, although not as disturbed as Marlborough, could not be left uncovered for long. The foot at Reading and Newbury were ordered to Marlborough, but were not to march until relieved by three companies of their own regiment from Windsor and Hampton Court. The latter in their turn could not move until relieved by the Foot Guards from London. In the event the Guards could not be moved immediately and Barrington had to send part of the 8th regiment from Chatham to relieve Reading and Newbury. Thus an intervention of infantry at Marlborough could only happen at the end of a series of movements, each depending on the completion of the previous one and occupying many days. Only the cavalry at Reading would have any chance of speedy action, and were ordered off at once. The mayor of Reading must have been sorry to see them go; he had expressed fears of a rising in his own town two days before.[47] It probably took them most of the day of 4 October to make the march; they then had to hold the town and area for upwards of a week until the infantry arrived.

Large areas remained troubled for a while, and the mobs had many successes before being dispersed. This does not imply a weakness in Barrington's plan: a much larger force than he could deploy would have been necessary for such a task. For some time the South and West was a scene of burning mills, warehouses and hay ricks, and many markets were temporarily taken over by mobs who sold foodstuffs at a regulated price, or for no price at all. There do not seem to have been many dangerous clashes between soldiers and rioters: in most cases the mob had done their work by the time the troops arrived, making the restoration of order easier. One stubbornly contested fight near Kidderminster ended with the death of eight rioters. Other deaths took place, but were the result of fighting between marching corn rioters and loyal mobs raised (and sometimes armed) by the now alarmed magistrates and proprietors. As a result of this fighting one death took place at Stroud – the owner who fired the shot being subsequently tried and acquitted – two at Frome and two at Beckington. Other battles of this sort took place outside the West Country, notably at Norwich, where the mayor called out the citizens, armed with staves, who succeeded after a long struggle in making thirty arrests. At Birmingham a loyal mob overpowered the rioters: another at Donnington was put to flight. Magistrates at Aylesbury made a number of arrests, and at Henley a mob was dispersed by the reading of the Riot Act alone, an uncommon occurrence. At Reading the authorities waited until a gang of bargement from Marlow were drunk before carrying them off to gaol. Barrington's frequently reiterated comment that the civil power could deal with riots except in the most extreme cases seemed justified on occasion in 1766.

Although the West Country was the area worst affected, violent clashes took place elsewhere between soldiers and rioters. At Derby a party of the 15th Light Dragoons were pelted with stones and their commander injured; 34 arrests were made. At Nottingham a detachment of the same regiment fought with a mob, and a farmer standing near by was killed. However the clashes and bloodshed in and out of the West Country that occurred seem proportionately light for such a widespread, prolonged and bitter outbreak.[48]

Altogether 51 arrests were made in Wiltshire, and 96 in Gloucestershire. Towards the end of October the riots began to die away. Prices fell a little. Some of the objectives of the mob, such as the destruction of mills and warehouses of hoarders, had been attained. So by a combination of heavy-handed repression, a slight amelioration of the dearth, and the usual loss of momentum characteristic of such outbreaks, one of the great risings of the people, perhaps the greatest of the century, died down.

Four special commissions were set up to try the rioters in Berkshire, Wiltshire, Gloucestershire and Norfolk. Some rioters were sentenced to death, but a good many were reprieved. Many others charged with less serious offences connected with rioting were tried at sessions.[49]

The autumn reviews proved impossible to hold. The Adjutant-General wrote to one of the reviewing generals at the end of September: 'As yet the generals can't set out, the troops being so much dispersed. It's to be hoped the rioters will soon be more temperate.'[50] Later he wrote:

Mordaunt's are separated.[51] It's very likely that more regiments may share the same fate. It's of no use your thinking to set out as yet, for the regiments can't assemble. I mentioned it yesterday to the K. He directs that no orders are to go at present for assembling, as such frequent requisitions arrive from the magistrates for protection.[52]

On 22 October, after several more postponements, it was recognized that the 1766 reviews could not be held.[53]

The riots of this year put the army to a severe test. They affected a surprising number of towns, they began in July and only died away in November, and they were very violent. In some places a number of people were killed, although in most cases not by soldiers, and before soldiers appeared. The bulk of the administrative work, alleviated partly by the creation of the independent command in the west of England, fell upon the War Office, which between August and the end of October issued 81 orders to units,[54] besides writing many other letters connected with the riots. The Secretary of State played only an intermittent part, and then only if by chance information came to his office. The sheriff of Gloucester reported the riots there to Seymour Conway; he discussed the position with Barrington, who then issued the necessary orders.[55] On 23 September Shelburne ordered the reinforcement of Trowbridge;[56] Barrington arrived back in the War Office on that day and at once took over the handling of the operation. Otherwise the Secretaries were content to allow the War Office to run the business, which it was well qualified to do. Their main part once again was confined to the arranging of the special assizes for the trial of rioters,[57] a part which lies outside the present study. Even here Barrington had advice to offer. A special commission was as necessary for Berkshire (where his own country house was situated) as for the other counties involved, and he passed on to the Treasury Solicitor copies of examinations taken under oath before the Abingdon justices.[58] When a special commission did issue for Berkshire as well as for the other counties, Barrington became bitter about the leniency showed to several of the rioters, and dissociated himself from such a policy. 'I find the Crown has been advised in that matter very differently from my ideas.'[59]

TABLE 9.1

Summary of Troop Movements and Interventions: 1766

Extracted from W.O. 4/80 and 4/81, W.O. 5/54. Comparison between Tables 9.1 and 9.2 shows many more riots than apparent interventions by troops. This is because in many cases troops, having gone to one town, assisted magistrates in another nearby. Also after 24 September when general orders to assist were issued many magistrates applied directly to the nearest troops and no marching orders appeared on the books of the War Office. Finally in a small number of cases magistrates restored order without military aid.

In some cases troops were already in the area of the riot; the order is then to intervene, not to march, but it is often to be found in the marching order book (W.O.5).

No table has been made for the numbers of troops used. Seven cavalry regiments and five infantry regiments were involved in whole or in part by orders from London, but the issue of general orders meant the intervention of many other units by local applications, of which there exists no record.

	Date	Unit	From	To	Remarks
	August				
1.	1	*3 Dragoons* 'detachments'	Dorchester	Ottery St Mary, Sidbury or Lyme	To march if requisitioned.
2.	8	*16 Light Dragoons* 2 troops	Epsom	Newbury	
3.	19	*3 Dragoons* 1 troop	Dorchester	Newbury	To relieve 16 L. Dragoons
	September				
4.	6	*3 Dragoons* 2 troops	Blandford	Cullompton and Ottery St Mary	
5.	19	*43 Foot* 2 companies	Winchester	Gloucester, Stroud, Hampton and Painswick	Distance Winchester – Gloucester is 80 miles or at least four days' march.
6.	19	*4 Dragoons* 'detachments'	Worcester	Gloucester, Stroud, Hampton and Painswick	To march if requisitioned
7.	20	*4 Dragoons* 2 troops	Worcester	Gloucester, Stroud, Hampton and Painswick	Cancelled order of the 19th.
8.	20	*43 Foot* 2 companies	Tiverton	Tiverton	In the town since 5 August, but not originally as a riot measure.

	Date	Unit	From	To	Remarks
	September				
9.	21	*13 Foot* 4 companies	Salisbury	Devizes	
10–19.	23	10 cavalry regiments to take up their horses from grass.			
20.	24	*13 Foot* 2 companies	Salisbury	Trowbridge	
21.	24	*13 Foot* 3 companies	Salisbury	Salisbury	To remain at request to War Office of the Mayor.
22.	24	*15 Light Dragoons* 20 men	Derby	Derby	To remain at request to War Office of the Mayor.
23.	24	*6 Dragoons*	Coventry	Coventry	To help Mayor and magistrates if requisitioned.
24–36.	24	General orders to 13 cavalry regiments and seven infantry regiments to assist magistrates if requisitioned.			
37–50.	27	Same order to 14 independent companies of invalids in garrison.			
51.	28	*2 Dragoon Guards* 2 Troops	Colchester	Norwich	
52.	28	*3 Dragoons* 2 Troops	Dorchester	Bradford and Trowbridge	See 20. above. Magistrates required additional force.
53.	28	Creation of Bradford area command – Lt.-Col. Bonham.			
54.	30	*13 Foot* 2 companies	Devizes	Chippenham (1 company) Calne (1 company)	
	October				
55.	1	*3 Dragoons* 1 Troop	Newbury	Reading	
56.	1	*43 Foot* 1 company	Hampton Court	Reading	When relieved by the Foot Guards.

	Date	Unit	From	To	Remarks
	October				
57.	1	*43 Foot* 2 companies	Windsor	Newbury	When relieved by the Foot Guards.
58.	2	*7 Dragoons* 'detachment'	Northampton	Leicester	To march if requisitioned.
59.	3	*8 Foot* 5 companies	Chatham	Reading (3 companies) Newbury (2 companies)	
60.	3	*43 Foot* 3 companies	Reading Newbury	Marlborough	When relieved by 8 Foot.
61.	3	*3 Dragoons* 2 troops	Reading	Marlborough	
62.	3	*3 Dragoons* 2 troops	Bradford	Frome	When relieved by 1 troop of 4 Dragoons.
63.	3	*4 Dragoons* 3 Troops	Gloucester	Devizes (2 troops) Bradford (1 troop)	
64.	3	Creation of West of England command Lt.-Col. Warde (to include Bradford command).			
65.	3	*4 Dragoons* 5 Troops	Worcester	Gloucester (2 troops) Stroud (1 troop) Hampton (1 troop) Painswick (1 troop)	When relived by three troops of 6 Dragoons.
66.	3	*6 Dragoons* 3 troops	Coventry	Worcester	
67.	3	*6 Dragoons* remainder	Coventry	Coventry	To remain at request of magistrates

	Date	Unit	From	To	Remarks
	October				
68.	5	*15 Light Dragoons* 'detachments'	Derby	Nottingham	To march if requisitioned
69.	5	*15 Light Dragoons* 2 troops	Derby	Birmingham	
70.	5	*6 Dragoons* 'detachments'	Coventry	Birmingham	O.C. to send detachments 'as you shall judge may conveniently be spared from the Service on which you are employed'.
71.	10	*15 Light Dragoons* 2 troops	Derby	Birmingham	To relieve two troops of same regiment already there (69 above).
72.	13	*15 Light Dragoons* Sergeant + 12 men	Birmingham	Stourbridge	
73.	21	*3 Dragoons* 2 troops	Marlborough	Bradford	
74.	21	*4 Dragoons* 2 troops	Devizes (1 troop) Bradford (1 troop)	Gloucester	Bradford troop not to move until relieved by 3 Dragoons.
75.	25	*49 Foot* 1 company	Woodbridge	Woodbridge	
76.	28	*2 Dragoon Guards* 1 troop	Colchester	Ipswich	
77.	29	*8 Foot* 1 company	Ipswich	Woodbridge	When relieved by 2 Dragoon Guards.

	Date	Unit	From	To	Remarks
	October				
78.	29	7 *Dragoons* 1 troop	Hinckley (Leics.)	Hinckley	To remain at requisition of Lord Denbigh
79.	29	7 *Dragoons* 1 troop	Northampton	Loughborough	
	November				
80.	16	4 *Foot* 1 company	Plymouth	Tiverton	To march if requisitioned.
81.	26	Lt.-Col. Warde to continue parties in Gloucestershire as required by magistrates.			

TABLE 9.2

Summary of Riots by County and Town: 1766

Berkshire	Newbury	*Northumberland*	Berwick
	Great Marlow	*Nottingham*	Nottingham
	Maidenhead	*Oxford*	Oxford
	Reading	*Somerset*	Bath
			Beckington
			Wincanton
Buckingham	Aylesbury	*Staffordshire*	Stoke
Cornwall	Redruth		Tipton
	St Austell		Wolverhampton
			Bromsgrove
Derby	Derby	*Suffolk*	Beccles
Devon	Crediton		Bungay
	Exeter		Ipswich
	Honiton		Woodbridge
	Silverton	*Warwick*	Birmingham
	Bradninch		Coventry
	Ottery St Mary		Alcester
	Lyme		Great Colton
	Sidbury	*Wiltshire*	Chippenham
	Cullompton		Calne
	Tiverton		Malmesbury
Gloucester	Gloucester		Marlborough
	Hampton		Bradley (near Trowbridge)
	Cirencester		Devizes
	Lechlade		Trowbridge
	Stroud		Salisbury
	Pagenwell		Bradford-on-Avon
	Tetbury		

TABLE 9.2 (*contd.*)

Hertford	St Albans	*Worcestershire*	Worcester
Leicester	Leicester		Bewdley
	Hinckley		Dudley
	Donnington		Halesowen
	Ashby de la Zouch		Kidderminster
	Loughborough		Stourbridge
Norfolk	Burnham Market	*Yorkshire*	Scarborough
	Norwich		
Northants	Wellingborough	20 counties	68 towns

TABLE 9.3

Forces under command of Lt.-Col. Warde, 3 October 1766 (W.O. 4/80)

Unit	Troop or Company	Place
3 Dragoons		
(Albemarle's)	2	Blandford
	2	Cullompton, Ottery
	2	Frome
	detachment	Marlborough
4 Dragoons		
(Rich's)	2	Gloucester
	1	Stroud, Hampton, Painswick
	1	Devizes
	1	Bradford
13 Foot		
(Duke of Gloucester's)	3	Salisbury
	2	Devizes
	2	Trowbridge
	1	Chippenham
	1	Calne
43 Foot		
(Cary's)	3	Marlborough
	2	Winchester
	2	Gloucester

10 The Problem of London

Eighteenth-century London, vast, sprawling and dangerous, produced riots which were in a class of their own, and the problems of dealing with them alarmed contemporaries. In the light of the events of 1765, and even more so of 1768 and 1780, the words of Sir John Fielding, urging the foundation of a proper police system in London, took on a prophetic ring:

> An attention to domestic quiet, especially in a metropolis, which is the seat of government, is, to the last degree, praiseworthy, as it is productive of the happiest effects; and when such a police is brought to due perfection, it will not only prevent common acts of violence between man and man, but such a vigilance will ever defeat any attempts that malice, extravagance or disappointed ambition may contrive against the government itself.[1]

Riots in this century, as we have already seen, were often difficult to deal with by virtue of their remoteness from the capital, but at least they usually lasted for some time and offered a fair mark to the forces marching towards the district. In London mobs often appeared, caused immense damage and vanished within a short time, giving no opportunity of interference from troops, and this within a mile or so of several military strong-points. Some of these riots were extremely difficult to forecast, arising from a sudden impulse of sheer devilment. Dire poverty and its horrors gave rise individually to crimes of robbery and violence and collectively to riotous situations, but often there was no direct element of social protest. In the countryside it was possible to ignore the poor, at least until they demanded sufficiently loudly to have their grievances noticed, but in the city the propertied classes could not fail to be made constantly uneasy by the vast underworld of men who made the streets so dangerous at night, composed the mobs which almost any unusual event seemed to conjure out of the ground, and who it seemed, having nothing to lose, could so easily make a bid for power. Henry Fielding wondered what the results of a general riot might be, when a small mob of chairmen or servants or thieves so easily got above the civil power.[2] The intelligent administrator had to expect the London riot at any time.

Some went so far as to make tentative strategic plans for some such outbreak, an unusual occurrence in this century, and itself a sufficient testimony to their alarm. In 1756 Lord Tyrawley, on being appointed to command the Coldstream Guards in London, submitted a paper[3] on the subject of the security of the capital to the Duke of Cumberland (who passed it on to Lord Holdernesse), apologising for some of his remarks 'which, as falling within the Civil Branch, may possibly be thought out of my sphere'. If any riot threatened, the Foot Guards, he wrote, should be ready to turn out at the first alarm, the barracks and armouries should be improved, Horse Guards and Horse Grenadier Guards should patrol, small detachments of men should be placed in the parish watch-houses, London and Westminster Bridges would require guards supported by field guns, and large boats should always be at hand (and guarded) at Whitehall and Somerset House stairs to take parties to danger points. The battalions stationed at St James's should regard the West End of the town as their care, and the Tower troops should watch the East End, the Bank and London Bridge. The parks should be closed to prevent the collecting of crowds. Private powder stores above a certain limited amount should be impounded, 'both for the safety of it and to prevent its falling into bad hands'. Communications through the City would be kept open by the trained bands of London and Westminster, 'was it only for the sake of keeping so many of these people employed that they may not mischievously employ themselves'. Roman Catholics should be sent away from London. He presumed that with the completion of such a system

> . . . the town, and the quiet of it, is secured from all tumults and riots, that people's fears or ill intentions might suggest to them on such an occasion, that the respect due to the Royal Family will be preserved, the Parliament and Courts of Justice protected in their sitting, and the shops and markets kept open, as in times of the most profound quiet.[4]

The measures suggested, many of which were hurriedly put into effect in 1780 and closely resemble those forming the basis of nineteenth-century planning on the subject, do not seem to have impressed Holdernesse, who filed the paper without comment.

Lord Barrington also wrote down his thoughts on the matter, although he had a more accurate sense of what was politically possible than Tyrawley. He wrote in 1776:

> In the years 1757 and 1758, when there was not the least difference of opinion in politics, within doors or without, a very numerous army was scarce sufficient to suppress insurrections in many places, on account of the militia, and a scarcity of corn: yet at that time everything was quiet, in and about the capital.
>
> On the contrary, at present, London is of all places in the island the most attentively to be watched, on account of the many actively desperate and ill-affected people who are in it. I need not say how little the magistracy of the City is to be trusted, or how much to be feared.[5]

This paper, which was presented to the King to urge against the denuding of Britain's garrison to supply the American theatre, suggested that no detachments from the Guards in London should be made, at least until an augmentation equal in numbers had been provided. The numbers of the Guards were in any case lower than they had ever been since 1763. He continued:

> When the weavers attacked Bedford House, the Guards were not deemed a sufficient force; and many regiments were assembled in the neighbourhood, as a reinforcement.
>
> It is not many years, since a mob at Madrid forced the King of Spain to fly from his capital; or many months, since another alarmed the King of France at Versailles: at the same time it was necessary that every baker's shop at Paris should be protected by soldiers. The governments, in almost all the provinces of North America, were overturned by insurrections last summer, because there was not a sufficient force to defend them.
>
> If an insurrection in London should be attended with the least success, or even to continue unquelled for any time, (a circumstance much to be apprehended, as the City Magistrates will not call for the assistance of troops) it is highly probable, there would also be risings in many parts of the kingdom. The present apparent quiet should not make it forgotten, that there is a very levelling spirit among the people.
>
> Repeated experience shows that no stops can be put anywhere to these risings, without the intervention of troops; and if there are not, within reasonable distance, sufficient troops to check them at the beginning, a large force becomes necessary for the purpose.[6]

The peace of London was threatened in 1765, 1768, and most seriously in 1780. Each of these outbreaks gave rise to movements of troops on a large scale, and to problems of planning and strategy. The first rising was of the weavers of the East End. They had already rioted in October 1763 and destroyed property. Four of their number were shot dead. The operation was handled by the Foot Guards and no problem deserving to be called strategical arose.[7] In 1765 they were more determined and created more complicated problems for the Secretary at War. The riots were violent but, largely as a result of a resolute use of military power, short-lived. They began on 16 May 1765 and had died away by 21 May, but were serious enough to make Horace Walpole believe that 'there is such a general spirit of mutiny and dissatisfaction in the lower people, that I think we are in danger of a rebellion in the heart of the capital in a week',[8] and to make use of the term 'civil war.'[9]

The tactics of mob-breaking by soldiers are discussed in Chapter 13. The strategical handling of the emergency by the War Office was a good example of promptly executed short-range action, where delays of only an hour or less would have had serious consequences.

The story of the rising has taken its place in the annals of eighteenth-century London, and needs no detailed description. The events[10] were as follows:

1. *Thursday 16 May.* The weavers assembled in Moorfields, broke the windows of several master weavers and threatened to pull down their houses. They then drew up their procession and marched towards Westminster in a crowd of several thousand to picket Parliament.

2. *17 May.* The weavers again surrounded the Palace of Westminster to the number of about 8000. Events wore a much more ugly air on this day, and in the evening part of the mob moved off to attack Bedford House, the Duke having become unpopular with them as being the only peer who spoke against increasing the duties on Italian silks. This mob was dispersed by the military with great violence.[11]

3. *18 May.* Palace Yard was again crowded with weavers, and peers could only get in with the help of Horse and Foot Guards. Rioters also damaged the house of a master weaver on Ludgate Hill.

4. *20 May.* Mobs again gathered in Bloomsbury Square but moved off when horse and foot appeared.

The danger points for the War Office to consider were Bloomsbury Square, Westminster, Spitalfields and Moorfields. The first two were within reach of the Guards at St James's, the Tiltyard, the Savoy and Somerset House. Spitalfields and Moorfields could be covered by the detachment of Foot Guards at the Tower. The first move of the Secretary at War was, as in 1763, to quarter soldiers in the riotous area. One hundred men of the Guards moved from the Tower into the parishes of St Matthew (Bethnal Green), Christchurch (Spitalfields), and St Leonard (Shoreditch), with power to move to any other spot suggested by the civil magistrates.[12] The master weavers had complained of being molested, whether to the Secretary at War or the Secretary of State is not clear; certainly the Secretaries of State, Halifax and Sandwich, issued a number of orders to Welbore Ellis on 16 May which in the interests of speed were never put into writing.[13] On the next day all three regiments of Foot Guards were ordered to be held ready to send without delay detachments if called upon by the civil magistrates.[14] In operations against destructive street mobs, where events moved very rapidly, considerable damage might be done in the time taken to turn out a detachment which was not ready to march. A similar order was sent to the 11th Dragoons, who were quartered at Lambeth, to have ready one squadron for immediate march.[15]

On 17 May the riots were much worse. Parties of horse and foot attended at Palace Yard, the squadron of dragoons alerted the previous day marched from Lambeth to Westminster Bridge, and a further detachment of 100 of the Guards were sent into Moorfields, where rioting had taken place.[16] The Secretaries of State were sufficiently alarmed to require more troops to be held ready;[17] the afternoon and evening were however occupied by the siege in Bloomsbury, and the Secretary at War did not issue orders for this until the morning of 18 May.

The orders of 17 May for troops to protect Bedford House were part of an efficient operation, in a situation where observers such as Horace Walpole thought that the least delay would have been fatal. Fortunately a detachment of 50 men of the Foot Guards was already there.[18] Two messengers came to Ellis, probably in the late afternoon, with news of the attack on the house. The squadron in readiness (90 men of the 11th Dragoons) with one troop of Horse Guards and one of Horse Grenadier Guards marched immediately, under the command of Colonel Warrender of the Dragoons, who was the senior officer present.[19] They arrived in time to save Bedford House.[20] Halifax believed that without them the house would have been levelled to the ground and the Duke and his company probably murdered.[21] During the evening the force of Foot Guards at the house was built up to 172. The total numbers (excluding magistrates and peace officers) required to guard one town house, admittedly an extensive property in this case, was therefore over 320, that is to say 172 guardsmen and five troops of cavalry. Later in the evening Colonel Warrender was authorised to use the entire regiment if the magistrates wanted it, but by then the riot had died down, at least in Bloomsbury.[22] The second troop of the Horse Grenadier Guards and a party of Foot Guards also did duty that night on Ludgate Hill at the requisition of the Lord Mayor to the Secretaries of State.[23] Between midnight and one o'clock in the morning of 18 May another requisition arrived from Sandwich for a party in Moorfields; the troops were evidently not in any readiness to march at once and did not leave their quarters until between 6 and 7 o'clock in the morning.[24]

This last circumstance gave point to the activities later the same morning of the Secretary at War, who began to put into effect the instructions of the Secretaries of State of the previous afternoon. The entire regiment of the 11th Dragoons, instead of detachments only, and all the Foot Guards were to hold themselves ready for immediate march.[25] The Secretaries continued to maintain a close hold over operations, and started to cast around for other reinforcements.

> The troops of Guards having been much harassed with the fatigue of yesterday, Lord Sandwich and Lord Halifax have thought it their duty to direct the Secretary at War to order Lord Waldegrave's and Sir John Mordaunt's Dragoons nearer London.[26]

Accordingly the War Office ordered the 2nd Dragoon Guards at Putney to quarter one squadron at Hoxton, Hackney and Bethnal Green, and one at Islington and St Pancras, after agreeing the exact posts with the magistrates.[27] The 10th Dragoons at Kingston were ordered to quarter one squadron at Kensington and Knightsbridge, and one at Paddington,

Lissing Green (i.e. Lisson Green), Marylebone and Tottenham Court.[28] These quarters were fixed upon after consulting with the quartermaster, Colonel Roy,[29] who no doubt expected the former regiment to cover the East End where the mobs arose, and the latter to cover Bloomsbury and Westminster. As a third reserve the 15th Light Dragoons were ordered to march from Staines to Fulham, Putney, Hammersmith, Kew Green, Turnham Green and Parsons Green.[30] The Royal Regiment of Horse Guards at Hertford were ordered to be ready to march immediately if an order should come 'which, it is judged, may be necessary to be sent for your advancing nearer to London'.[31]

By 20 May the government, unaware that the worst was now past, was considering placing the operations in and around London under a single commander. Lord Granby, the Duke of Richmond and Lord Waldegrave were all proposed, and the Adjutant-General proposed himself. The King wrote:

Lord Granby is a very popular man and might save the lives of these deluded wretches which may be exposed and sacrificed by another commander equally well intentioned but less a favourite of the people.[32]

The Adjutant-General's opinion was based more on a logistic than a human appreciation of the problem:

. . . it may be attended with some convenience to have one officer have the command of the whole, by which means the duty may be better regulated, and the civil magistrates, by knowing what particular person to apply to, may be more expeditiously furnished with the whole, or any number that may be necessary. As I am on the staff, and not employed as Adjutant General in this affair, I think it incumbent on me to offer myself for this duty.[33]

The King eventually fixed upon the Duke of Cumberland to be Captain General; the Duke was not pleased at the prospect: 'I shall ever obey your orders with obedience and readiness: all I hope is I am only ordered and expected on this occasion.'[34]

A number of orders issued from the War Office on 20 May; altogether during that day Ellis wrote eighteen letters of orders or directions which appear on the letter books. They may be summarised as follows:

1. *Orders for the security of the House of Lords.*

The house was to meet this day, and orders went to the entire corps of Horse and Horse Grenadier Guards to be ready for instant call in terms similar to those already given to the Foot Guards two days before.[35] The 11th Dragoons at Lambeth, the battalion of the 1st Guards at the Tower (apart from the parties in Spitalfields), the 2nd Dragoon Guards at Islington, and the 10th Dragoons at Kensington were all similarly ordered.[36] The authorities expected riots to begin in the neighbourhood of Westminster, and to be transmitted rapidly around Westminster and the City.

2. *Orders to watch Spitalfields and Bedford House.*

Two hundred men of the Guards in Spitalfields were to be at the disposal of the Lord Mayor together with the troops of the 2nd Dragoon Guards dispersed in Hoxton, Hackney and Bethnal Green (three troops) and Islington and St Pancras (three troops).[37] Saunders Welch, the J.P. on duty at Bedford House, asked for another 100 Horse and Horse Grenadier Guards, which were provided;[38] and a detachment of the 2nd Dragoon Guards, whose numbers were to be at the discretion of the regiment's commander, was to patrol the New Road (now Marylebone and Euston Roads) and the Duke's private road, and give notice to Saunders Welch of any approach of rioters.[39] A similar patrol at Marylebone was ordered for the 10th Dragoons.[40]

3. *Orders for the collection and receipt of firearms.*

In 1768 and 1780 plans were made to stop private firearms from falling into the hands of the mob. In 1765 the chief fear was for the arms of the Middlesex Militia, which had been lodged in the Savoy, where they were in a place of indifferent security, the more so if the Guards there should be called out. The Secretary at War arranged for their removal with the Duke of Northumberland, who commanded the Militia, and with the Master General of the Ordnance.[41] Boats were hired and they were transported by water to the Tower.[42]

This outbreak ceased as suddenly as it had begun. Some precautions were taken on 21 May, but they were unnecessary. Ellis proposed to the King to hold in readiness only one squadron each at Lambeth, Hackney and Marylebone,

> which with a picquet of fifty Footguards at the Savoy and fifty at the Horse Guards, together with the hundred quartered in Moorfields and one hundred quartered in Spitalfields may, as it is presumed, secure the peace of the town for this night.[43]

This letter was endorsed in the King's hand 'Approved if the Adj. G. is of that opinion'.

The government at first thought the tranquillity after 20 May illusory and ominous, and kept the troops on duty for several more days, after which they were marched back to quarters.[44] Nothing further was done to appoint a commander for the troops in the area of London.

This short but reasonably well organised military intervention was a fair example of King, War Office and Secretary of State's Office working together without ambiguity. Welbore Ellis, a man of little experience in such matters, was agitated but by no means overcome by the situation, and was probably relieved to have tactful help from a staff with experience under Barrington, and active and close supervision from the government, who directed affairs in these riots to a degree not observable in riots outside London. The handling of the 1768 riots, admittedly much more widespread among many different groups of workers in and outside London, and more violent, was less happy in its results. As will be shown, an experienced administrator of Barrington's type would have managed better in 1768 without the constant interference of the King and the incompetent, petulant Lord Weymouth.

11 The London Riots of 1768

The London riots of 1768 were the most severe test of the system of public order which eighteenth-century London had yet experienced, with the possible exception of the Sacheverell riots. Although the Wilkite mobs have had the most attention from historians there were disturbances in many parts of the country, and some of the riots in and around London had nothing to do with Wilkes and precede his appearance as a parliamentary candidate. Bad harvests for several years, followed by a severe winter in 1767–8, had caused much hardship, and the coal heavers and weavers of the East End had rioted in January even before Wilkes had returned to England.[1] By the middle of 1768, in addition to the Wilkes riots, there had occurred (or were still occurring) riots in the London area on the part of the Spitalfields weavers, the coal heavers of Wapping and Shadwell, the hatters, the tailors and the glass-grinders; and in the provinces, among the sailors and keelmen of Newcastle and Sunderland, and the poor of Tenterden, Maidstone, Hastings, Norwich, Great Yarmouth, Melton, Boston, Pontefract, Gloucester, and many parts of Cornwall. Most of these did not affect the handling of operations in London. The events which made up the problem there for the War Office can briefly be summarised:[2]

1. *28 March.* After the election for the County of Middlesex at Brentford the mob returned through Westminster and the City, breaking windows not illuminated in honour of Wilkes' victory.

2. *29 March.* Rioting became more violent, in spite of precautions on the part of the government.

3. *31 March.* Sir John Fielding, chairman of the Westminster Quarter Sessions, felt compelled to ask for troops.

The early days of April saw a lull in London, although few nights were free from some sort of disturbance. The government turned its attention to the provincial disturbances, of which there were many.

4. *20 April.* This was the first day of the law term, when Wilkes had undertaken publicly to surrender to his outlawry. In the event he was released when it became clear that he had been served with a defective process. The government made many preparations, with magistrates and peace officers in attendance, and soldiers on call, but the day was an anticlimax and no mob appeared around Westminster Hall. An unconnected but serious riot occurred however at the other end of the town, where the Guards and the Shadwell coal heavers fought together.[3]

5. *22 April.* A riot at Goodman Fields, which seems to have arisen out of

an abduction, needed 100 soldiers to disperse it.[4]

6. *26 April*. The coal heavers of Wapping rose, and three people were killed before the Guards appeared. Alderman Beckford distributed 100 guineas among them and promised them fair wages for their labour.

7. *27 April*. Wilkes was now properly served and brought into court, but on his committal was carried off into the City by a rescue mob. Subsequently he wisely surrendered himself to the Marshal and was confined in the King's Bench Prison.

8. *28 April*. Riots in the neighbourhood of the King's Bench Prison were too much for the civil power, and soldiers cleared the precincts. The rioters then compelled the houses of Borough High Street to illuminate their windows.

9. *29 April*. Riots again occurred around the prison. After this day a comparative lull again ensued, until

10. *6 May*, when the Surrey magistrates asked for a permanent guard at the prison. By this date the port of London had almost ceased to function, thousands of sailors had stopped work and deliberately disabled ships from sailing, and the coal heavers had joined forces with them.

11. *10 May*. The riot of St George's Fields, one of the most notorious of the century, took place. Soldiers pursued and shot dead a young man during the morning. In the afternoon, after the Riot Act had been read, soldiers fired on the crowd and a number of people were killed or wounded. The rioting in London died down, probably as a result of this sobering experience.

12. *8 June*. Wilkes appeared in court (and again on 18 June); on each occasion security precautions were taken but no riots developed. For the government these riots produced dangerous situations not only at both ends of the town, as in 1765, but also on the Surrey side of the river. And whereas the riots of 1765 were contained within a single week, those of 1768 lasted for nearly three months, apart from the provincial risings, which occupied a large part of the whole year.

Once again the Secretary of State kept a tight control on the operation, a circumstance not always favourable to efficiency and speed, but unavoidable because the magistrates looked to his office for guidance. The intervention of the office of the Secretary of State in 1768 was frequently amateurish and impeding, a contrast with its role in 1765, and with that of the War Office, which by this date had developed a technique for the swift handling of riots. Of the two secretaries Shelburne appeared very little, and the Wilkes riots were handled by Viscount Weymouth. Weymouth, one of Bedford's protégés, has not had much praise from contemporaries or historians. Horace Walpole calls him an 'inconsiderable, debauched young man',[5] and said that he seldom rose before midday and that his secretary Robert Wood transacted much of the business of the office while his master was gaming at White's.[6] Certainly most of the letters during the emergency went out over Wood's signature.

The events of 28 March did not entirely take the government by surprise, as some thought at the time,[7] but certainly Barrington, from long experience of this sort of thing, was much better prepared than Weymouth. He wrote to the King, probably in the early afternoon:

> A very great and riotous mob having gone this morning to Brentford, it is not unreasonable to suppose they may attempt to do more mischief on their return: I have therefore given a hint to Lt. Col. Hollingsworth, who is the officer on guard, to be alert; and I have desired Lords Gower and Weymouth (who called on me, the same idea having struck them) to take the proper measures for having a civil magistrate in the way this evening. There is no sort of intelligence to create the least suspicion of any formed design, but the mob if not prevented often does mischief which it did not intend.[8]

The King wrote back that he would not stir from home so that Barrington could come or send to him if necessary.[9]

In fact the military were hardly used that night. This was not their fault; they were obliged to wait for a request from a magistrate, and they waited, for the most part, in vain. Two companies of the Guards were sent to the Mansion House, but the greater part of the damage to windows had been done before they arrived. This and other checks were of local and minor effect, and the mob was almost unchallenged that night. The King stayed up all night 'full of indignation at the insult', and to those who expressed fears that the rioters would approach the Queen's House he said 'he wished they would push their insolence so far, he should then be justified in repelling it, and giving proper orders to the Guards'.[10] He wrote indignantly to Barrington on the morning of 29 March:

> Considering the riotous conduct of the populace last night, it becomes the more highly necessary that every precaution be used that the military be ready this evening to keep the peace if the civil magistrate should call for their aid.[11]

On the same morning Weymouth wrote to Barrington with the King's command to hold troops in readiness to intervene at the shortest notice if the magistrates applied.[12]

It is likely that this letter was written to regularise verbal instructions, and that the idea of alerting troops, a commonplace one for the War Office by 1768, originated from Barrington at the consultation with Weymouth the previous day.[13]

Weymouth also wrote – directly, not through the War Office, which must have confused the situation – to Lord Cadogan to ask him to give orders to the Horse Grenadier Guards to be similarly ready, adding:

your Lordship should give the orders with as little appearance of alarm as possible, for though it is intended to provide effectually against mischief which may possibly happen, it is to he hoped there will be no occasion to come to such extremities.[14]

Barrington wrote to the King: 'Your majesty may be assured that proper and sufficient military assistance will not be wanting, nor was it wanting yesterday',[15] a tactful reminder that however well-laid War Office plans might be, the initiative lay with the magistrates. He then wrote orders for the Guards at the Savoy to make detachments as required by the magistrates.[16] At 4 p.m. he wrote again to the King to say that the battalion at the Savoy was ready to march at short notice, and that the battalion at the Tower would help if the Lord Mayor and the City magistrates wanted.

> Colonel Matthews, a very good officer, is on guard today: I have seen him, and he will keep a very good look out.
> I am myself persuaded that a very small force will if properly directed keep the peace: but as no precaution should be omitted, I have desired Colonel Morrison to draw up a proper plan for bringing the troops within three score miles nearer to the capital. . . .
> I have fully apprised Lord Weymouth of everything I have done and I acquainted him where military aid may be had at a moment's notice.[17]

On the same day Weymouth wrote to the Duke of Northumberland, the Lord Lieutenant of Middlesex, encouraging him to call for a military force if necessary.[18]

In spite of all these preparations the mischief on the evening of 29 March far outstripped anything seen on the previous night. Once again mobs met with little resistance save from a few spiritied constables. The magistrates did not call for soldiers and War Office plans were therefore unavoidably abortive. Not until 31 March did Sir John Fielding ask for soldiers. Fielding disliked the use of troops, but his force of 80 constables for the whole of London and Westminster was clearly insufficient to deal with large crowds, usually in the dark hours, and with appeals for help from owners of threatened houses.

No information survives of any conversations between Barrington and the Quarter-Master General, Colonel Morrison, about concentrating troops near London, but it must soon have become clear to them that a circle of 60 miles around London was insufficient and that troops would have to come from further afield. On 4 April orders were sent to Burgoyne's Light Dragoons at Lincoln to march south, avoiding election towns, and to take up quarters at Epsom, Ewell, Beddington and Carshalton.[19] As the danger increased one troop was brought in to Richmond and two troops to Wimbledon, Tooting, Wandsworth, Clapham and Clapham Common.[20]

Within the next five weeks the following regiments were brought into the London area as a result of riots:

1. *25th Foot (Lennox's)* from St Albans to Hampstead, Highgate and Kentish Town, to march on 23 April.[21]
2. *1st Light Dragoons (Elliott's)* from Egham to Richmond, Kew, Kew Green, Chiswick, Putney, Fulham, Parson's Green and Walham Green, to march on 23 April.[22]
3. *2nd Light Dragoons (Burgoyne's)* from Epsom and Beddington to Wimbledon, Tooting, Wandsworth, Clapham, and Clapham Common, to arrive on 29 April.[23]
4. *3rd Dragoons (Albemarle's)* from Lewes to Deptford and Lewisham, in two divisions, the second to arrive on 7 May.[24]
5. *2nd or Royal North British Dragoons (Argyll's)* from Canterbury to Greenwich and Blackheath, to arrive on 7 May.[25]
6. *6th or Inniskilling Dragoons (Cholmondeley's)* from Henley and Maidenhead to Lambeth, Vauxhall, Kennington, Newington Butts, Battersea, Streatham, Clapham and Clapham Common.[26]
7. *Royal Regiment of Horse Guards or Blues (Granby's)* from Barnet to Greenwich, Blackheath, Deptford and Lewisham.[27]

This plan, which had the effect of laying a considerable military cordon around London without making the presence of soldiers felt within the capital, was in accordance with Barrington's usual principle to have troops on hand but not on display.

It was realised that careful preparations would have to be made for the first day of the legal term. The government felt that it had been made to look ineffective and ridiculous, and a harder note creeps into new preparations; magistrates are urged not to hesitate to call for troops, and use them, in the knowledge that the ministers would give their support to officers and men. This tendency culminated in Weymouth's letter to the Surrey magistrates on 17 April,[28] and Barrington's letter of congratulation to the Guards after the killings in St George's Fields,[29] both of which were published in newspapers, and gave the handling of the operation an air which was brutal and sinister rather than merely inept.

On the afternoon of 9 April the King, knowing that Grafton was to meet his ministers in the evening, wrote to him at length; his letter shows that the King had as clear an apprehension of the dangers of using the military as had his government, and had also in his mind the legal problems arising from the use of force:

> I am of opinion, that those conversant in the law must first declare what can legally be done; that once ascertained, I incline much to following that with vigour that licentiousness may be curbed; and a general resolution to this effect is all I wish to be come to this evening. . . . if it

should afterwards appear necessary, that additional troops be brought to the Capital, that can easily be effected and I have already taken some steps on that head that cannot spread alarm. I am averse to making any show of troops in the streets on the day of opening the term, for that naturally would draw a concourse of people together but the battalion in barrack at the Savoy may be kept there in readiness to be called upon at a minute's warning; the same precaution may be had with regard to the Horse and Grenadier Guards without any noise.[30]

On 14 April the Duke of Northumberland wrote to both Secretaries of State to point out that the arms of the Middlesex militia were deposited in vestry rooms and other places in Westminster easily accessible to the mob, and ought to be taken to the Tower.[31] Weymouth merely recommended greater vigilance in guarding the arms; the military could be called in if the mob attempted to seize them. Northumberland, dissatisfied with the obvious inadequacy of such an arrangement, on his own account ordered the guns to be rendered temporarily useless by removal of the locks.[32]

As the first day of term approached preparation increased. Barrington sent a memorandum to the Secretary of State's office saying that the civil magistrates might have military assistance on 20 April by sending for it to the Tower, Savoy or War Office,[33] a piece of information which Weymouth passed on to Sir John Fielding and to Daniel Ponton, the Chairman of Lambeth Sessions,in whose jurisdiction the King's Bench Prison lay.[34] Barrington had by then done all he could to protect the capital; by 20 April there were regiments or parts of regiments at many points in villages outside London and this cordon was increased after the episode of 27 April. More forces could not be spared, due to the disorders elsewhere in England; Norwich, Manchester, Newcastle and most of Northumberland and Durham had been affected by riots for weeks. Two regiments of cavalry were on riot duty in the area of Newcastle alone.

Weymouth wrote to Northumberland enclosing a report of the Adjutant-General on the disposition of troops. Detachments were ready to march at a moment's notice from the Tower, Savoy or Tiltyard, and the names of the responsible officers to whom the magistrates' requisitions were to be addressed were all set down.

If more troops are wanted than what the Tower, Savoy, Tiltyard Guard and Horse Guards can supply, on application to the Secretary at War at the War Office, orders will be issued immediately.[35]

As the Horse Guards will be in readiness to march to the Surrey side General Harvey thinks that it may be better not to quarter light troops on the other side of Westminster Bridge, which can't be done privately; he has ordered Burgoyne's to halt a day as they will be more in readiness to assist should anything happen on Wednesday than if they went through that morning to Croydon as was intended.[36]

Other letters to Ponton and Fielding on 19 April left them in no doubt as to where to obtain troops, even if the advice on their employment was as usual vague. A more realistic view was expressed in the Lord Mayor's letter to Weymouth on the same day; he pointed out that as the business would be over early in the day nothing much need be feared, 'as from observation I have found very few daring enough to commit an open breach of the peace in daylight'.[37] He was right, for the appearance of Wilkes before Mansfield was an anticlimax. He left the court at 2 p.m.; large crowds were on the streets but no violence was offered. There was nothing for the military to do, and apart from a few arrests very little for the magistrates.

A few days later the kidnapping of Wilkes by the populace took place. He had now been properly served and brought to Westminster Hall, but on his committal to the King's Bench Prison his carriage was in the late afternoon carried off into the city 'with an expedition beyond conception' in the words of a shaken Fielding.[38] This tactical defeat of the forces of order arose from a combination of strategic failure and accident. The Surrey constables should have been on the bridge to receive Wilkes into their district but were not there. The documents show that Middlesex was better informed than Surrey,[39] but that in the course of the day Fielding, realising how matters were developing, sent an express to warn Ponton and his justices. In the event it was too late. Wilkes emerged from court at 6.30 p.m., giving ample time for a mob to develop. Earlier in the day matters might have been different, but the hearing was delayed by a long case which occupied most of the day. The whole incident was described by Lord Weymouth as 'a disgrace to civil government',[40] and certainly an eighteenth-century government can seldom have been made to appear so ridiculous. No arrests were even made, and although the War Office had made careful preparations events had rendered them null. It is arguable that if strategical plans fail to set up a system in which tactics can be successful then that is a strategical failure, but for this the War Office could hardly be blamed. Its plans were only one half of an overall scheme of which the civil officers were part – and constitutionally the part holding the initiative, and over which the Secretary of State on this occasion was determined to keep a tight control. The preparations of the Secretary of State's office, which were careful for 20 April, seemed to have been relaxed in the days before 27 April. The rescue of Wilkes was so sudden that only a plan involving numerous troops actually in attendance, however provocative this might be, would have prevented it, and this could only be arranged if Weymouth had ordered it. Barrington could not possibly have ordered it on his own. The War Office letter-book shows that he had given orders to the Horse and Foot Guards to be prepared for instant call on that day, but not to be actually present. The copy of the letter was inserted after several letters of 28 and 29 April, but Barrington was determined, however awkwardly, to have his personal record straight. He was going to be blameless and to be seen to be blameless.[41] Later he went to the trouble of drawing up an abstract of all his transactions connected with the St George's Fields riot as far back as 29 March and extending forward to 7 September, and added a note of the judges' summing up in the trial of the magistrates on duty on 10 May.[42] By 1768 Barrington was too experienced to be caught unbriefed.

No further plans were called for during the riots of the next few days. The troops in London continued under orders to help if magistrates requisitioned them, and they waited in vain to be requisitioned. Not all the requests were felt to be wise and proper. At the end of April Ponton wrote to Barrington describing the riots of 28 and 29 April near the King's Bench Prison, and asking for horse to be quartered in the inns of the Borough so as to be close at hand.[43] Barrington, harassed but cautious, replied that he felt unable to order this; assistance would be sent across the river if the magistrates really needed it,[44] but he believed that the inevitable delay was preferable to aggravating the feelings of the people by quartering cavalry on them. This does not mean that the danger across the river was underestimated. The War Office realised that the King's Bench Prison with its famous inmate would be the scene of even worse riots. The Adjutant-General wrote: 'It is not impossible but that the Spitalfields Powers may take the field, and lie on their arms in that neighbourhood.'[45] But the provocative and irritating effect of troops parading in a threatening manner in the streets was a factor by now well appreciated at the War Office.

For a few days the riots abated a little,[46] but by 6 May they had worsened and Weymouth asked Barrington to arrange for a guard of 100 men to do duty at the prison until further notice, 'in such manner as General Harvey shall judge proper'.[47] It was not easy to provide this number of men immediately, and as a temporary measure an officer and 30 men quitted the Tiltyard and remained on duty until relieved by the larger party.[48] The marshal of the prison had the task of deciding upon the best stations for the men.

The rioting increased. The placing of a body of soldiers at the prison had the worst possible effect upon an aggressive crowd, which by then had scored so many successes. The answer of the magistrates was to call for more soldiers, and that of the government to provide them. On 9 May Ponton wrote to the Secretary of State:

> . . . the magistrates find themselves under the necessity of desiring that such a respectable body of soldiers may do constant duty there as shall be thought necessary for the protection of the prison, which the marshal represents to be in the utmost danger.[49]

Wood wrote back on the same day:

> . . . Lord Weymouth wishes much to know from you if you are prepared

to point out a proper distribution of a farther reinforcement of troops in order to preserve the peace, and whether you think that a hundred men more, or what number, may be sufficient to answer the purpose.[50]

It was feared that the riots would reach their height on the first day of Parliament, for it had been widely rumoured among the poor that, even though in custody, Wilkes would take his seat. Thus was the scene prepared for the massacre of 10 May in St George's Fields, the events of which belong outside a study of planning.[51] On the one hand there was a mob flushed with recent triumphs, on the other an overstrained and inadequate magistracy increasingly goaded by an alarmed and humiliated Secretary of State, and most ominously, an exasperated military, nominally under the direction of a Secretary at War who in reality had almost no freedom of action.

The last appearances of Wilkes in court on 8 and 18 June were from the point of view of public disorder an anticlimax. On each occasion elaborate precautions were taken. On 8 June there was a great deal of play-acting on the part of the constables of Surrey and Westminster, who met on the bridge, Wilkes being meanwhile brought by water.[52] Similar plans to ensure the smooth delivery of the prisoner from one division of peace officers to another, with massive guards of foot soldiers in attendance, were concerted for 18 June.[53] Cavalry was also made available, at Weymouth's request. His secretary wrote:

> . . . as the sentence will be pronounced and the prisoner sent back perhaps before ten o'clock, if it could be contrived to have some horse in the way under any pretence it would be effectual.[54]

In the event no attempts at rescue were made. It is difficult to know whether this was due to the display of force (which itself must have been gratifying and entertaining for Wilkes) or whether in fact there was no danger anyway. The government were probably convinced that their plans were responsible. Certainly such displays of force in advance of any actual disturbance were foreign to Barrington's theory and to his preference for keeping troops in ambush but out of sight. He came up from Claremont in time for 18 June and found horse and foot in readiness, but recorded 'happily there was no occasion for them'.[55]

Matters quietened down in the summer, although trouble flared up intermittently at Shadwell and Wapping, where a guard of 100 men was maintained until the autumn, and in the Pool. The following winter, when Wilkes was brought to the bar of the House of Commons, efficient security precautions were taken; the magistrates met at the Westminster Guildhall at midday and stayed there to be on call until 1 a.m. next day. Troops were in readiness but not on the streets, and all peace officers in London and

Westminster were on duty around the Houses of Parliament.[56] No arrests were made and no disturbances occurred; the system had reached its high point of excellence at a time when the need for it had largely subsided.

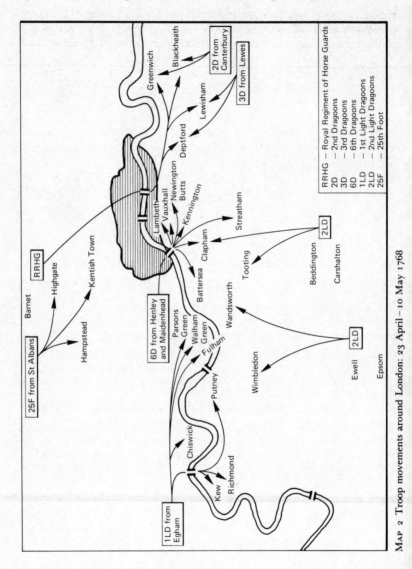

MAP 2 Troop movements around London: 23 April – 10 May 1768

12 The London Riots of 1780

The events of 1780 had so many features which were unusual, and in some cases novel, that they deserve separate treatment. The story of the riot, the most dangerous of the century, is well known;[1] the events may be briefly outlined:

(1) *Friday 2 June.* The march of the Protestant Association to Westminster began at 2.30 p.m. The Palace of Westminster was besieged by the mob for many hours until horse and foot arrived. The mob dispersed to sack Catholic chapels and property.

(2) *Saturday 3 June.* A short interval of comparative calm. A minor riot in Moorfields was dispersed by J.P.s and peace officers unaided by the military.

(3) *Sunday 4 June.* Riots in Moorfields were beyond the civil power. The military arrived but were not allowed to act.

(4) *Monday 5 June.* Riots occurred in many parts, including Wapping and Smithfield. Sir George Savile's house was attacked.

(5) *Tuesday 6 June.* Rioting increased. Parties of soldiers were sent out to protect Parliament and a number of private houses.

(6) *Wednesday 7 June ('Black Wednesday').* Widespread riots and fires. The Fleet, Newgate, Bridewell, King's Bench prisons and others destroyed, also watch-houses, bridge tollgates and other buildings; attacks on the Bank of England and the Navy Pay Office. Rumours circulated of plans by the mob to release the convicts from the hulks, the lions from the Tower and the lunatics from Bedlam, to seize arms from the Artillery Ground, and to interfere with the metropolitan water supply. Troops began to converge on London, later to be encamped in the Parks. The Privy Council met and passed the Order in Council from which derived the General Order to troops to act without magistrates. The conduct of the operation passed into the hands of the Commander-in-Chief, Lord Amherst. That evening mobs were met and defeated in many quarters.

(7) *Thursday 8 June.* Rioting began to die down and troops were now in control.

The unpreparedness of the authorities undoubtedly gave the mob a fair start. The opposition said later that the government was not ready at all; they accused it of 'ludicrous complacency' on the approach of an advertised demonstration. Lord Hillsborough, one of the Secretaries of State, afterwards assured Parliament that the magistrates had been told to attend at the Palace of Westminster on 2 June, but the magistrates insisted they never received any instructions.[2] This confusion was never cleared up. No reference to the events of 2 June appears in the State Papers until the late evening of 2 June, when the other Secretary of State, Lord Stormont, who had just escaped from the House of Lords, wrote to the magistrates of Bow Street and Lichfield Street to suppress the riot,[3] and to the War Office to hold sufficient forces in readiness.[4]

At the War Office there was no apprehension of danger before 2 June; the Secretary at War, Charles Jenkinson, was in the country, and did not return until 4 June. This was a far cry from the days of Barrington, who was usually sensitive to the approach of disorder in London and made preparations for it. When the civil power wanted help he was often ready to provide it at short notice. His otherwise excellent system was however in some ways personal to himself, and on his resignation in 1778 it seems not to have been kept up in the same way by his successor.

It is difficult to discern who, at any one time, was really in control of the peace-keeping operation. Generally between June 2 and June 5 the Secretaries of State attempted to use the traditional methods, as in 1765 and 1768, that is to say they gave instructions to magistrates, told the War Office to be ready with forces, and even issued direct instructions (because of the absence of Jenkinson) to Major General Wynyard of the 3rd Foot Guards at Somerset House for a detachment.[5] Most of these instructions came from Stormont rather than Hillsborough. After 5 June their function atrophied, their out-letters became less frequent, and they acted as a post office, passing on reports and appeals for help to the military authorities. Between 2 and 5 June they wrote nine letters to magistrates outside the City, five to the Lord Mayor, and two to the Lord Lieutenant of Middlesex. After 5 June, apart from writing three letters to the Lord Mayor, the wretched Kennett, they sent no more letters at all to magistrates. On the other hand their letters to the Commander-in-Chief increase: on 7 June they wrote nine to him, and a further seven on 8 June. But with the exception of one letter from Hillsborough recommending the arrest of persons wearing blue cockades (the badge of the Protestant Association) in the street, these were letters not of instructions but of information, usually of riots impending in certain areas. After 6 June the Commander-in-Chief, Lord Amherst, had unfettered control. The Secretaries were prepared to acquiesce in this unusual procedure to save time in such an unprecedented emergency. On 6 June they added their voice to the rest of the cabinet advising the King to use 'other methods' to preserve the peace in cases where magistrates would not act, and to place the whole military force under one command immediately.[6]

The records of the War Office emphasize how quickly its own role diminished. There are no out-letters at all on the riots before 5 June. Before that date movement of troops had been informal, by direct application of magistrates on 2 June, and by magistrates' application by way of the

Secretary of State's office on 3 and 4 June. After 5 June matters were passing away from the Secretary at War and into the hands of the Commander-in-Chief. Apart from sending some Chelsea pensioners to defend Drummond's Bank,[7] Jenkinson played little part in the actual suppression of riots in London, his task being confined to arranging marches of regulars and militia into the area of the capital and arranging quarters for them. After 7 June he relayed calls for help to the office of the Commander-in-Chief. The appointment of a military commander in such a context was in fact so novel that members of the public and magistrates naturally continued to send reports to the Secretary of State or the Secretary at War, and their transmission wasted valuable time. Thus the semi-independent status acquired over the years by Barrington, partly lost in 1768 for a time, was for a single week in 1780 by stress of circumstances entirely destroyed. The Secretary at War during the emergency reverted to the role of a mere adjutant or military secretary, and was no doubt thankful to do so.

Apart from one isolated letter on 3 June Amherst's correspondence began on 6 June when he began to take control; his position was not formally recognised until 7 June, when the defence of London passed to the military.

As the initiative passed from hand to hand the beginnings of longer-term planning can be detected growing up alongside day-to-day handling of immediate emergencies. Stormont's instructions to the magistrates on 2 June were merely to use 'every effective legal method' to keep the peace and to ensure the attendance of justices, constables and peace officers at Westminster the next day to allow access to the Houses of Parliament.[8] His instructions to the War Office were to hold in readiness a sufficient force in case the magistrates wanted it. Soon after midnight Stormont heard of the attacks on the chapels of the Sardinian and Bavarian embassies; he sent for magistrates, but gave no further orders for soldiers.[9] In fact there was little for Stormont and Hillsborough to do but give the magistrates information and encouragement,[10] and wait for them to do their part. In 1780, as is well known, they did not, but Stormont for some time continued to act in the belief that they would use troops, and in the absence of Jenkinson wrote to the officer in charge of the Foot Guards about the security of Catholic chapels,

> . . . which happen all to lie at so great a distance from the Tiltyard and the Savoy, being situated in and about Hanover, Portman and Grosvenor Squares, that much mischief may be done before any military aid could arrive to support the civil magistrates, in case they should find themselves forced to apply for such assistance; under these circumstances would it not be proper to have a guard placed in that part of the town so as to be more immediately within the reach of the civil magistrates.[11]

The officer commanding suggested that the men be quartered in the chapels 'as they cannot be supposed to lay all night in the open air'.[12]

Otherwise most of the correspondence of 3 June concerned arrangements to post magistrates, who were now watching Catholic chapels and houses in several parts of the town. In many cases they had Guards with them, although they did not use them.[13] Jenkinson was still out of London, and these escorts were provided by the commander of the Horse Guards on direct application from Hillsborough, thus by-passing the War Office.[14] With a great deal of effort on the part of constables and magistrates order was restored on 3 June, and at 3 a.m. the following day all was quiet. It is noteworthy that in spite of rumours of further risings no orders were yet given for bringing troops nearer to London.

The riots of 4 June were more violent, and were clearly becoming impossible for a handful of magistrates and peace officers to suppress, even if they had the will to do so. Stormont wrote three letters to the Secretary at War, commanding him

1. to augment the guard at the Tiltyard and the Savoy on the following day;[15]

2. at eleven at night, to tell the commander of troops at the Tower to take all steps to help magistrates as he thought proper;[16] and

3. at midnight, to ensure that all Guards should be ready for immediate march.[17]

Matthew Lewis, Jenkinson's secretary, sent orders arising out of letter 2 above to the Tower at 1 a.m. on 5 June;[18] the Tower letter-book records that the message arrived at 3 a.m.[19]

Jenkinson, in his office by the evening of 4 June, wrote to General Craig of the Guards, to Gold Stick of the Horse Guards and to the Adjutant General:

I will trouble you, Sir, to meet me immediately at the War Office that I may consult with you upon the measures which it may be proper to take in consequence of the King's Orders before mentioned, so that nothing may be omitted which it is proper for us to do for the purpose of preserving the public tranquillity.[20]

He met these officers during the morning, and with Amherst's concurrence sent orders to the 16th Light Dragoons at Kensington to march three troops into Southwark and one troop into Lambeth, where riots had also occurred.[21]

For a space Jenkinson seemed to be about to play a leading part in the operation.[22] But within a short time Amherst had stepped in, a tribute to the seriousness of matters: there had never been any suggestion that the

Commander-in-Chief in 1768, Lord Granby, should have control of the Wilkes riots.

There are two large letter-books on the riots in the Amherst Papers.[23] The first volume, which runs from 5 June to 12 June, contains over 340 items, the majority on 7 and 8 June.It is quite clear that the minute secretariat kept by Amherst at his office at the Horse Guards was overwhelmed by this mass of paper, and this must have materially affected the success of the peace-keeping operation.

His problems began almost at once. At 12.40 a.m. on 6 June he received a hurried note from both Secretaries, saying that the magistrates felt unable to keep the peace unless they could call upon 'a very considerable body of horse', which they had thought more useful than the Foot Guards.[24] They wrote of widespread attacks on houses and chapels. It seems to have been borne in upon the authorities at this stage that they were dealing with a situation quite beyond the ordinary methods of control. The original sectarian character of the riot was becoming blurred; it was now a mere plundering mob, but on a huge scale. The *Annual Register* wrote afterwards: 'This mob was much more powerful and numerous, as well as dangerous, than any other in remembrance'.[25]

After digesting this letter Amherst called the dragoons at Lambeth back across the river, telling them to call at Whitehall for orders.[26] He then set about the task of reinforcing the capital. On the same day he sent orders to three dragoon regiments to march 'with all the expedition you can, consistently with a due care not to render the regiment unserviceable'.[27]

The other troop movements in or into London during these riots are summarised below. After the orders to the cavalry at Lambeth, which issued from his own office, Amherst sent all orders through (and no doubt after consultation with) Jenkinson.

TABLE 12.1

REGULAR ARMY[28]

7 June

	From	To
1st Foot (2nd Battn.)	Hertford	Hyde Park
18th Foot	Woburn	Hyde Park
11 Dragoons	Newbury	Hammersmith, Fulham, Kensington, Turnham Green and Knightsbridge
3rd Dragoons	Croydon	Kensington, Chelsea and Knightsbridge

TABLE 12.1 *(contd.)*

8 June			
	52nd Foot (5 companies)	Dartford	Greenwich and Deptford

MILITIA[29]

5 June			
	North Hampshire (first division)	Staines	Hammersmith and Fulham
6 June	South Hampshire	Lambeth	to remain
7 June	Hertfordshire	Barnet	Hyde Park
	Northumberland	Islington	to enlarge quarters to Hampstead and Highgate
	Northamptonshire (first division)	Lambeth	to remain
	Northamptonshire (second division)	Uxbridge	Hammersmith, Fulham and Putney
8 June			
	Northamptonshire (second division)	Fulham	Lambeth, Vauxhall and Wandsworth
	Buckinghamshire (5 companies)	Bromley	Woolwich Docks
	Buckinghamshire (5 companies)	Kingston	Deptford
	Middlesex (first division)	Staines	Old and New Brentford, Kew and Kew Green (to arrive on 10 June)
	Cambridge (100 men)	Barnet	Kenwood (to relieve Northumberlands)
	Cambridge (remainder)	Barnet	Hampstead, Highgate and Kentish Town
9 June	2nd West Yorkshire	Hyde Park	British Museum

These dispositions thus involved a total of two-and-a-half regular regiments of foot and four of cavalry, and seven of militia. There were also the Horse and Foot Guards.

In spite of these preparations rioting was even worse on 6 June. Newgate Prison was sacked and burnt, and the houses of Sir George Savile, Sir John Fielding, Lord Mansfield, and of several justices who had exerted themselves conspicuously were also sacked. It was clear that unity of command by itself was not enough. Troops were present in sufficient numbers; tactics to enable them successfully to face the mob were now needed. The advice of Wedderburn, the Attorney-General, to the King at the famous Privy Council meeting, which dispelled the fog of ignorance of many years, has already been mentioned. After the issuing of the General Order the tactical as well as the planning problem was solved. The effect of this order is discussed elsewhere.[30]

The strategy for 7 June was the same as for previous days. Troops continued to march aimlessly about during the day and the Order did not issue until the evening. In any case it did not affect strategy, which was still defensive. the traditional military strokes of manœuvre and surprise could not be applicable. The mob still had the initiative and could appear where it chose. It probably also worked on a shift basis with continual departures and fresh arrivals. The soldiers could not go out and hunt it: they could only guard threatened points. At least they could now do so effectively.

These points fall into several categories. Embassies with Catholic Chapels were still an obvious mark, as also were private houses of Catholics. But as the scope of the riot widened it was felt that any foreign embassy was in danger, as also were the private houses of people other than Catholics. Shops, warehouses, distilleries and other commercial undertakings were attacked, also institutions (e.g. the Bank of England, the East India Company) and public utilities (e.g. the water works). Then there were whole areas of London which either launched mobs, such as Wapping, Moorfields, or Southwark, or attracted them, such as Whitehall or, later in the riot, Bloomsbury and the area of the Bank and the Mansion House in the City. The list of places grew hourly as information came in to the Horse Guards.[31] The defence of these places was a daunting task, for many of the troops had not yet arrived, or were still coming in exhausted from forced marches.

By the evening of 7 June planning began to take a more definite shape. Even so a great deal of damage was done by mobs unhindered in their work. Critics of Amherst's strategy at the time said that this was because he concentrated his troops in a few places and left large areas unprotected. One wrote:

You will think it strange that Lord Amherst, out of near 12,000 men, should have only 300 men in the City, beside those stationed at and not to leave the Tower, but such was the case.[32]

This impression is worth examining critically, for many believed it at the time. Unfortunately it is not easy to determine what the exact dispositions of troops were. Amherst's own letter-book[33] has letters of reassurance about the provision of guards for the protection of property, but does not contain the orders which placed those guards on 6 and 7 June. Statistical returns only show where the troops were in detail from 8 June. The reports of individual officers give an earlier picture, though it is one with many gaps in it. The plan seems to have been to place a few large detachments at or near places particularly threatened, with power to make smaller detachments if necessary and if, in the opinion of the commander, it was safe. Chief among these was the enormous force of Foot Guards based on the Bank of England, which was besieged and repeatedly attacked on evening of 7 June. By 8 June the numbers there had risen to 534, under Lt.-Col. Twisleton, assisted by Lt.-Col. Hugh Debbieg, an officer of engineers. A further 100 men of the Guards lay in reserve in St Paul's Churchyard. Outside the City detachments were at Burlington Gardens (150), at the Tiltyard (61) and the Savoy (52), but the greater part of the Guards were placed in a hurriedly arranged camp in St James's Park. More men of the Guards at the houses of Lord Stormont, Sir George Savile, Count Haslang, Lord Rockingham, Lord George Germain, Samson Rainforth and Lord North, at Warwick Street Chapel, Metcalfe's mills at Bromley, at the Sardinian embassy and at the Admiralty accounted for a further 226. The garrison at the Tower could not move in case the fortress was attacked, neither could the Queen's guard (32) or the King's guard (104). Altogether 1517 men of the Foot Guards were involved in doing duty at these posts (and a few minor ones not mentioned).[34] The total numbers of the seven battalions of Foot Guards in London was however 3724 men, and it is clear that a number were not used at all on the evening of 7 June. The other units in London, again according to a return of 8 June, numbered as follows:

TABLE 12.2

CAVALRY[35]

Horse Guards	St James's	292
Horse Grenadier Guards	St James's	244
3rd Dragoon Guards	Whitechapel, Islington, Tottenham, Marylebone, Paddington	212
3rd Dragoons	Kensington, Knightsbridge, Chelsea	215

TABLE 12.2 (*contd.*)

4th Dragoons	Lambeth,	
	Vauxhall,	
	Camberwell	216
11th Dragoons	Hammersmith,	
	Turnham Green,	
	Fulham,	
	Putney,	
	Brentford	221
16th Light Dragoons	King's Mews	323
	Total	1723

INFANTRY[36]

2nd Battn. of 1st Foot		646
2nd or Queen's Regiment		591
Militia	Hyde Park Camp	
Hertfordshire		560
North Hants		538
2nd West Yorks		578
Northumberland	Lincolns Inn Fields	500[37]
	Kenwood	100
South Hants	Kent St. Bridewell	461
	Total	3974

It is clear then that the forces of guards, regulars and militia, even if they did not total 12,000 as alleged in Colonel Stuart's letter, did amount to nearly 9500, a respectable force apparently will placed within striking distance of many troubled areas.[38] They cannot all have been exhausted by marches. It is also clear that the criticism remains unanswered, and that the City at least was poorly protected. It is true that it was not possible to station troops in every street of a large town, and that troops have to be billeted somewhere. Even so it was in the City that most of the real mischief was done on the night of 7 June, and here the success of the system constituted by Amherst depended on whether parties could be sent out by the garrisons posted in the city, and how quickly they would arrive. Such parties as were sent for arrived quickly, and some patrols were sent. At the Bank however Colonel Twisleton felt able to hold on and no more, and appeals for help to him fell upon deaf ears. His letter to Amherst on the subject contains a hint of criticism:

I have given a general refusal, and told them I would not detach a single man. If a considerable force, and the more troops the better, were immediately sent into the City, much mischief might be prevented, and the town cleared of these rioters.[39]

The result was that after the attacks on the Bank had been repulsed the mob dispersed to attack houses in the City, in which course they met with little hindrance. The Middlesex Militia drove away a mob in Broad Street and other streets nearby,[40] but a number of such groups taken from the mass of unengaged troops outside and in London would have done more service in the City that night.

Once the plan of dispositions, which converted so much of his force into a reserve, had been crystallised in his mind Amherst became reluctant to deal with calls for help, seeming to be more concerned with keeping his reserve in being than with using it. When Jenkinson wrote enclosing a letter from the Dean of the Arches and the Judge of the Admiralty Court about the security of Doctors Commons he replied:

> The application is a very proper one, but the detachments already made are so numerous it is impossible to comply with their request. The number indeed now left on the parade will not admit of being any further lessened.[41]

Jenkinson took the hint, and during the evening replied in the same spirit when his office received a similar appeal for help:

> In consequence of an Order in Council the whole defence of the Town is devolved upon the military. A proper disposition of all the force that can be got will be made for every man's security, and it would be inconsistent with this to grant guards for the protection of any particular place, which would only weaken that power which is necessary for the safety of the whole.[42]

Evidently the failure was partly due to logistical factors arising from the confusion of an overworked office, and partly from a certain inelasticity of mind in a Commander-in-Chief unable to keep pace with the speed of events. Some people complained afterwards that their applications for help were ignored. In the House of Commons Sir Philip Jennings Clerke alleged that the King's Bench Prison need never have been destroyed.[43] He sent a message to Amherst at noon that the prison and Thrale's brewhouse nearby were in danger.[44] The letter was endorsed on the back in Amherst's hand 'If this can be supplied it must be from Lambeth', but soldiers did not arrive until 9 p.m. They saved the brewery but the prison was burnt. The Bishop of St David's wrote to ask for a guard for his house, which was threatened. His servant received no answer and the bishop had to write again.[45] Stormont wrote at 10.30 a.m. on 7 June to warn Amherst of the danger to Mansfield's house at Kenwood; getting no answer he wrote again at 1.30 p.m.[46] The Northumberland Militia arrived in time to save the place.[47] There is a local tradition that the landlord of the Spaniards Inn near by sent for troops, and delayed the rioters in their march by a politic distribution of free liquor.[48] If true this was more effective than Amherst's order.

All these and many other signs of the dislocation at the Horse Guards may account for the mixed success of the troops on the night of Black Wednesday. On 6 June Amherst received nine letters, on 7 June 34, and on 8 June 80. There may have been more but they have not survived. The out-letter book shows that on the first day he answered four letters, on the second 23, and on the third 31. In cases where these letters were appeals for help Amherst generally gave it to peers and other Members of Parliament, and to places of public importance such as the Navy Pay Office and the Victualling Office. The humbler people, especially those who addressed joint petitions, got no help, and as far as can be judged from the letter-books, not even any answer.[49]

The government afterwards replied to criticisms by saying that

the services were so numerous, and the applications so continual, and from such various quarters, for protection or assistance, as the apprehensions or danger of the people increased, that the troops at hand were not half sufficient to answer the demands, until the arrival of the regulars and militia from the country.[50]

They adhered to this interpretation of events, but the figures for troop concentrations in War Office files do not support it. Perhaps the newspaper which reported Amherst as 'running about, and wringing his hands with fear, not knowing what orders to give',[51] was more accurate, if unkindly expressed.

As in 1768 the system became effective when the need had ceased. Two great camps were now in being in Hyde Park and St James's Park, and the machinery for keeping them and the City garrisons supplied with ammunition, bread, meat, porter, firewood and blankets was set in motion.[52] In these camps and in barracks and billets, there were on 8 June nearly 10,000 troops, provided with lethal instructions which they well understood. Cannon guarded the arsenal at Woolwich and the Bank, and were even given to the South Hants militia.[53] Even more drastic plans were discussed. Lord Hillsborough wrote to Amherst on 7 June to recommend securing the Surrey ends of London and Blackfriars bridges to prevent the junction of the City and Southwark mobs. If the mob, as was rumoured, had possessed themselves of artillery, then mortars loaded with grapeshot should also be placed on each bridge. The Tower ditch should be filled with water.[54] This plan was not Hillsborough's, but was suggested to him:

. . . I could not help proposing a plan to my uncle for the defence of this side of the river, and he insisted on my stating it to Lord Hillsborough. That the three bridges should be held with considerable detachments and a cannon, that the Tower should cover the right flank, the Parks the left; in the Parks two thousand men; on the six stations between, a thousand men at each, viz. Whitechapel, Moorfields, Charter House, Gray's Inn, Soho Square, Leicester Fields – commanded by six generals, who would send constant patrols, maintaining communications between each station.[55]

If the emergency had continued a more radical plan resembling the above would no doubt have been put into effect for, apart from bizarre details such as artillery, it was only a more tidy version of the strategy towards which Amherst had been groping uncertainly from day to day. Its chief difference was in the proposal to put more men in the City. However, after the terrible retaliations of the night of Black Wednesday, 8 June was comparatively quiet. Twisleton wrote from the Bank:

After the arrival of the troops at the different places ordered by your Lordship in the evening there was a chain of detachments and patrols all over the City, and the utmost tranquillity took place.[56]

As in previous years the authorities took steps to prevent stocks of arms falling into the hands of the mob. There are many letters in the Amherst Papers at this stage on the subject. The City gunsmiths prudently surrendered their stocks to the Tower, which recorded on its books the receipt of 9670 firearms by 9 June,[57] and the arms of the volunteer companies were soon impounded or rendered useless by the removal of the locks. Some pistols were used by the rioters, but the report which reached the government that they had cannon was untrue. The magazine at Purfleet, which might have been attacked for its powder, was provided with artillery (2-pounders) ferried across from Woolwich by Captain Congreve and a reinforcement of 50 men.[58]

Troops remained in and around London for some time after 8 June. In fact orders issued at the height of the riots kept them marching in for several days after the need for them had ceased. The 18th (Royal Irish) Foot appeared in London on 8 June but were too much fatigued by a forced march from Woburn to be of any service immediately. The Hertfordshire, Westminster (Middlesex) and Cambridge regiments of militia also were not ordered into London until 8 June. On 12 June the numbers in the London area had risen to 12,000 of whom nearly 3600 were employed on guard duties.

Halfway through July the camps of St James's Park and Hyde Park were broken up, to be replaced by more remote camps at Blackheath and

Finchley.[59] They remained there until the summer camps broke up on 24 October.

Shaken as they were by this appalling episode the government made no contingency plan for the defence of London; for the future the expertise gathered in June 1780 would have to suffice. The riots however gave rise to two interesting plans for the protection of particular places:

1. Lt.-Col. Hugh Debbieg, an experienced engineer officer under Twisleton's command, submitted his thoughts on the defence of the Bank. His plan envisaged the building of flanking towers sufficiently high to command the roof, with communicating passages between for patrols. To make the building safe from fire and other forms of attack from all sides he proposed buying up a number of contiguous properties and demolishing them.[60] This last part of the plan, which he estimated would cost £30,000, caused the directors of the Bank to lose interest and they returned a non-committal answer;[61] the only result was the institution of the Bank guard, which persisted until modern times.

2. Debbieg also became alarmed for the New River Company, and submitted a more complex plan for its security. On 8 June he had dispatched a guard of 40 men (increased the next day to 65) to guard the waterworks. The Surveyor undertook to provide for the wants of the detachment.[62] Debbieg thought it should remain and encamp for a time, in view of the seriousness of the matter, notwithstanding 'what I have the honour to know of your Lordship's wishes to keep the military separate as much as possible from the populace'.[63] After the riots had died down he went to examine in detail for himself the system whereby much of London's water arrived.[64] In view of recent events he was astonished at its vulnerability. Part of the river near Bush Hill crossed a valley by means of a wooden-framed trough lined with lead, the structure of which, in his view, might be destroyed in a quarter of an hour by a few boys. The sluices and many other works were open to the attack of a few men with tools, who could in less than an hour let out the water into the fields. He went about the task of preparing a report with enthusiasm, but again his proposals for remedying the situation were felt to be overambitious; 'guard rooms of a particular construction like the American block-houses, judiciously placed' and a guard of 700 men for the 40 miles of river would have been too costly for the company.[65]

TABLE 12.3

By 8 June 1780 the following had been attacked, or had been directly threatened by the mob, or believing themselves to be in danger had applied for a guard (extracted from W.O. 34/103).

(i) *Foreign Embassies or Residencies*

Sardinia	Marquis de Cordon	Lincoln's Inn Fields
The Empire	Count Belgioso	Portman Square
Naples	Count Pignatelli	Lower Brook Street
Portugal	Chevalier de Pinto	South Audley Street
Venice	M. de Cavalli	Soho Square
Bavaria	Count Haslang	Golden Square
Genoa	M. d'Agena	Green Street
Russia	M. de Simolin	Hanover Square
Denmark	M. Dreyer	Highgate

(ii) *Institutions, companies, etc.*

Bank of England
South Sea Company
East India Company
Excise Office
Customs Office
Navy Pay Office
Victualling Office
King's Bench Prison
Clerkenwell Prison
Bridewell
New Prison
Prison Hulks (Deptford)
Tollgates on the Bridges
Waterworks (London Bridge) and pipes of New River Company
Freemasons Hall – Queen Street
The Temple
New Inn
Clements Inn
Thomas Coutts
Thelusson's Bank
Drummond's Bank
Loughborough House School
Langdale's Distillery
Thrale's Brewery
Metcalfe's Distillery – West Ham
Sanders & Henniker – Tower Wharf
Brymant Barnett – Stockwell

TABLE 12.3 (*contd.*)

(iii) *Private Houses*

Lord Petre – Park Lane
Lord North – Downing Street
Duke of Norfolk – St James's Square
Lord Thurlow – Great Ormonde Street
Lord Townshend – Portman Square
Lord Stormont – Portland Place
Lord Bathurst – Piccadilly
Lord Mansfield – Bloomsbury Square and Kenwood
Lord Rockingham   :
Lord Lascelles – Portman Square
Lord Ashburnham – Dover Street
Lord Milburne – Burlington Gardens
Duke of Queensbury – Piccadilly
Lord Fauconberg
Lord Macclesfield
Archbishop of Canterbury
Archbishop of York
Bishop of St Davids
Sir George Savile – Leicester Fields
Sir John Fielding – Bow Street
Mr Wilmot – Bloomsbury Square
Mr Maberley – Little Queen Street
Mr Rainforth – Clare Market
Dr Trotter – Swallow Street
Edmund Burke – Charles Street
John Dunning
General Seymour Conway – Little Warwick Street
Justice Cox – Great Queen Street
George Grenville

(iv) *The inhabitants of*

Newman Street
Berners Street
Bedford Street (Covent Garden)
Wells Street
Oxford Street
Lant Street (Southwark)
Devonshire Street (Red Lion Square)
Bruton Street
Cavendish Street
Gloucester Street (Queen's Square)
Woodstock Street
Bartlett's Buildings (Holborn)

These last submitted petitions with a number of signatures.

PART III
Tactics

13 Tactical Methods of Troops

INTRODUCTION

Householders might complain, magistrates make their reports, and politicians their plans, but ultimately it was the army which came into physical contact with the riot. The fog of war descends upon this as upon the more orthodox tactical situations of real warfare, creating obvious problems for the researcher. A mêlée with a crowd, particularly at night, is inevitably a confused and scrambling affair, and versions of it will vary even at the time. Public documents, so useful a source for plans beforehand, contain little in the way of reports afterwards by officers on the spot which might have given a clue as to how troops conducted themselves in the presence of a riot. Occasional references in the War Office letter-books show that such reports were made,[1] but either it was thought that no lessons might be learnt from them and they suffered the fate of many other categories of ephemera of the time, or if they were copied the letter-books have perished. This is known to have happened to a large part of the in-correspondence of the eighteenth-century War Office.

Two valuable exceptions to this lack exist. In 1757 Barrington began to keep a file of officers' reports. He had already struggled through a year of rioting, and at this stage, even amidst the frequent emergencies of wartime, he must have realised what a significant part of his task the riot duty was, and also perhaps how important such material might be if he was called upon to defend himself at a public level. The reports were kept for two years; there may have been others that were discarded later.[2] Also there exist a large number of reports from officers during the Gordon Riots, contained in the series known as the Amherst Papers in the Public Record Office.[3] Again there may have been sound reasons for the careful keeping of these records. The suppression, however necessary, of a great riot in the metropolis would be jealously scrutinised in all its details. The memory of Burke's attacks in 1768 and 1769 after the Wilkes riot was still fresh. Amherst was determined to be personally cognisant of all these details; if he should come to be attacked in the House of Lords there were going to be no surprises, and a specific order was given for every officer exercising an independent command, however small, to make a report. This order never appeared on the letter-books, but seems to have been given verbally, probably through Amherst's brother William, who was Adjutant-General. Many of the reports begin by referring to it,[4] however. Bound together and preceded by a lengthy statement of the legal position about riot-duty as understood by the War Office, they constitute Amherst's brief for his defence. The most informative of these reports were by regimental commanders, but a good many were made by young ensigns in command of no more than twenty or thirty men, and as such are unusual among eighteenth-century peacetime records. In the event Amherst was not attacked upon the severity of the military intervention he had arranged, but rather upon his alleged infringement of the ancient rights of the people of the City of London, in rejecting their offers to help in defending themselves, and in countenancing the disarming by his troops of many private citizens.[5]

Apart from these exceptions, methods used by troops against mobs have often to be inferred indirectly from the evidence in documents, picked up from the not always reliable evidence in newspapers, or occasionally found in contemporary diaries and memoirs.

A great contrast in success is at once evident between the strategy and the tactics of crowd control in the eighteenth century. The frequent failure of the agencies of control was not so much one of strategic action, which was often well conceived and carried out, but in the ineffectiveness of troops on arrival in the riot area, and this of course stemmed from the unfortunate legal ambiguity discussed above.[6] It is true that the appearance of troops, although it sometimes angered one crowd, could be enough to disperse another, but a mob, especially one engaged in food rioting, often showed fight, and officers and men were uncertain of their powers. Such vacillation and delay was always regarded as weakness, and increased the violence and sense of elated power often noticed in crowds. During the riot at the King's Bench prison on 10 May 1768 it appeared at the subsequent trial that the soldiers threatened to fire several times, kneeling and presenting their firelocks, but to no purpose; the excitement of the crowd increased greatly as a result, and the soldiers were bombarded with stones so as scarcely to be able to keep their ranks. A captain's threat to fire was treated as bluff. Similar occurrences in 1780 convinced the Gordon rioters that they had nothing to fear from the troops, and their violence increased accordingly. The disastrous result was that counter-measures, when eventually resorted to, had to be proportionably more violent.

While many officers were either convinced that their hands were tied, or were humane, or were just of poor quality, it should not be concluded from the above that troop intervention was always ineffective. In fact their action was often forceful, sometimes too forceful, and firearms were often used in desperate situations. However there were many ways in which troops might operate short of ultimate force.

(1) Control.

Although in some circumstances the red coat might have the same effect on a crowd as upon a bull, there were also many cases where the mere appearance of a disciplined, armed body of men under orders was in itself enough to overawe a crowd and cause it to disperse. The mob of Spitalfields weavers in 1765 was deterred from renewing its assaults on Bedford House and the premises of the master weavers on 20 May by a great show of military force alone. A display of warlike panoply was designed on this occasion to intimidate and prevent the junction of large bodies of weavers:

> Two troops of horse were drawn up in Moorfields in order of battle, with colours, standards etc. In the centre was a battalion of the guards; they continued under arms all day. A troop of horse was stationed at the foot of London bridge to prevent their passing that way, and another troop of horse did duty at the foot of Westminster Bridge.[7]

None of these men drew trigger or sabre all day; they merely indicated by the threat of their presence and by their disposition in certain places what would happen if the peace were broken.[8] This was the same mob which had besieged Bedford House a few days earlier and had been driven off by force, although by the 20th it had lost a good deal (but not all) of its violence. When Horace Walpole visited the Duke to congratulate him on his escape he found the square still filled with people, several days later. The crowd, he recorded, grew so riotous while he was there that 'they were forced to make both horse and foot parade the square before the tumult was dispersed'.[9]

Similar successes in mob-breaking occurred in the same year before the violence of the crowd had reached its apex. On 16 May, the day before the assault on Bedford House, another body of weavers estimated at 8000 marched towards St James's, 'in consequence whereof the guards were ordered out to prevent the like outrages for the future. This precaution had the desired effect, and no violence was offered on the part of the weavers.'[10]

A small force might also act as a steadying influence rather than as a threat, even if it were clear to soldiers and mob that the force was not strong enough to go on to the offensive. In 1727 a serious corn riot at Falmouth was the subject of correspondence between the Pelham brothers.[11] Eventually four companies of Harrison's regiment were sent from Exeter to keep the peace,[12] but in the meantime the magistrates had to do what they could with the assistance of a weak force. Captain Massey, the commander of the garrison of invalids at Pendennis Castle, came to help them each day with a party of thirty men, 'which was as large a party as could consistently with the safety of the garrison be drawn out'. They could get no help from the townsfolk, and the rioters threatened to reduce the town to ashes if one of their number was harmed, so 'it was not thought advisable to come to blows with the rioters or to attempt with the small force we had to suppress or apprehend any of them'.[13] All that this small force could do was to remain in observation and restrain the rioters from worse excesses until a more respectable party arrived.

At other times the mere threat of the approach of troops sufficed, but crowds were not often warned off so easily. During the Nottingham corn riots of 1756 the Mayor wrote to the Secretary of State[14] to record his satisfaction at the speed with which the cavalry had appeared at his request.[15]

> The very rumour of these troops, which are thought to have dropt into this town from the clouds, may not only stop their progress, but give us and the country justices an opportunity to take up and imprison some of the most mischievous of the offenders.[16]

The Mayor was right; the mob, which a few days before had paraded armed through Nottingham, had rescued three of their number from the custody of the magistrates, and had badly damaged three flour mills, dispersed on the approach of the dragoons. The Mayor spent the next few days making arrests with the help of the troops. He was convinced that the continuing peace of the area depended on the toops, having no confidence in his own force of constables.[17]

However, the situation deteriorated in the next few days and provided an example of another form of mob control without actual force, involving a confrontation, either conciliatory or threatening, with a dangerous crowd. The Mayor's letter to Lord Holdernesse, the Secretary of State, gave an account.

> A body of them drew in view of the town about noon; upon which the Colonel beat to arms, and a division of the troops being immediately mounted and in a posture to receive them; the mob stopt, and after some time retired to a village about a mile from Nottingham. The colliers returned again about 3, and were just entering this town; whereupon the Colonel beat to arms, and having a party instantly mounted; he rode with a man or two to meet them; and upon his drawing near the mob fell back: and the Colonel sent to them and desired to talk with anyone they would appoint to meet him on a promise that he should go back unhurt. This was agreed to: and the Colonel desired to know their design. It was, they said, to have back their comrades.[18] The Colonel expostulated with them about the wrong method that had been taken; they might have told their complaints first to the justices; they replied those should not be their Lords: they might apply to Parliament, they answered, it was too late for that. He desired them to desist, he should be sorry to fight against his country men; that the way they were taking would do their comrades

no good nor leave room to show them any lenity. . . .
And returning into the town, the Colonel ordered his troop to the gaol,
there to wait for them. Sentinels were stationed; the constables were
ordered to give notice to the inhabitants to keep off at a certain distance
lest they should be fired upon. . . . And many were in fear all the night
long, of the consequences that would follow either from the colliers
attempting the gaol; or the demolishing the houses of the magistrates, or
such other inhabitants as gave assistance upon this occasion.

I took the liberty with another justice, in order to prevent sitting up all
night which might have overset us to authorize and request Colonel
Harvey by writing under our hands and seals in case of any real actual
attempt upon the gaol, or an actual beginning to demolish any house or
outhouse, to repel force with force; and if he thought fit, to fire upon
them. We take him to be a very prudent as well as a courageous
commander and that it was the best service we could do his Majesty to
leave the matter to his discretion: to which we owe it, that we are
hitherto safe.[19]

It is difficult to decide at this distance of time whether quitting the scene
and leaving such a heavy load on the officer was an act of confidence or of
cowardice on the part of the magistrates, but the prudence of the officer
cannot be doubted. In the event the colliers did not come.

Although as in any age some officers were to be found wanting in
courage, there must have been many occasions when this sort of prudence
and spirit availed to save bloodshed, and justified the War Office in their
trust in the man on the spot. In the 1765 riots a crowd in the City was
pacified by a troop of Horse Grenadier Guards who were returning from
Ludgate Hill to Westminster on 18 May (i.e. the day after the savage riots
in Bloomsbury Square),

. . . not the least accident having happened to any person from the time
of their first arrival; the genteel behaviour of their commanding officer
cannot, on this occasion be sufficiently applauded, who made a
handsome speech to the populace, in which he pathetically exhorted
them not to put either his humanity or his duty to so severe a trial as to
oblige him to proceed to extremities.[20]

N.C.O.s also tried to be tactful and conciliatory, though not always with
success. In October 1763 a crowd of sailors in Shoreditch besieged the
alehouse of one Kelly who had incurred their resentment. A lieutenant's
guard was called for and the crowd dispersed. On Kelly's plea a sergeant's
guard (i.e. twelve men) was left. The sailors returned 'more desperate than
before. The sergeant met them singly, before they had reached the house
and pulling off his hat, requested that they would not proceed to break the
king's peace.' The subsequent course of this riot belongs to another

section;[21] it is sufficient here to note that they paid no heed to the sergeant's words.

During the Wilkes riots of 1768 several newspapers carried with evident approval accounts of individuals whose determined behaviour succeeded against mobs. A single sentinel on duty before a house in Whitehall which had not been illuminated made clear to a threatening mob that the throwing of the first stone would be the signal for him to fire, whereupon the crowd drew off.[22] Even civilians could play their part: an 'eminent hosier of Smithfield' managed to quiet another mob by a speech. The editor who reported it, evidently a friend to the 'moral force' theory, wrote that he had included the piece to show the public 'how easy it is to appease the rage of a tumultuous mob by giving them good words, and how an whole street may very often be saved from destruction by a few seasonable expressions'.[23]

Some officers were more than tactful – as far as their position allowed them to be they were sympathetic and reluctant to use force for reasons of humanity. The useful bundle of James Wolfe's letters[24] written when he was on riot duty in the West Country show his anxiety to avert bloodshed and his pity for the unfortunate clothworkers of the area. Elsewhere he wrote with a kind of humorous disdain:

> What kind of duty do you think I am engaged on and what enemy am I opposed to? Hungry weavers! a dishonour to our arms; and they have had the impudence to make assaults, and commit riots *à ma barbe* – but as the poor devils are half starved, and as their masters have agreed to mend their wages, I have hopes that they will return to work, rather than proceed to hostilities; for one or other they must do, in a very few days.[25]

Elsewhere he describes the weavers as 'a good deal oppressed by their masters, who have reduced their wages so low, that they cannot live by their labour'. Trade, he said, was in decline and provisions dear, and this 'makes the condition of many of them extremely wretched and miserable, though they are of the greatest use to the public'.[26] Wolfe, a thoughtful and apparently humane officer,[27] played his part with care, and used his troops as an instrument of control rather than of outright suppression, content to wait on events whilst clothiers and J.P.s negotiated about wages, and reserving his force to prevent actual breaches of the peace. 'I am persuaded that the presence of the troops has prevented a good deal of mischief, and may continue to do so, if the civil Magistrates are not wanting in their duty.' Later in the same letter he raises the question of the importance of Hampton, the centre of the clothing country; he had evidently quickly grasped the pattern of the disturbances:[28]

> [It] is the place of rendezvous of the seditious, it is a much fitter place to

quarter a company, than Tetbury, where there are few weavers and no disturbances. . . . I believe it would be for his Majesty's service, and for the quiet of the country, that I should have it in my power to quarter Captain Parr's company at Hampton, whenever things seem to require it, and to prevent the possibility of any illtimed delays.[29]

A kind of uneasy peace fell upon the area (although the new rates agreed between masters and men were not entirely satisfactory), and an ugly crisis had been averted. This sort of action on the part of troops (whenever it was possible) was obviously the wisest course, indicating to the inhabitants of an area that the troops were quartered upon them to protect and not to brutalise them. In the following year during the militia riots Lord Royston wrote

> I shall take care to have it known that I do not send for soldiers to enforce the Militia Bill, but to protect everybody, farmers as well as gentlemen, in the peaceable enjoyment of their property.[30]

Even during the Gordon riots, the most ferocious of the century, the mere appearance of troops was sometimes sufficient to preserve or to restore order. Rockingham believed so; in asking for a guard for his house he said: 'My object is that by intimidation – rather than by actual *repelling* – that this house may be secure.'[31] The arrival of 150 men of the 3rd Battalion of the 1st Foot Guards frightened away a destructive mob from Sir George Savile's house.[32] Light dragoons and militia surrounded Lord Mansfield's country house at Kenwood, and the mob declined to attack.[33] In the same month the magistrates of Norwich feared a similar rising, as there were many Catholics in the town and the Norwich crowd was easily roused 'as is usual in large manufacturing cities'.[34] The outbreak was however prevented, at least in the opinion of the magistrates, by the mere presence of dragoons in the town.[35]

As the riots in London died down the task of the soldiers became easier. On the morning of 9 June (i.e. soon after the bloodbath) a threatening mob again appeared, 'but the appearance of the soldiers, who have conducted themselves with the greatest regularity and attention to their duty, soon dispelled the alarm'.[36] The commander of the City garrison, Colonel Twisleton, wrote to Lord Amherst that a profound quiet fell upon London once the troops had reached their stations on the evening of 8 June.[37] After 8 June Twisleton's daily reports back to the Commander-in-Chief constantly say 'The patroles went as usual', a reminder to the crowd of his strength. The soldiers took on another role, that of making arrests. There are many accounts in the public documents of help given to constables in rounding up suspects and in providing prison guards. The largest bag of arrests was made by a patrol of the 1st Foot Guards, who took 80 prisoners in one swoop; they must have been over-zealous, because some were released on the spot, only 59 being brought in.[38] Their enthusiasm aroused resentment. One newspaper wrote: 'When this paper went to press the City had a most dismal aspect. Almost every street had more or less of the military in it, who were chasing the populace.'[39]

The task of pursuit and arrest was usually the last job of the troops in a long-lasting riot;[40] it rarely involved violence, and the assistance of informers was often important. Ringleaders were particularly looked for. To prevent a recrudescence of rioting, troops were often deliberately left in or within short marching distance of a riot area, as far as the always thorny problem of billeting would allow. In 1768 the Shadwell coalheavers' riots had been suppressed by the military in April; a guard of 100 men was still quartered there in, October. The City of London was garrisoned for months after the Gordon riots, and the nightly protection of the well-known Bank Guard was only discontinued in recent times.

(2) The Defensive Role.

Akin to the role of mere non-violent control was that of the defensive, already touched upon above. Troops would often be sent to guard a particular object or area, and, even though forbidden to use force, might be exposed to the mob's violence. During the riots of 1766 guards were placed at the doors of bakehouses in Newbury.[41] Guard duties of this sort were wearisome and disliked by officers and men alike, but were often very necessary. During a turnpike riot at Leeds in 1753 a magistrate anxiously wrote to the Secretary of State fearing lest a forthcoming review of troops might lead to a calling in of outlying detachments; he hoped this might be avoided, 'for if the turnpikes (which since the riots have been guarded) are left unguarded for but one night, I am very sure they will be demolished; for the spirit of rebellion, which rages amongst the lower sort of people in this county, is inconceivable.'[42]

The unpopularity of a purely defensive position needs no explanation; soldiers compelled to stand their ground under insults and blows tend to become sulky. Such a state of affairs however was common; a cautious War Office was determined never to allow its soldiers to be left in the presence of a mob without the assistance and orders of a civil magistrate, who was himself usually in a confusion of mind as to what his powers were. The present-day statement of law and practice for the guidance of officers[43] takes care of this situation; no sympathy will be shown, it implies, to an officer who attempts to shelter behind the cowardice of a magistrate:

> A commander on the spot, while attaching great weight to the opinion of the magistrate, must himself decide whether military intervention is necessary.
> . . . On the other hand, a commander will not be performing his duty if, from fear of responsibility, he takes no action, and allows outrages to be

committed which it is in his power to check, merely on the ground that there is no magistrate to direct him to take action.[44]

In the eighteenth century, however, no officer believed he had such a power of unilateral action, and consequently defensive situations were common. During the early stages of the Gordon riots, before the Order of 7 June, the troops remained on the defensive and so were able to achieve little. A party of the Coldstream guards formed a ring around a bonfire in Moorfields on 4 June; the crowd merely hurled furniture and other fuel over their heads from upper windows, 'which we could not prevent them from doing as the Magistrate would not permit us to act'.[45] Eventually reinforcements arrived and were more effective. The Lord Mayor's orders were 'for me to enlarge the circle and to prevent the mob pressing in on the fire, and to hinder any more persons entering the chapel and houses – These orders I immediately executed.' Later a fire engine put the fire out.[46]

Another detachment tried to protect a chapel on the Ratcliff Highway,

but the Magistrates not ordering me to act, the mob pulled down the chapel; as soon as it was down, a squadron of light horse coming up, the Riot Act was read by Justice Staples, upon which the mob shortly dispersed.[47]

This appears at first sight to be a rare victory for the Riot Act, but it seems more likely that the crowd, having done all that it wished to do, made off on the approach of the light cavalry.

Some detachments in 1780 recorded meagre successes in defending buildings[48] and hindering the mob from cutting the pipes of fire-engines,[49] but in most cases their position was so impossible that, after waiting in vain for a magistrate to arrive (or if present, for orders from him), they marched away from the scene of destruction.

In the long term also it is not surprising to find that troops on the defensive were gravely disadvantaged. The deterrent effect of a defence-guard was not likely to last for long after its departure. We have already noticed the anxiety of the magistrate for his turnpikes. Other guards which had to be permanent or at least of long standing to be effective included the Haymarket Theatre guard, and the Navy Pay Office Guard which attended monthly at Broad Street to convey coin to Portsmouth. The curious Loughborough rabbit-warren riots, a species of organised poaching in which as many as 2000 people participated, flared up as often as the soldiery were taken away from the neighbourhood.[50] So also did the activities of the nearby inhabitants, who cut down and carried off firewood and destroyed the deer of Salcey and Whittlewood Forests whenever the authorities were not looking.[51] Prison officers had similar problems. Many provincial prisons at this date, such as the one described in the *Vicar of*

Wakefield, were places of scant security, and a heavy crop of arrests following a riot was often more than they could cope with; soldiers were then called for as a gaol guard, at least until the trials were over.[52]

It is clear therefore that although there were some situations in which a threat of intervention was enough (and even some in which tact might soothe a crowd), this was not likely to be enough to disperse many of the riots of these times. It is probably difficult to imagine in present-day England what an eighteenth-century riot could be, although some idea can be gathered from the contemporary accounts of the Gordon riots (which have been described as the worst disaster London suffered since the Great Fire), when ferocious mobs attacked guarded strong-points again and again as in a regular battle and were met with volley after volley from the army. This is not the only action left to troops, however, and other courses short of ultimate force must first be considered.

(3) The Limited Offensive Role.

The methods here varied from the mere pushing scrimmage, in which on the face of it, apart from the greater solidarity of their formation and their readiness to order, soldiers were likely to have very little advantage over civilians, through various grades of force up to the use of clubbed muskets or the flat of sword-blades. The Tower detachment of Foot Guards, sent on 4 January 1768 to deal with the City disturbances, was opposed by rioters armed with old swords, sticks and bludgeons; they returned the blows but did not use firearms, and made some arrests. The riot was quelled.[53] Again in 1765 the army used force, but not excessive force, in Bloomsbury Square. The Secretary at War reported:

> The Justice[54] ordered his troop to charge upon them; which it accordingly did, but with orders to his men not to cut with their swords nor to draw a pistol. This charge broke the mob and threw many down and the rest ran into courts and the openings of the streets, where, there being some houses rebuilding, the mob with the bricks pelted the Guards very severely and hurt several men and horses, but there was but one man of the first troop who was very materially wounded by a cut in his head from the stroke of a brick.[55]

The Secretary at War claimed that none of the mob had been much hurt 'as had been heard of', and the action of these troops falls short of ultimate force, but it cannot be supposed that a cavalry charge, even without the use of arms, would be unattended by some serious injuries. Horace Walpole described the first attack of the mob which nearly forced an entry into Bedford House before another party of foot guards arrived to reinforce the 50 men already on guard.[56] 'At last after reading the proclamation, the gates of the court were thrown open and sixty foot soldiers marched out; the mob fled, but being met by a party of horse were much cut and trampled, but no lives were lost.'[57]Elsewhere Horace Walpole again asserts that the mob were slashed with sabres, so it seems that the instruction to use the flat of the sword was not obeyed by all the men.[58] A newspaper reported the death of a woman in the crowd, but this seems to have been mere rumour.[59] The *Gentleman's Magazine*, which appeared at the end of the month and was in a better position to check such stories, makes no mention of any fatalities in its account of the riots.[60] It might have turned out otherwise, for according to the regimental history the Foot Guards had been issued with six rounds of ball cartridge in case of need.[61]

Sometimes no physical collision took place and troops merely chased a mob; this seems to have happened more often in the countryside where troops, particularly cavalry, had the advantage, than in the streets of a town, and for the same reason, more often by daylight. During the 1757 militia riots

a party of country fellows were marching towards Sir H. Menoux's house at Wotton to demolish it, upon which Lord Ossory, Sir H. Menoux and some other gentlemen, attended by 10 of the dragoons, got on horseback and went after them.[62]

In their pursuit they came up with three separate parties of rioters on the road, who fled into hedges and ditches begging for mercy.[63]

In 1780 some small successes were achieved by troops acting in a limited offensive capacity before the general order. A mob, which admittedly was not large and probably so drunk as to show little resistance, was routed in Clare Market by an officer who secured all the avenues of escape, divided his force and approached from two directions. After a brawl in which no arms were used a few arrests were made.[64] A determined captain of the same regiment pursued another mob from Leicester Fields to Golden Square and deprived them of their iron bars, sticks and colours, whereupon they dispersed.[65] Horse were used in the same way as in 1765; the place was once again Bloomsbury Square, where the object of the mob's hatred was the town house of Lord Mansfield. A party of light dragoons arrived first:

Not having a magistrate, or orders to act offensively I ordered the men to form and charge[66] through the mob, which was done three times, without any effect; unfortunately the last time, one of the men's horses fell down, by which he had his arm broke.[67]

This account raises serious doubts as to the value of cavalry, at least of the value of the shock action of a conventional cavalry charge.[68]

(4) The Unlimited Offensive Role

The final resort of unlimited force was used with a frequency that is surprising when the constitutional, political and legal dangers of such a course are remembered. The riots of 1768 and 1780 are well known, but the mid-eighteenth-century records are remarkable for the number of riots which ended fatally for several of the participants; similar incidents were quite common in the equally burdensome smuggling duty, in which pitched battles were sometimes joined with large gangs of runners.

The methods previously discussed were often complementary to and usually previous to the use of *force majeure*. Naturally no officer however contemptuous of rioters would risk firing on them until all else had been tried. There was usually a long preliminary stage in which attempts were made to placate a crowd, or if the officer in charge was not enterprising, during which the detachment took no action of any sort. At this stage the troops might have to endure much provocation and insult. Sometimes, in spite of the tight rein kept upon the private men, soldiers were stung into retaliating without orders. During the Nottingham corn riots of 1756 Barrington wrote to Colonel Harvey of the Inniskilling Dragoons

> . . . [I] am sorry that the populace by throwing stones provoked two of your men to fire upon them by which a young man of the town was shot through the knee, and a good deal hurt, but am glad the firing (as it was not directed from a civil magistrate) was not from any orders given by the officers; and H.R.H.[69] very much approves of your having endeavoured (though unsuccessfully) to find out the persons that fired, as likewise of your conduct and proceedings on the present occasion.[70]

This letter and many like it also told the officer of the time all he needed to know about the Secretary at War's determination to subordinate military initiative to the civil arm.

Usually however officers were quick enough to restrain their men from acting independently. In 1780 a mob followed a party of guards escorting some arrested rioters from Bow Street to Newgate pelting them with large stones, whereat 'one of the soldiers turned and presented his piece, but the officer very humanely would not permit him to fire'.[71]

The army was of course often placed in situations where humanity became a luxury, and firearms would have to be used to disperse a crowd. At times the safety of the soldiers and officers of the law was in jeopardy. In the savage struggle between the Manchester crowd and the invalids at Shudehill in November 1757 one of the soldiers was killed and a number of others hurt before they opened fire. Several civilians were killed. The invalids presented and took aim several times, but without firing their numbers were too small to overawe the crowd.[72] In 1761 the mob at Hexham, numbering some eight or nine thousand, in their efforts to get the militia ballot lists from the magistrates, made no secret of their murderous intentions:

> No words would pacify them. The Riot Act was read several times, all to no purpose. The mob came to the very points of the bayonets endeavouring to break in upon our men, who bore the greatest insults for over two hours. At last they were commanded to fire. The mob took to their heels, leaving about twenty dead upon the spot, and several wounded. Ensign Hart of our battalion was shot through the body in the confusion by our own men, but was not dead when the accounts came away. There were one private man of Captain Blomburg's company killed and two wounded. The mob detachment will march back hither today, the mob being dispersed, and all being quiet. According to all accounts both officers and men behaved with the greatest steadiness and resolution.[73]

In a postscript Lt.-Col. Duncombe, the commander of the regiment, reported that Ensign Hart had since died, and that in fact he and three private men had all been hit by pistol bullets from the mob.[74] In a confused and bitter struggle of this type, with a determined and armed mob, the officer in charge must have felt that he had little choice but to fire. Twenty-one of the mob were killed, according to Holdernesse's information.[75] The magistrates were not so confident as Duncombe, and asked for a detachment of light horse in case of a fresh outburst.[76] The War Office sent two troops of cavalry and authorised their commander to call for reinforcements from other more distant detachments in Yorkshire if necessary.[77]

This savage riot seems largely to have derived its violence from the weak behaviour of the magistrates nearby at Morpeth and Gateshead, who had been terrorised into surrendering their ballot lists. The news of this success soon reached Hexham with predictable results. This sort of weakness, fairly common among magistrates,[78] was always heartily censured by the government. Vacillation arising from a feeling that force was illegal was treated by them with more leniency because they in part shared this feeling themselves.

During the riot of 17 October 1763, already mentioned above,[79] in which a Shoreditch public house underwent a siege by a body of sailors, the soldiers were again obliged to fire, as much to defend themselves as to suppress the riot. In spite of the presence of troops[80] the building was damaged, and a struggle began in which at first no firearms were used. The sergeant who had tried to pacify the mob with fair words was seized and became separated from his men. He called on his men to charge 'and the engagement soon began to be bloody. The men fired as if at an enemy; the people began to drop, and in a few minutes four men were killed.'[81] Two innocent bystanders were among those killed; this was to happen again in

1768 and 1780. There were no political repercussions after this incident, but the *Public Advertiser* noted meaningly: 'There did not appear to be either a Justice of Peace or constable present when the soldiers fired', and insisted (although it seems unlikely on the facts) that 'the whole mischief was done in a few minutes after the sailors came to the publican's House.'[82] The crowd, made furious by the repulse and, a few days later, by the verdict of homicide by misadventure instead of murder by the coroner's jury, threatened to return. The unfortunate sergeant had to call for reinforcements,[83] which was sufficient to prevent a further attack on the building.

After the Porteous affair and the Gordon riots the riot of 10 May 1768 ranks as the most notorious example of the use of military power in support of the civil arm in the century. It was also an important stage in the development by the army of a rougher but more effective line of action against crowds. The creation by Burke of a political issue out of the events, and the trial for murder of the magistrate who gave the order to fire helps to explain why this technique was not developed and perhaps made more efficient and more careful, a sad lack in the early stages of the Gordon riots.

The story, due to the persistence of Burke and the fame of Wilkes, has often been told. It is noteworthy that by 10 May the government had been dealing with what had been almost a continuous riot in London since 28 March, when the elections for the county of Middlesex had been held, and that the whole of 1768 had been remarkable for riots, beginning in January[84] and arising largely from a run of bad harvests and a severe winter. The actions of the government and army in May 1768 must not be isolated from this background, nor from the events which more recently preceded it.

From the date of the Middlesex elections the London rioters had been a source of mounting concern and irritation to ministers, War Office and army. The magistracy had in many cases proved inadequate to their task, and those of the Surrey side of the river in particular came out with a bad record. In spite of all that the authorities could do the mob seemed unchecked. Sheer exasperation accounted for much of what happened on the fatal day of the massacre in St George's Fields. Also the letter written by Weymouth on 17 April 1768 to Daniel Ponton, Chairman of the Surrey Quarter Sessions, the purport of which would be passed to his brother magistrates, was an important encouragement:

> As I have no reason to doubt your caution and discretion in not calling for troops till they are wanted, so on the other hand, I hope you will not delay a moment calling for their aid and making use of them effectually where there is occasion. That occasion always presents itself when the
> · civil power is trifled with and insulted, nor can a military force ever be employed to a more constitutional purpose than in support of the authority and dignity of magistracy.[85]

This letter,[86] which at first appears to say little, needs to be compared with many other similar letters from Secretaries to J.P.s. It is in fact the nearest to an overt invitation to use force that the man on the spot was ever likely to get from an eighteenth-century government. Conscious as he was of all the dangers, Weymouth was expressing the exasperation of an administration at the end of its tether. The final words of his letter show his awareness of the constitutional argument against force, and his rejection of it.

The contemporary accounts of the riots of 10 May in letter-books, memoirs, newspapers, depositions at the subsequent trials, and even prints, are confused and difficult to disentangle, but the events of the day seem to have been as follows. The riot began outside the King's Bench prison early in the day, itself an unusual and ominous sign, and there was a good deal of stone-throwing between 11 and 12 o'clock. Shortly after midday Ponton read the Riot Act proclamation, and soon afterwards an ensign and three soldiers left the ranks and pursued a young man whose behaviour they thought particularly insulting. They lost sight of him during the chase; it was a long one, giving the impression later of an excessively vengeful pursuit. About a quarter of a mile away they came up with and shot dead a man whom they believed to be their quarry; on the evidence it seems that the man they shot, one William Allen, was the wrong one, and that their real tormentor escaped. All three of the soldiers who had pursued him were Scottish, a fact which did not escape notice:

> The thinking and unprejudiced part of the world are of opinion that it was very imprudent (to say no worse of it) to order out any party from the third regiment on such an occasion as that in St. George's Fields, because the major part of this regiment, officers as well as private men, consists of Scotchmen, in whom it might very reasonably be supposed, the seeds of resentment, respecting Mr. Wilkes and his opposition of the Scots, were still remaining, and ready the first opportunity to vegetate into action.[87]

At about 1 o'clock one of Ponton's justices, Samuel Gillam, approached the mob and told them that the proclamation had been read upwards of an hour. Upon the mob expressing disbelief Gillam, to satisfy them, read it again. Between 2 and 3 o'clock he again begged them to go away, saying that the Riot Act had been read, and that 'they were every soul liable to be taken up'.[88] The crowd replied with a shower of stones, mainly directed at the soldiers. Gillam continued: 'For God's sake, good people, go away: if I see any more stones thrown I will order the guards to fire.' He was almost immediately struck on the temple by a stone, causing him to reel back several paces. He then told the officer to give the order to fire. The soldiers were in two rows to protect as much of the front of the prison as possible; they fell back into four ranks and began to fire in pairs. According to one deponent[89] at the subsequent trial, some of them fired several times and 'seemed to enjoy their fire, which I thought a great cruelty'. The horse guards also rode up and discharged their pistols into the crowd. Gillam, shaken by the experience, was heard to say anxiously to the commanding officer that he hoped there was no harm done. The officer replied: 'You may depend upon it, there is no mischief done, because we always fire in the air.'[90] However this may be, a number of people were killed or wounded,[91] but perhaps the officer's statement was correct, for the casualities appear to have occurred at some distance from the prison, and in some cases at a higher level along the causeway which carried the road across St George's Fields, which would be a result consistent with an order to fire high. Eighteen soldiers were injured in the confrontation, apparently from stones.[92]

Another witness stated that he heard Gillam say after the death of Allen, but before the firing upon the crowd, that 'he had orders from the ministry to fire upon the people, and there must be some killed, and it was better to kill five and twenty today than have a hundred killed tomorrow.'[93]

If the government was shaken so was the populace, and no further rioting in the St George's Fields area was reported after 10 May. Unpalatable though it may be, it is difficult to avoid the conclusion that suppression involving bloodshed did have a sobering effect, for a time at least, upon a riotous mob, although they would be likely to emerge to fight again at a later date as long as their grievances remained unsolved. The army and the government had in fact been made to feel that no sooner had they used an obviously effective method than they were forced to abandon it by the public outcry.

The years that followed saw the occasional use of force by troops,[94] but on the whole few lives were lost when it is remembered how widespread rioting was in times of dearth. The natural caution of politicians and officers, so long tempered by custom and experience, and particularly by the jolt of 1768, no doubt explained this. The uncertainty became paralysis in 1780, followed in the space of a single day by a complete about-face, in which for the first time the army was ordered not only to use unlimited force, but to do so whether assisted by a magistrate or not.

Some of the activities of detachments before the issuing of general orders on 7 June 1780 have been alluded to above.[95] There were however a few instances of force properly so called (but without the sanction of government orders) before 7 June. A mob offering to attack the Prime Minister's house was charged by a detachment of the Queens Light Dragoons. Three people were cut down but no lives were lost.[96] The only large-scale action of this type was in Bloomsbury Square on 6 June, during the attack on Lord Mansfield's house. After the unsuccessful operations of the troop of light horse mentioned above, which it appears caused more injury to the men than to the mob, a reinforcement of the Horse Grenadier

Guards and Foot Guards arrived under the command of Lt.-Col. Woodford, 'who by firing killed seven and wounded others, dispersed the rioters'.[97] Woodford's own report shows that he was taken to the square by one of the magistrates from the Lichfield Street office, where they found a party of the Third Guards being very roughly handled. The proclamation in the Riot Act was read but the crowd continued to insult and pelt the men. The soldiers bore it all very patiently, and when eventually the order was given to fire only a few at first obeyed. More joined in as the mob refused at first to be intimidated, but continued to throw stones; one fired a blunderbuss, although it seems to have hurt no one.[98] 'The firing was not ordered till the mob determined to rescue, and had effected the same, of some men taken in the house by the civil magistrate.'[99] The mob stood the fire for a minute or so before breaking up and retreating. If a full volley had been accurately discharged at the first order the result would have been more effective, but it seems clear on the evidence that the fire was straggling and took a little time to depress the crowd's morale. Any student of eighteenth-century military operations is aware of the effect of musketry at close range on packed masses of humanity, and there are during the period many indirect proofs, from the low casualty rate after a good deal of firing, that officers must have told their men to fire high, or even if they did not, the soldiers did so deliberately against orders, unwilling to injure people with whose grievance they secretly sympathised.[100]

The earlier stages of the above incident[101] shows that cavalry was not always as effective as it was supposed to be by contemporaries. Horse was useful to catch up with mobs of the quicksilver type already discussed, where contact was always difficult. There are many reports in June 1780 from detachments of foot soldiers, who returned to quarters after a useless patrol of the streets, during which they saw nothing:

> The mischief is done before your Lordship can send troops. The riot bursts forth at different places and times – from the distance and paucity of magistrates it is only followed, and we call out why does not Government prevent?[102]

So it is not surprising that cavalry were preferred and regarded as more effective; the magistrates asked for more on 5 June, saying that they would be in difficulties

> unless there is a very considerable body of horse which they can call in to their assistance. They find that assistance much more effectual than any that can be given by the Foot Guards.[103]

'Assistance' again means patrolling at this stage; the problem with the night mobs of 2–5 June had been to catch them. It is true that horsemen were far more useful for patrol duty than the slow-moving infantry, and when it came to a struggle they were sometimes, but not always, of more service than foot soldiers, at least foot soldiers who were not allowed to fire. On 7 June the War Office received an appeal for more horse-guards 'as the mob do not mind the foot'[104] but this was before the publication of the Order and the infantry had not yet become effective; twenty-four hours later the case was otherwise. The deciding factor was the behaviour of a mob rather than the action of the troops; a mob was sometimes so constituted (physically and psychologically) and situated that it could be dispersed with cavalry, but if it was dense, armed and determined, and in a confined space, the horses would no more face it than they would a square of infantry in battle, and would by their reaction become a liability to their riders. In fact the London streets of the eighteenth century were not the place for the classic cavalry manoeuvre, and the horse often got into scrapes – a favourite trick of the mob was to throw firebrands at the horses. Therefore in spite of the widespread impression of the superiority of cavalry over infantry, the truth was that it often did not know what to do with a mob once it had caught it. The brunt of the fighting of 7 June fell on the infantry.

However if foot were more effective than horse, horse and foot operating together could be even more so, and some officers realised this. They had of course no way of instructing themselves in the theory of riot suppression in advance, but some learned quickly and adapted recognised tactical forms learned in battle. The letter-book of Lt.-General Rainsford,[105] commander of the camp set up in Hyde Park during the riots, shows that he was careful to provide cavalry escorts for all infantry detachments sent out from his camp, so that they could act in concert. They did so in dealing with the Fleet Market mob of 7 June:

> Colonel Lake . . . as well as myself were separately with the mob for at least a quarter of an hour endeavouring by every fair means we could think of to persuade them to disperse, advising them with the consequences if they persisted in staying; this had not the least effect.[106]

At last the officer commanding the footguard detachment (i.e. the senior officer present) ordered his men to fire.[107] The mob wavered and began to panic, and the dragoons followed up the advantage with a charge of a quarter rank in front. An infantry volley followed by a cavalry charge to cause a disintegrating opponent to break in rout was standard battle practice; employed in the streets of London on 7 June the results were effective and tragic, and forty or fifty of the mob were killed.[108]

FORBEARANCE OF TROOPS

It is clear from the above, with its account of two officers pleading with the mob at risk to themselves, that some commanders were not happy about firing, and felt sorry for the victims.[109] Similar examples of forbearance occurred during the night of 7 June, and this in spite of the irritation of government, property-owners and particularly army, and in spite of having received specific orders to use force. Lord Algernon Percy's militia (the Northumberlands) was praised for their caution:

> It is a known fact, that even after they had fired, this corps twice presented and twice recovered their arms, without a single man discharging his piece, although the mob were at that time using every means to irritate and provoke them.[110]

There was a similar scene on the final night of the tragedy in Broad Street: 'We were very merciful to them, by firing only one gun at once, instead of a volley, thereby giving time to many to get off.'[111]

The last account is anonymous and need not have been written by an officer but the orders must have been given for these tactics. The sympathy of the soldier in the ranks for the crowd has already been discussed; it was always a source of apprehension to the War Office and government. Many doubted on 7 June if soldiers would fire at all when called upon to do so, if it was to protect Catholics and their property. Wraxall wrote:

> A great nobleman, now alive, who like myself, was a spectator of all the scenes of devastation committed on that night, told me that he felt strong doubts whether de Burgh's Regiment would actually draw the trigger.[112]

A guardsman observing a burning chapel on 4 June was heard to observe 'Great fools! Why didn't they pull down the building! Fire might hurt their neighbours.'[113] Several of the newspapers thought that the regular soldiers were partial to the mob and compared them unfavourably with the militia:

> Whether it was owing to the pusillanimous conduct of the magistrates, that the riots were not quelled in their infancy, or that the soldiery of the Guards had too much fellow feeling for a banditti, with whom they must have unavoidably long associated, we will not presume to say; the fact however is clear, that had some of the battalions of militia been on the spot at the commencement of the business, its termination had not been so long procrastinated.[114]

Another, describing the riot in Clare Market, wrote: 'Some soldiers both horse and foot, attended, but neither in sufficient numbers, nor were they seemingly much disposed to impede the proceedings of the mob.'[115]

The possibility of soldiers being tampered with had arisen in 1768; in 1780 at least one dangerous doctrine had got abroad among the soldiery, that having taken the oath to uphold the Protestant succession it would be a breach of it to assist the Catholics and protect their property by firing on Protestant crowds.

In spite of all these libels the officers seem to have had little cause to complain of the men's behaviour; no records exist of any overt insubordination. Lord Barrington wrote after the riots to Charles Jenkinson, praising their conduct.[116]

In any case the issue was never in doubt after the general orders of 7 June; these came from the office of the Adjutant-General: 'In obedience to an order of the King in Council, the military to act without waiting for directions from the Civil Magistrates, and to use force for dispersing the illegal and tumultuous assemblies of the people.'[117]

Unfortunately by that stage the ineffectiveness of troops not permitted to fire had encouraged the crowd to regard itself as invulnerable, and a bitter struggle was inevitable. War Office orders after the publication of the Order begin to include the words 'to attack and disperse' mobs, a far cry from the cautious formula 'but not to repel force with force etc.'. Even twentyfour hours earlier orders to troops have the same vagueness and readiness to place all responsibility upon the civil arm, e.g.: 'You will therefore assemble such troops as you can and follow the directions of the Civil Magistrate.'[118] It was the failure of the magistracy which had compelled the government to do without them, and for the first time in the century the military were given the opportunity of unfettered action. The scenes that followed are difficult to imagine. An anonymous member of the London Military Association wrote:

> We had not been in this position above ten minutes before mobs approached us down Cheapside, and were fired upon. Soon after another mob came down towards the bank, and were also fired upon. Within the lines all was perfectly still and silent, but on all sides the air was rent with huzzas. The mob, consisting of thieves of every species, had some pistols, which were fired, but felt no inclination to stay when they felt the musket balls amongst them.[119]

This detachment was then ordered to disperse the Broad Street riot,[120] for the Guards could not be spared from their duty of guarding the Bank; this mob also fled after a good deal of bloodshed. During this terrible night the crowds began to realise that the authorities were in earnest; on their third foray this detachment observed that the mob would not face them but fled at their approach.[121]

The commander at the Bank, Col. Twisleton, took similar action: 'I acted without civil magistrates and was obliged to fire upon the rioters, being attacked in front, rear and left flank by them; some were killed and wounded which had a good effect.'[122] A young lieutenant in the Foot

Guards under Twisleton's command wrote to his family:

> The dash with which the men went out last night, to rescue an house, that the mob had attacked, was as apparent as the sulkiness they before went out with, knowing they were to be ill used, and not to defend themselves; and after the first fire they were all very cool; so cool as to fire single shots.[123]

The garrison of the Tower had been doubled on 4 June. The Lieutenant expected an attack and gave some thought to the tactical problem involved. Although long obsolete as a regular fortress, and only looked upon as a barracks, it would have been an unforgettable disgrace if by some accident the mob had obtained entrance. The Lieutenant's orders of 7 June show his anxiety. In an emergency all companies were to repair to the alarm posts:

> In case of a mob assembling upon the hill on any side of the Tower, the sentries in the line or the batteries are to fire at any man who shall get into the ditch . . . if they are attacked it will be by a lawless, outrageous and undisciplined mob, whom a battalion of guards in this situation ought to despise; he therefore begs leave to recommend to them to keep themselves cool and sober, to be attentive on their posts; and if things should be brought to that extremity that they shall be obliged to fire, he hopes they will not throw it away.[124]

The Lieutenant's obvious desire to instil a contempt for the crowd (and his anxiety for economy in the use of army material) proved unnecessary, for no attempt was made upon the Tower.

USE OF ARTILLERY

The Gordon riots also raised the question of the use of artillery on mobs, a surprising and alarming novelty, which fortunately was not carried out. The destruction in Paris in 1795 (and 1871) show the logical results of military force used to an unlimited degree with all weapons, but cannon have never been used in the streets of London. Apart from Lord Tyrawley's plan in 1756, its use was never even discussed in the eighteenth century except during this great emergency, and then mainly as a defensive measure.

Much of Amherst's correspondence in the critical days of June 1780 was with Major-General Belford of the Royal Artillery, about the security of Woolwich and other places containing powder stores and arms. Both were aware of the incalculable effects of the mob gaining access to powder. On 6 June Belford reported that he had brought out and emparked in front of the new barracks at Woolwich twelve battalion guns, (that is to say, light six-pounders which would be easy to transport), with ten round shot and fifty rounds of case shot for each, 'so that should those riotous rascals choose to come here or oblige us to come to them, we are prepared at a minute's warning'.[125] Belford was clearly in favour of the latter course of seeking out what he regarded as an enemy; his provision of five times as much case shot would seem to show that he looked forward to in-fighting. He expected orders to march and added: 'If there should be occasion to send orders for these guns to march Your Lordship will at the same time send down 36 horses'; and added an aggressive postscript, 'I must insist on having the direction of this little command without regard to rank.'[126]

A few fire-eaters of this calibre in the City on 7 June would have taken many more lives. In the event the use of Belford's guns was not called for in any defensive or offensive capacity by the government, although some artillery was moved from the Tower to the South Hants Militia at Lambeth. They were sent by river, as being the quietest way: 'The motion of artillery would be very alarming through the City, and better to avoid it,' wrote Amherst.[127] The commander of the militia, Sir Richard Worsley, was thinking in terms of defence. 'If it was possible for us to receive some canister shot, it might be serviceable in case of an attack.'[128] In the event the militia never used their cannon. On the other hand the Commander-in-Chief was not prepared to risk releasing artillery to the unreliable Lord Mayor Kennett, who, anxious to erase the impression of his earlier conduct, wrote asking for four cannon, but his requisition was not complied with.[129] Clearly however artillery would have been used had the riots gone on for longer; on 7 June Amherst was sending for artillerymen from Woolwich to serve the guns being placed in Hyde Park.[130]

The proposal on the part of Lord Hillsborough to post howitzers on Blackfriars Bridge, though drastic, was also a defensive idea,[131] but it is enough to show us how desperate they thought the situation. The camp at Hyde Park was provided with battalion guns, but these were intended for the defence of the camp itself. They seem to have caused its commander, General Rainsford, more anxiety than peace of mind; after making all detachments of men called for at the height of the riots he was left with 150 men to guard the camp with baggage and six pieces of cannon.

Even without the use of cannon the casualties were high. Estimates vary, but several hundred were certainly killed. Wraxall, an eye-witness, wrote of the concealment by the mob of many bodies,[132] and believed the number killed to be not less than 700,[133] a much greater figure than the government admitted to. This unusual factor alone makes the Gordon riots unique in the history of riots in this country, and resembling more the events of 1795 and 1871 in Paris.

Appendix 1

A Marching Route for a regiment of foot: Exeter to Newcastle. Christopher D'Oyly to O.C. 43rd Foot at Exeter, 16 May, 1768. W.O. 5/55, 339. Approximate mileages are added.

[Exeter to Cullompton 13 miles]

Sunday May	22	Cullompton	19		8	Loughborough	15
	23	Taunton Dean	11		9	*Halt*	
	24	Bridgwater	9		10	Nottingham	14
	25	*Halt*			11	Mansfield	13
	26	Axbridge	17	Sunday	12	*Halt*	
	27	Bristol	10		13	Worksop and Blythe	17
	28	Iron Acton	12		14	Doncaster	22
Sunday	29	*Halt*			15	*Halt*	
	30	Dursley	15		16	Ferrybridge	18
	31	Gloucester	16		17	York	21
June	1	*Halt*			18	Boroughbridge	16
	2	Wincombe	12	Sunday	19	*Halt.*	
	3	Chipping Camden	15		20	Northallerton	16
	4	Stratford	19		21	Darlington	18
Sunday	5	*Halt*			22	Durham	15
	6	Coventry	11		23	*Halt*	
	7	Wolvey	24		24	Newcastle	

Summary: 25 Marching days, 9 halts, 375 miles: average day's march, 15 miles.

Appendix 2

A Marching Order for riot duty. W.O. 5/55, 276. (Original form – capitals, punctuation etc.)

It having been represented to His Majesty that a number of disorderly Persons assembled themselves last Night, and committed divers Outrages in several of the principal Streets in the Liberty of Westminster & in Places adjacent, and it having been likewise represented that a Military Force is absolutely necessary for preventing these Disorders, it is H[is] M[ajesty's] P[leasure] that upon Application made by any of the Magistrates of the City & Liberty of Westminster, or of the County of Middlesex, you cause such Detachments as shall be judged necessary to be made from the Battalion of Foot Guards doing Duty in the Savoy (under Your Command) and march, and be aiding and assisting to the Civil Magistrates upon their Requisition, in suppressing any Riots or Tumults that shall happen, in preserving the Public Peace, and in seizing the Rioters; but not to repel Force with Force unless in Case of absolute Necessity, or being thereunto required by the Civil Magistrates
      Wherein etc*

Given at the War Office, 29 March 1768

By H.M.C.

Field Officer in Staff Waiting   Barrington.
for the three Regiments of Foot
Guards

*This is the usual form at the end of a marching order: in full it would run: 'Wherein the Civil Magistrates and all others concerned are to be assisting in providing Quarters, impressing Carriages, and otherwise as there shall be Occasion.'

A Note on Sources

The principal source for War Office policy is the series known as W.O.4 in the Public Record Office, i.e. the Secretary at War's out-letters. These need to be supplemented with W.O.5 (marching orders). In normal cases the two are sent together: the marching order contains no more than a formal confirmation of the request referred to in the letter with it. However it is not safe to rely on this, and marching orders can be found without any trace of a covering letter in W.O.4, and (less frequently) vice versa. For a large part of the period of this study additional information is forthcoming from the Barrington Papers in the East Suffolk Record Office. Interventions and policies of the Secretaries of State in the period studied can be followed from the S.P. series in the Public Record Office, particularly S.P. 36, 37, 41 and 44, and from the Newcastle, Holdernesse and other papers in the British Museum.

Apart from the collection in the East Suffolk Record Office, which has many tantalising gaps, there appears to exist no good run of Barrington papers. Individual items can, however, be found in other places (e.g. the Chatham MSS.). As a result he remains, as in his lifetime, a somewhat vague and reticent figure. It is possible to say what he did: less often is it clear why he did it.

Notes

1. C. V. F. Townshend, *The Military Life of Field-Marshal George First Marquess Townshend*, (1901), 317.

1. See Chapters 2 and 3.
2. Savile to John Hewitt, November 1779. Savile Foljambe MSS., *H.M.C.*, XV. 5, 153.
3. Sir William Holdsworth, *A History of English Law*, 17 vols (1903–72), X, 705; Ian Brownlie *The Law Relating to Public Order*, (1968), 37–52.
4. These were women, clergy, and persons decrepit or under 15 years of age. 2 Henry V, c.8.
5. Sir Matthew Hale, *The History of the Pleas of the Crown*, 2 vols (1800), I, 495.
6. Such a riot had to show a wide-ranging political purpose for a prosecution to succeed, e.g. *R. v. Dammaree and Purchase* (1709), 15 *State Trials*, 522. Another attempt to resurrect the treason-felony charge was made in 1780 in Lord George Gordon's case, but the jury again showed their distaste for the doctrine by acquitting him. 21 *State Trials*, 485.
7. 1 Geo I st.2, c.5. It was a restatement of several similar earlier acts: 3, 4 Edw. VI, c.5; 1 Mar. sess. 2, c.12; 1 Eliz.I, c.16.
8. *Gent. Mag.* (1768), 323–5.
9. *P.H.*, XXI, 694–8.
10. *R. v. Gordon* (1781), *21 State Trials*, 493.
11. 'On the Suppression of Riots by Military Interference', *Law Magazine*, IX (1833), 66.
12. *Per* Gould J., Recorder, Parker C.B. and Aston J. concurring. The latter added that if assistance was wanted 'none could be more proper than the military, who are always in readiness, more easily collected, more subject to command, and more capable of defence, than any other parts of the people'. *Gent. Mag.* (1768), 325.
13. 19 June 1780, *P.H.*, XXI, 696.
14. *P.H.*, X, 207, 209.
15. i.e. Samuel Gillam, the magistrate present.
16. *Sub. nom.* 'Englishman'. *Gazetteer*, 20 May 1768. Similar letters appeared in the *Westminster Journal*, 21 and 28 May, and the *St. James' Chronicle*, 5–7 May.
17. Weymouth to Sir John Fielding, 15 April 1768. S.P.44/142, 57.
18. *C.J.*, XXXII, 296. The debate is in Cavendish, *Debates*, I, 307–37, and in

History, Debates and Proceedings of Both Houses of Parliament of Great Britain, V, 78.

19. Ibid.
20. W.O. 34/103, ff.1 – 12. A further bundle of copies is also to be found in W.O. 34/109, ff.23 – 9.
21. Opinion of Edward Northey, 26 October 1717. S.P. 35/10, f.37.
22. Opinion of Robert Raymond, 10 January 1722; Carteret to Secretary at War, 11 January 1722. W.O. 34/103, ff.5 – 6r, 7.
23. Opinion of Philip Yorke, 2 January 1733; Secretary at War to Major-General Gore, 12 May 1733. Ibid., ff.8 – 9r, 10.
24. Richard Arnold to O. C. Honeywood's Dragoons, 25 April 1734. W.O.5/31, 25.
25. Same to O. C. Tatton's Foot, 23 April 1734. Ibid., 23.
26. Opinion of Sir J. Willes and Sir D. Ryder, 10 May 1735. W.O. 34/103, f. 11r.
27. William Yonge to the Lord in Gold Staff Waiting for His Majesty's Four Troops of Horse Guards, 31 July 1736. W.O. 4/34, 219.
28. Henry Fox to O. C. Bland's Dragoons, 12 September 1747; same to O. C. Harrison's Foot, 11 October 1748. W.O. 5/39, 11, 323.
29. Welbore Ellis to O. C. Guards at the Tower, 16 May 1765. W.O. 5/53, 313.
30. Murray to Lord Holdernesse, 12 October 1753; Holdernesse to Lord Mayor and Recorder of Leeds, 13 October; same to Lord Irwin, 13 October. S.P. 36/123, ff. 135 – 6r, 137 – 8, 140.
31. Fox to O. C. Companies of Welch Fusiliers at Bristol, 4 September 1753. W.O. 5/41, 479.
32. Barrington to Attorney-General, n.d. (1773). Barrington MSS. HA174: 1026/6a(2).
33. Report of Sir John Scott and Sir John Mitford to the Duke of Portland, 19 December 1796. Quoted in Clode, II, 637.
34. Report of Attorney-General. Ibid., 649.
35. Wellington to Lord Anglesey, 17 June 1848. W.O. 30/111.
36. W.O. 34/103, f. 2r.

CHAPTER 2

1. E.g. S. and B. Webb, *The Parish and the County* (1923), vol. 1 of *English Local Government, from the Revolution to the Municipal Corporations Act* (9 vols), 319–82.
2. Richard Burn, *The Justice of the Peace, and Parish Officer* (1755).
3. W. Nelson, *The Office and Authority of a Justice of Peace* (1718).
4. William Lambarde, *Eirenarcha: or the Office of the Justice of Peace, in Foure Bookes* (1599).
5. M. Dalton, *The Country Justice* (1635), 110. There were numerous reprintings. The British Museum lists 17 editions between 1618 and 1746.
6. Saunders Welch, *Observations on the Office of Constable* (1754), 6.
7. *Gent. Mag.* (1757), 430.
8. Ibid. (1768), 323 – 5.
9. Ibid. (1757), 592.
10. Nathanial Cholmley to the Duke of Newcastle, 4 October 1757. Add. MSS. 32874, f. 444r.
11. *Lloyd's Evening Post,* 28 – 30 March 1768.

12. John Hewitt, *A Journal of the Proceedings of J. Hewitt, Mayor, and One of His Majesty's Justices of the Peace for the City and County of Coventry, in the Year 1756* etc. (1779), 2–3.
13. Ibid., 4.
14. *C.J.*, XXXII, 12–13.
15. N. Cholmley to Newcastle, 14 September, 1757. Add. MSS. 32874, f. 46r.
16. W. Osbaldeston to Newcastle, 16 September 1757. Ibid., f. 88.
17. He believed that the government 'teach the magistrate to look to the military power as its first instrument, and not as the final and desperate resource in case of necessity'. 8 March 1769. Cavendish, *Debates*, I, 308.

CHAPTER 3

1. Fortescue, II, 15–16.
2. Lois G. Schwoerer, *No Standing Armies* (Baltimore and London, 1974), Chapter 9, surveys some of the literature on the subject.
3. Cavendish, *Debates*, I, 10.
4. Fortescue, II, 17.
5. *P.H.*, X, 376.
6. 1 William and Mary, c.5. In fact there were several years when the Act was not passed.
7. James Craggs to Colonel Fane, 13 August 1717. W.O. 4/20, 250.
8. Barrington to the Earl of Home, 28 September 1756. W.O. 4/52, 266.
9. Shelburne to General Gage (in America), 13 September 1766. C.O. 5/220, 3.
10. Colonel Anstruther to Barrington, 18 March 1757. W.O. 1/973, 45; Barrington to Colonel Howard, 22 March 1757. W.O. 4/53, 382.
11. Barrington to Mayor of Sudbury, 18 March 1761.W.O. 4/63, 625.
12. *Gent. Mag.* (1771), 471.
13. James Craggs to Thomas Palmer, 21 August 1717. W.O. 4/20, 196–7.
14. Sir John Fortescue, 'The Army', in *Johnson's England*, ed. A. S. Tuberville, 2 vols (1933), I, 81.
15. Clode, I, 398.
16. Corelli Barnett, *Britain and Her Army, 1509–1970* (1970), 165.
17. Clode, I, 398.
18. Ibid.
19. Ibid.
20. Fortescue, II, 529–30.
21. Barrington to Benjamin Woodroffe at Winchester, 1 February 1757. W.O. 4/53, 150.
22. Prince Frederick to Lord Amherst, 8 June 1780. W.O. 34/103, f. 16or.
23. *C.J.*, XXIX, 666; *P.H.*, XV, 1328–9.
24. Duke of Northumberland to Lord Shelburne and Lord Weymouth, 12 April; Weymouth to Lord Barrington, 12 April 1768. S.P. 44/142, 47–9, 50–1.
25. Barrington to O.C. 2nd Dragoon Guards, 12 April. W.O. 5/55, 290–1.
26. Barrington to Weymouth, 13 April. S.P. 44/142, 54.
27. Barrington to Morrison, 15 April. W.O. 4/83, 302.
28. Report of Lt.-Col. Morrison, enclosed with Barrington to Weymouth, 18 April. Ibid., 318–19.

29. Edward Harvey to Colonel Skene, 21 April. W.O. 3/24, 32.
30. Barrington to Lord North, 23 December 1774. Barrington MSS. HA 174: 1026/107, 281-2.
31. See Chapter 13. The light dragoons were to be men of 5'5" to 5'7" on horses of 14 hands 3 to 15-0, while the ordinary dragoons were 5'8" to 5'10" on horses of 15-0 to 15-1. Welbore Ellis to Earl of Drogheda, 5 December 1764. W.O. 4/1044, 23-4.
32. See below, Chapter 13.
33. B. P. Hughes, *Firepower. Weapons Effectiveness on the Battlefield, 1630-1850* (1974).
34. *General Wolfe's Instructions to Young Officers* (1780), 49.
35. Examination of Lord Provost of Edinburgh, 10 March 1736. Add. MSS. 33049, f. 27r.
36. For a routine marching route see Appendix 1. In emergencies the route was sometimes left to the local commanders.
37. E.g. from Newcastle to suppress a riot at York. Barrington to Major Scott, 20 September 1757. W.O. 4/54, 448.
38. See Chapter 7.
39. C. Gill, *History of Birmingham* (1952), 145. The subject of horses at grass is discussed in Chapter 6.
40. Peter Young and J. P. Lawford (ed.), *History of the British Army* (1970), 47. Young remarks significantly: 'It seems these old battles were not quite such drill parades as we are sometimes asked to believe.'
41. *Gent. Mag.* (1763), 516.
42. *Public Advertiser*, 2 April 1768.
43. J. F. C. Fuller, *British Light Infantry in the Eighteenth Century* (1925), 56.
44. See above p. 183.
45. Quoted by E. P. Thompson, *The Making of the English Working Class* (1963), 562.
46. Shute Barrington, 115-18. This author doubted if the men of the relieving force due to march to the King's Bench Prison the next day would have obeyed their officers if it had not been for the good effect of this letter.
47. May, 1768, 244.
48. 11 May 1768. W.O. 4/83, 379-80.
49. *Public Advertiser*, 19 May 1768 (*sub. nom.* 'Fiat Justitia').
50. Barrington to Lt.-Col. Sloper, 26 August 1765. W.O. 4/77, 377-8. Similar orders were given to forces in North America.
51. Barrington to John and Robert Andrew, 1 August 1765. W.O. 4/77, 276; see also same to John Meredith of Brecon, 4 November 1768. W.O. 4/84, 323; same to Thomas Vivian of Truro, 25 February 1773. W.O. 4/90, 417.
52. See Chapter 1.
53. See Chapter 2.
54. H. Bland, *A Treatise of Military Discipline* (1727). Eight more editions appeared up to 1762.
55. Barrington to Thomas Bradshaw, 12 October 1768. Barrington MSS. H.A. 174: 1026/107, 104-7.
56. Soldiers were called upon to collect customs by 14 Car. II, c.11, and to suppress conventicles by 22 Car. II, c.1.
57. 'Employment of Troops in Aid of the Civil Power', *Manual of Military Law* (9th Edition, 1968), Part II, Section V, 501-12.

58. *The Queen's Regulations for the Army* (1961), paragraphs 1164–83.

59. Some sort of guidance was later to be found in *Standing Orders for the Light Horse Volunteers of London and Westminster* (1805), 165–72, under 'Street Duty'. The articles of this section however were all concerned with elementary tactics, not law.

60. Richard Arnold to Field Officer in Staff Waiting, 9 November 1723. W.O. 4/ 29, 336.

61. Barrington to OC 4th Dragoons at Romney, 26 May 1768. W.O. 4/83, 412. In 1756 he wrote to Lord Egremont about a detachment sent to Taunton: 'I have ordered that this detachment be sent under the command of a very discreet captain.' 20 November 1756. W.O. 4/52, 416.

62. Harvey to Lt.-Col. Warde, 10 October 1766. W.O. 4/1044, 94.

63. Barrington to Wolfe, 8 January 1757. W.O. 4/53, 40.

64. Wolfe to the Duke of Richmond, 19 January 1757, in *Wolfe to the Duke of Richmond. Unpublished Letters*, ed. P. L. Carver. (Reprint from *University of Toronto Quarterly*, VIII, No. 1 (1938).)

65. Thomas Tyrwhitt to Marlborough, 30 June 1757. W.O. 4/54, 178.

66. Barrington to Lord Dartmouth, 12 November 1774. H.A. 174: 1026/107, 280–1.

67. Same to same, 24 February 1775. Ibid., 293–4.

68. Same to same, 28 March 1775. Ibid., 298.

69. Colonel Francis Leighton to General Wade, 24 September 1740. SP 41/12.

70. Clode, Vol. II, 615–17.

71. R. Delafaye to Newcastle, 1 December 1725. S.P. 35/60, f. 1.

72. Commissioners in Scotland to Lords Justices. 16 February 1728. S.P. 36/5, f. 108v.

73. Lt.-Col. Fitzwilliam to Col. Fleming, 4 June 1743. S.P. 36/61.

74. See Chapter 12.

75. See Chapter 2.

76. Rainsford to Barrington 23 May, 1768. W.O. 1/874, 85–6.

77. W.O. 1/874, 85–6, 89, 97.

78. Weymouth's secretary.

79. 24 May 1768. W.O. 1/874, 105–6.

80. E.g. W. Lecky, *A History of England in the Eighteenth Century*, 8 vols (1878–90), III, 516.

81. See Chapter 13.

82. General Mostyn's inspection returns of the 4th Foot (of which five companies were absent on riot duty) at Plymouth, 3 October, and the 10th Dragoons (of which four troops were away for the same reason) at Northampton, 27 October 1757. W.O. 27/5.

83. The returns of inspections in W.O. 27/13 show that very few autumn reviews could be held.

84. Edward Harvey to Marquess of Granby, 25 October 1766. Rutland MSS. *H.M.C.*, 12 V, 288; Edward Harvey to Major-General Keppell, Major-General Parslow, and Lord Pembroke, 22 October 1766. W.O. 4/1044, 97. See below Chapter 9.

85. Barrington to Lt.-Col. Sloper at York, 26 August 1765. W.O. 4/77, 377. See also Barrington to Lord Edgecumbe, 28 April 1773. W.O. 4/91, 42, and Major-General Byng to Mayor of Kendal, 1 March 1818. H.O. 50/462,

bundle 4.

86. Lt.-Col. La Fausille to Barrington, 9 April 1757. W.O. 1/973, 662.

87. E.g. 'The regiment having been on coast duty has been very sickly.' Review of 3rd Dragoons in 1768. W.O. 27/12.

88. See above p. 23 for the Quarter-Master General's views in 1768 upon the decline of army discipline as a result of the riot duty.

89. See Barrington's paper presented to the King in January 1776, quoted in Shute Barrington, 153–7.

90. 'Four out of the seven battalions of Foot Guards which are necessary to preserve the peace in London . . .' (from a paper of army statistics) 27 July 1757. Add MSS. 33047, f. 99r.

91. From a memoir on the defence of Britain by 'M.G.L.', no date but apparently 1796–97. W.O. 30/58, bundle 18. See also 'General Arrangements for Defence of the Capital, 1779', W.O. 1/1137, bundle 7; 'Precautions in case of an alarm in London', in General Rainsford's letter book (1778), Add MSS. 23655, ff. 19–20r; Lt.-Col. George Hanger, *Military Reflections on the Attack and Defence of London* (1795).

CHAPTER 4

1. G. Rudé, *The Crowd In History* (New York, 1964), 37.

2. Brief of Evidence in the Walsall riot, 29 May 1750. S.P. 36/113, ff. 88–101r; Lord Dupplin to Duke of Newcastle, 26 September 1757. Add MSS. 32874, ff. 304–5.

3. Anon. 'Observations on the present spirit of rioting'. *Gent. Mag.* (1757), 591.

4. Grenville to Lord Amherst, 28 June 1780. W.O. 34/125, f. 180r.

5. Macclesfield to Charles Jenkinson, 15 June 1780. Add. MSS. 38214, f. 23r.

6. Sarah Hoare to Mrs Bland, 10 June 1780. *Memoirs of Samuel Hoare*, ed. F. J. Pryor (1911), 60.

7. *Paris and London in the 18th Century: Studies in Popular Protest* (1969), 19–21.

8. John Hewitt, *A Journal of the Proceedings of J. Hewitt, Mayor, and One of His Majesty's Justices of the Peace for the City and County of Coventry in the Year 1756* (1779), 16.

9. Mayor and Corporation of Falmouth to the Duke of Newcastle, 26 November 1727. S.P. 44/125, ff. 184–5.

10. Cavendish, *Debates*, I, 312.

11. *Gent. Mag.* (1749), 329.

12. H. Walpole, *The Last Journals of Horace Walpole During the Reign of George III from 1771–1783, 2 vols (1910),* II, 36.

13. L. T. C. Rolt, *The Aeronauts. A History of Ballooning, 1783–1903* (1966), 63, 66, 69.

14. *Gent. Mag.,* (1763), 517.

15. A useful but not exhaustive list of these outbreaks, based on some of the State Papers and the *Gentleman's Magazine*, can be found in Robert F. Wearmouth, *Methodism and the Common People of the Eighteenth Century* (1945), 19–50. Some of them have received a more critical treatment from G. Rudé, *The Crowd in History* (1964), and *Paris and London in the 18th Century: Studies in Popular Protest* (1969), E. P. Thompson, *The Making of the English Working Class* (1963), and,

for militia riots, J. R. Western, *The English Militia in the Eighteenth Century* (1965).

16. Hannah Darby to Rachel Thompson, n.d. [1756], in A. Raistrick, *Dynasty of Ironfounders. The Darbys and Coalbrookdale* (1953).

17. See below p. 179.

18. 'The Scots Victory', F. G. Stephens and E. Hawkins, *Catalogue of Prints and Drawings in the British Museum. Political and Personal Satires*, IV, no. 4196.

19. Fielding to Robert Wood, 31 March 1768. S.P. 44/142, 104.

20. John Creed to Newcastle, 19 May 1740. S.P. 36/50, f. 418r.

21. J. D. Chambers, *Nottinghamshire in the Eighteenth Century: A Study of Life and Labour under the Squirearchy* (1932), 41–2.

CHAPTER 5

1. These have been discussed, although not at any great length, by M. A. Thomson, *The Secretaries of State 1681–1782* (1968), 107–9.

2. See below pp. 52–3.

3. Daniel Defoe, *A Tour through the whole Island of Great Britain*, 2 Vols., (1962), II, 118.

4. Arthur Young, *A Six Month's Tour through the North of England*, 4 Vols (1771), IV, 423–31.

5. Edwin Gay, 'Arthur Young on English Roads', *Quarterly Journal of Economics*, XLI (1927), 545–51, at 551.

6. W. Albert, *The Turnpike Road System in England, 1663–1840* (1972), 139.

7. Ibid., 49.

8. Ibid., 31.

9. J. L. McAdam, *Remarks on the Present System of Road Making* (5th ed. enlarged, 1822), 10.

10. *The Natural History and Antiquities of Selbourne* (1789), 174.

11. *Gent. Mag.* (1752), 517.

12. E. A. Pratt, *A History of Inland Transportation in England* (1912), 55.

13. Howard Robinson, *Britain's Post Office. A History of Development from the Beginnings to the Present Day* (1953), 103.

14. On the effect of weather on the economy generally see T. S. Ashton, *Economic Fluctuations in England, 1700–1800* (1959), Chapter 1.

15. Sarah Osborn to Sir John Osborn, July, 1766. *The Letters of Sarah Byng Osborn, 1721–1773*, ed. John McClelland (1930), 105–6.

16. Same to same, 8 September 1768. Ibid., 142.

17. W. Marshall, *A Review of the Reports to the Board of Agriculture*, (1815), I, 77–8.

18. E. L. Jones, *Seasons and Prices: The Role of the Weather in English Agricultural History* (1964), 144.

19. See Chapter 6.

20. Col. Prescott (7th Foot) to Barrington, 10 February 1773. W.O. 40/16.

21. Barrington to Reverend Dr Parry of Market Harborough, Leicestershire, 17 February 1773. W.O. 4/90, 402–3.

22. Paper on the state of the army in 1764. Add. MSS. 40759, f. 231.

CHAPTER 6

1. Clode, II, Chapter XXI; Olive Anderson, 'The Constitutional Position of the Secretary at War, 1643–1855', *Journal of the Society of Army Historical Research*, XXXVI (1958), 165.
2. *The Secretaries of State, 1681–1782* (1968), Chapter II.
3. (Charles Jenkinson), *P.H.*, XX, 1253. See Olive Anderson, loc. cit., who emphasized the limited and technical nature of most of the duties of the office, asserting that only in the sphere of army finance did he have much scope.
4. 'A secretary at war must obey the King's orders signified by a secretary of state or resign. He is only a ministerial officer. He is not a proper judge of the propriety of a measure.' Speech of Lord Barrington, in *Brickdale's Debates*, 9 December 1770.
5. He was Secretary at War from 1683 to 1704. *D.N.B.* See also G. A. Jacobson, *William Blathwayt, a Late Seventeenth Century Administrator* (New Haven, 1932)
6. R. G. Scouller, *The Armies of Queen Anne* (1966), 18.
7. I. F. Burton, *The Secretary at War and the Administration of the Army during the War of the Spanish Succession* (unpublished London Ph.D. thesis, 1960), 45.
8. He could be and often was asked to be present on particular occasions.
9. I. F. Burton, op. cit., 255, 273.
10. All eighteenth century Secretaries at War were members except for R. Pringle (1718). In 1776, when Barrington expressed a wish to retire from the Commons the King suggested that he give up his seat but stay on at the War Office, but North thought a Secretary at War must be in Parliament, and vetoed this as a permanent arrangement, although Barrington gave up his seat in the Commons in March 1778 and did not quit the War Office until December. Shute Barrington, 167.
11. E.g. in Sir Lewis Namier and John Brooke, *The House of Commons 1754–1790*, 3 vols (1964), II, 58.
12. See below pp. 70–1.
13. He took office in November 1755 and was replaced by Charles Townshend in March 1761. In November 1762 Welbore Ellis became Secretary at War, and Barrington returned in August 1765, remaining at the War Office until driven out by the many disagreements he had with colleagues over the conduct of the American war, in December 1778. The remainder of the period (i.e. to 1780) is covered by the tenure of Charles Jenkinson.
14. Namier and Brooke, op. cit., I, 140.
15. Namier and Brooke, op. cit., II, 55.
16. Ibid., 56.
17. Lord of Admiralty, 1746–54, Master of the Great Wardrobe, 1754–5, Chancellor of the Exchequer, 1761–2, Treasurer of the Navy, 1762–5.
18. Barrington to Andrew Mitchell, 3 March 1761. Sir H. Ellis, *Original Letters illustrative of English History*, 4 vols (1827), IV, 432.
19. *Memoirs of the Reign of King George II*, 3 vols (1847), II, 144.
20. Barrington to Charles Gould, 8 February 1766. Shute Barrington, 137.
21. See his letter to General Elliott, who had solicited some favour for his son, 25 November 1767. Ibid., 122.
22. Barrington to Lieut. Daniel Roche (on half pay), 20 May 1767. Barrington MSS. H.A. 174: 1026/107, 32.

23. Same to Lord North, 5 May 1776. Ibid. H.A. 174: 1026/6c (3).

24. Barrington to Wolfe, 21 February 1757. W.O. 4/53, 265.

25. Barrington to Wolfe, 8 January 1757, W. O. 4/53, 40. See above pp. 30–1.

26. See below p. 186.

27. *Gent. Mag.* (1756), 395–6.

28. *Memoirs of the Reign of King George the Second*, 3 vols (1846), II, 142.

29. *Court and City Register* (1757), 174.

30. Ibid. (1766), 194.

31. Ibid. (1768), 200.

32. *The Royal Kalendar for 1773*, 165.

33. *The Court and City Register* (1777), 163.

34. M. A. Thomson, op. cit., 132.

35. *D.N.B.*

36. Ibid.

37. Ibid.

38. See below p. 40.

39. *D.N.B.*

40. 21 December 1771. Joseph Parkes and Herman Merivale, *Memoirs of Sir Philip Francis, K.C.B., with Correspondence and Journals*, 2 vols (1867), I, 274.

41. *Public Advertiser*, 23 March 1772.

42. Charles Dupin, *View of the History and Actual State of the Military Force of Great Britain* (London, 1822), 172. Clerks in the office of the Secretary of State seem not to have been overworked either. M. A. Thomson, op. cit., 134.

43. Barrington MSS. H. A. 174: 1026/107, 167–8.

44. Barrington to Bowlby, 27 September 1759. W.O. 4/59, 82.

45. John Ogilby, *Mr. Ogilby's Tables of his Measur'd Roads, etc.* (1676).

46. *Mr. Ogilby's and Mr. Morgan's Pocket Book of the Roads, etc.* (1680).

47. *England and Wales, or Ogilby Improved* (1720).

48. 8 Geo. II, c.30.

49. Fortescue, I, 24.

50. See above, Chapter 5.

51. See above, Chapter 9.

52. E.g. William Blackett of Coventry to Henry Fox described the miseries of his district and hinted at impending trouble: 26 October 1756. S.P. 44/136, 393–4. A mayor and corporation became anxious about their prisoners of war and wrote for help: Mayor and five magistrates of Helston to Barrington, 20 May 1758. W.O. 1/976, 597.

53. Welbore Ellis to Field Officer in Waiting, 18 May; to O.C. 11th Dragoons (Lambeth), 18 May; to O.C. Royal Regiment of Horse Guards (Hertford), 18 May; to Gold Stick in Waiting, 20 May; to O.C. 1st Guards (Tower), 20 May; to O.C. 10th Dragoons (Kensington), 20 May; to O.C. 2nd Dragoon Guards (Islington), 20 May 1765. W.O. 4/77, 16, 21, 23, 30, 31, 32, 43.

54. 29 March, 27 April 1768. W.O. 5/55, 276, 316; see also Sir John Fielding to Robert Wood, 15 June 1768. S.P. 44/142, 147–50.

55. Barrington to Pitt, 1 July 1758. P.R.O. 30/8/18, f. 188r.

56. Edward Harvey to O.sC. 13 regiments of cavalry, 9 October 1766. W.O. 4/1044, 93.

57. W. Yonge to O.C. detachment of Lord Mark Kerr's regiment, 12 July 1740. W.O. 4/36, 54.

58. C. D'Oyly to Lt.-Col. Warde (4th Dragoons), 20 September 1776. W.O. 4/80, 287.
59. Seymour Conway to the King, 20 September 1766. Fortescue, *Correspondence*, I, no. 388.
60. Barrington to Earl Waldegrave or OC 2nd or Queen's Dragoon Guards at Colchester (and ten other cavalry regiments), 23 September 1766, W.O. 4/80, 293–4. See below p. 117.
61. The Secretary of State wrote to a Gloucester J.P. telling him of the orders to move troops into his area, 'and I could have wished their horses had not been at grass'. Seymour Conway to William Dellaway, 22 September 1766, S.P. 44/142, 5.
62. Barrington to OC 1st or King's Dragoon Guards, (and six other cavalry regiments), 14 April, 14 May 1768. W.O. 4/83, 296.
63. Barrington to Lt.-Col. Harvey, 26 and 27 August 1756. W.O. 5/43, 363, 365–6.
64. Holdernesse to Barrington, 26 August 1756. S.P. 44/134, 381–2.
65. S.P. 36/135 contains twelve letters from magistrates and eye-witnesses in the Midlands to the Secretary of State's office describing riots and/or asking for help between 19 August and 7 September. Ff. 226–9, 238–9, 256–7, 260–1, 266–8, 271–4, 281–8, 289–91, 299–300, 301–2, 303–4, 305–6.
66. 'The Marquis of Rockingham having sent me, by express, the proceedings of the rioters at Sheffield.' Barrington to Lt.-Col. Harvey, 31 August 1756. W.O. 4/52, 188.
67. Holdernesse to Rockingham, 31 August 1756. Egerton 3436, f. 91r.
68. Rockingham to Holdernesse, 13 September. Ibid., ff. 93r–94r.
69. Ibid., f. 94v.
70. An unfulfilled promise. In fact wheat rose from 4/6 a bushel in 1755 to 6/9 in 1756 (Michaelmas prices). T. S. Ashton, *Economic Fluctuations in England, 1700–1800* (1959), 181.
71. Holdernesse to Newcastle, 25 August 1756. Add. MSS. 32867, f. 48.
72. 'All applications for troops which come to Lord Barrington on similar occasions he will constantly transmit to the Secretaries of State.' Barrington to Holdernesse, 31 August 1756. Egerton 3432, f. 5r.
73. The account is set out in more detail in Chapter 8.
74. At this date he took many of his instructions from Cumberland. See Barrington to Sir J. Molesworth, 15 March 1757. W.O. 4/53, 347.
75. Hardwicke to Royston, 18 September 1757. Add. MSS. 35352, f. 417r.
76. Bedford to Holdernesse, 1 September 1757. S.P. 36/138, f. 1r.
77. W. Ellis to Nathaniel Ryder, 4 June 1765. W.O. 1/982, 146.
78. T. Duncombe to Holdernesse, 10 March 1761. Egerton 3436.
79. 12 March 1761. S.P. 44/139, 9–10.
80. 13 March 1761. W.O. 4/63, 568.
81. 17 March 1763. W.O. 1/870, 437.
82. 23 and 28 March 1764. W.O. 1/988, 415–16, 419–20.
83. Welbore Ellis to O.C. Battalion of Foot Guards, and to the Constable of the Tower, 16 May 1765. W.O. 4/77, 7, 8, W.O. 5/53, 312–13.
84. Same to Field Officer in Waiting for the Regiments of Foot Guards, 17 May 1765. W.O. 5/53, 315.
85. Same to O.C. 11th Dragoons, 17 May. Ibid., 315.

86. i.e. the 11th Dragoons.
87. Welbore Ellis to the King, 17 May 1765. Fortescue, *Correspondence*, I, no. 62.
88. Welbore Ellis to O.C. 2nd or Queen's Dragoon Guards at Putney and to O.C. 10th Dragoons at Kingston, 18 May 1765. W.O. 5/53, 323, 324.
89. Welbore Ellis to the King 11.30 a.m., 18 May 1765. Fortescue, *Correspondence*, I, no. 68.
90. Seymour Conway to William Dellaway, 22 September 1766. S.P. 44/142, 5; Same to the King, 20 September 1766. Fortescue, *Correspondence*, I, no. 388; C. D'Oyly to Lt.-Col. Warde, 20 September 1766. W.O. 4/80, 287, W.O. 5/54, 306–7.
91. C. D'Oyly to Charles Garth and James Sutton at Devizes, 22 September 1766: W.O. 4/80, 289; Shelburne to the King, 21 September 1766: Fortescue, *Correspondence*, I, no. 392.
92. See below p. 142.
93. Henry Pelham to the Colonels of the three regiments of Foot Guards, 12 October 1727. W.O. 5/27, 294.
94. Same to same, 25 June 1727. W.O. 4/28, 335.
95. Same to O. C. two troops of Royal Regiment of Horse Guards, 24 June 1727. W.O. 5/27, 205.
96. Same to O.C. a troop of same, 24 June 1727. Ibid., 206: See also *Mist's Weekly Journal*, 1 July 1727.
97. H. Pelham to Major Erskine of Campbell's Regiment, 24 August 1727. W.O. 4/29, 36.
98. Mayor and Recorder of Leeds to Holdernesse, 25 June 1753. Egerton 3436, f. 31r.
99. E.g. several of Barrington's replies to such letters in June 1757. W.O. 4/54, 130, 137, 141, 144.
100. See Appendix 2.
101. Barrington to O. C. Troops of 4th Dragoons at Manchester, and nine other officers commanding, 22 January 1766. W.O. 40/17.
102. See Chapter 9.
103. Barrington to Warde, 23 September 1766. W.O. 4/80, 296.
104. Cavendish, *Debates*, I, 70.
105. Barrington to Lt.-Col. Harvey (Nottingham), 31 August 1756; same to same, 4 September; same to Lt.-Col. Dalrymple, 8 September: W.O. 4/52, 188, 202, 218; same to Harvey, 27 August: W.O. 5/43, 365.
106. Barrington to Lt.-Col. Bonham, 20 September 1766; to O. C. Companies of 13th Regiment at Devizes and at Trowbridge, 29 September 1766. W.O. 4/80, 345–6, 347.
107. Barrington to O.C. Companies of 13th Regiment, 30 September 1766. W.O. 5/54, 330.
108. Barrington to Major Hill, 1 October 1766; to Lt.-Col. Bonham, 1 October 1766. Ibid., W.O. 4/80, 364, 363.
109. Barrington to Lt.-Col. Warde, 3 October 1766. Ibid., 384.
110. Barrington to Major Hill, 4 October 1766. Ibid., 387.
111. 'Disposition', n. d. Barrington·MSS. H.A. 174: 1026/6c (4).
112. Barrington to Shelburne, 3 November 1766.W.O. 4/80, 478.
113. The King to Halifax, same to Cumberland, Cumberland to same, 20 May 1765. Fortescue, *Correspondence*, I, nos. 72, 74, 75. Edward Harvey to

Secretary at War, 20 May. W.O. 4/1044, 26.

114. Barrington to Daniel Ponton, 29 April 1768. W.O. 4/83, 354. See below p. 143.

115. 'Memoranda by the Duke of Wellington, with statements showing distribution of the troops', 5 April 1848. W.O. 30/81, Bundle 28/1.

116. Barrington to Charles Jenkinson, 9 June 1780. Add. MSS. 38214, ff. 10r–11.

117. Barrington MSS. H.A. 174: 1026/7, passim.

CHAPTER 7

1. They lasted for more than a month, and involved the march of 150 men from Reading to Bristol, and thence by sea to Carmarthen. W.O. 4/51, 83, 84, 85, 87, 110, 202.

2. Sir John Fielding and Saunders Welch to Newcastle, 14 October 1756. Add. MSS. 32868, f. 296r. All dates in this chapter are 1756 unless otherwise stated.

3. T. S. Ashton, *Economic Fluctuations in England, 1700–1800* (1959), 21.

4. There were two regiments (called 'troops') each of the Horse Guards and Horse Grenadier Guards.

5. Totalling eight battalions (1st Guards three battalions, Coldstreams two battalions, 3rd Guards three battalions).

6. Barrington to Marquis of Lorne, 26 April 1768. W.O. 4/83, 340.

7. 'List and quarters of H. M. Forces on 14 February, 1756.' Add. MSS. 33047, f. 10r.

8. 'French & English Army & Fleet, 1756.' 10 September. Ibid., ff. 73v–74r.

9. 'Advices Received: 1 February, 1756, dated January 20 from The Hague.' W.O. 30/54.

10. 'Advices Received: 14 February, 1756, dated 10 February from The Hague.' Ibid.

11. *Whitehall Evening Post*, 19–21 August; *Gent. Mag.* (to which some of the places were clearly not familiar, e.g. 'Badgeley' and 'Heartfall'), 408–9.

12. *Whitehall Evening Post*, 19–21 August.

13. W. Wright to Henry Fox, 19 August. S.P. 36/135, f. 226r.

14. Statement of Henry Eames of Earl Shilton, Leicestershire, enclosed with above. S.P. 36/135, f. 227r.

15. E. F. to Holdernesse, 21 August. S.P. 36/135, f. 238r. The corn prices recorded by the *Gentleman's Magazine* for the bushel in Birmingham were: July 4/6, August 6/8, September 5/6, October 6/6, November 6/6, December 7/0.

16. Lord Justice Willes to Newcastle, 21 August. Add. MSS. 32867, ff. 3–4.

17. The 6th or Inniskilling Dragoons.

18. Barrington to Lt.-Col. Harvey, 24 August. W.O. 5/43, 359.

19. Same to Capt. Burton, 25 August. Ibid.

20. Holdernesse to Newcastle, 25 August. Add. MSS. 32867, f. 48. See above p. 66.

21. Holdernesse to Earl Gower and Earl Brooke, 25 August. S.P. 44/134, 379–380.

22. Holdernesse to Post Master General, 25 August. Ibid., ff. 380–1. He wrote to Newcastle asking him to make similar enquiries through the Customs and Excise, 25 August. Add. MSS. 32867, f. 50r.

23. Mayor and J.P.s of Nottingham to Holdernesse, 25 August (an express, sent out at 9 that evening; it arrived at 7 pm on the 26th). S.P. 36/135, ff. 256–7.

24. ' . . . which I conceive is owing to the great and just spirit of my Lord Justice Willes . . . A Justice of Peace, who lives near Atherstone, informs me, they are pretty well dispersed, and returned most of them to their own houses.' W. Wright to Fox, 26 August (received 28). S.P. 36/135, ff. 260–1.

25. Holdernesse to Barrington, 26 August. S.P. 44/134, 381–2.

26. Holdernesse to Mayor of Nottingham, 26 August. Ibid., 382.

27. Holdernesse to Newcastle, 26 August. Add. MSS. 32867, f. 74r.

28. Barrington to Lt.-Col. Harvey, 27 August. W.O. 5/43, 365.

29. Same to same, 27 August. W.O. 4/52, 184.

30. Barrington to Willes, 27 August. Barrington MSS. H.A. 174: 1026/3 (a).

31. Harvey to Barrington, 7 September. Ibid.

32. Barrington to Major Hepburne, 29 August. W.O. 5/43, 367.

33. Lord Willes to Newcastle, 29 August. Add. MSS. 32867, f. 149v.

34. Lt.-Col. Harvey to Barrington, 30 August (enclosed in a packet from Barrington to Newcastle, 2 September). Ibid., f. 189.

35. Samuel Fellows and John Burton to Holdernesse, 28 August. S.P. 36/135, ff. 266–8.

36. John Hewitt to Holdernesse, 30 August (received 31). Ibid., ff. 271–4.

37. Ibid., f. 272v.

38. Newcastle to Hardwick, 28 August. Add. MSS. 35415, f. 261v.

39. Barrington to Major Hepburne, 31 August. W.O. 4/52, 187; W.O. 5/43, 375.

40. Barrington to N.C.O.s of 6th Dragoons (at Newhaven), 31 August. W.O. 5/43, 375.

41. Holdernesse to Mayor of Coventry, 31 August. S.P. 44/134, 383.

42. Barrington to O.C. detachment of Kings Own Dragoons at Reading, same to same at Henley, 4 September. W.O. 5/43, 379–80; *Gent. Mag.* (1756), 447–8.

43. E. F. to Holdernesse, 30 August. S.P. 36/135, f. 281. See Chapter 5.

44. Samuel Fellows to Holdernesse, 30 August (received 1 September). Ibid., f. 289r.

45. Same to same, 5 September. Ibid., f. 299v.

46. See Chapter 13; same to same, 7 September. Ibid., ff. 305–6. The next day was quiet. Same to same, 8 September. Egerton 3437, f. 374r.

47. Samuel Fellows and John Burton to Holdernesse, 11 October; W. Murray to Holdernesse, 22 October; Holdernesse to Fellows and Burton, 24 October; Burton and Fellows to Holdernesse, 3 November. S.P. 36/136, ff. 24, 37–8r, 39–40r, 73r.

48. J. Hewitt to Holdernesse, 5 September. S.P. 36/135, f. 301r.

49. J. Hewitt, *A Journal of the Proceedings of J. Hewitt, Mayor. One of His Majesty's Justices of the Peace for the City and County of Coventry, in the Year 1756, in the Suppressing of Riots and Tumults etc.* (1779), 10.

50. E. F. to Holdernesse, 5 September. S.P. 36/135, f. 303.

51. Barrington to Harvey, 4 September; Thomas Sherwin to Hepburne, 4 September. W.O. 4/52, 202, 205. Barrington to Hepburne, 4 September. W.O. 5/43, 379.

52. Barrington to Adjutant of Albemarle's Regiment, 7 September; Thomas Sherwin to Captain St. Leger, n.d. Ibid., 413.

53. Barrington to O.C. 3rd Dragoons, 8 September. W.O. 4/52, 218.

54. *Whitehall Evening Post*, 4–7 September; Barrington to Harvey, 8 September. W.O. 4/52, 217.
55. E. S. Lindley, *A History of Wotton under Edge* (1962), 103–4.
56. Presumably verbally; no letter survives in Fox's letter books. Ducie's request for troops is mentioned in a letter written after Fox's resignation by Barrington to Holdernesse, 21 November. Egerton 3432, f. 7r.
57. Barrington to Sir John Mordaunt or Lt.-Col. Wolfe, 18 October. W.O. 5/43, 417.
58. Julia de Lacy Mann, 'Textile Industries since 1550', in *The Victoria History of the Counties of England: A History of Wiltshire*, 9 vols (1957–69) Vol. IV, 166. See also W. Minchington, 'The Petitions of Weavers and Clothiers in 1756', *Bristol and Gloucester Archaeological Society*, LXXIII, 215.
59. Wolfe to his father, 19 October Beckles Willson, *The Life and Letters of James Wolfe* (1909), 303–4.
60. Barrington to Holdernesse, 21 November. Egerton 3432, f. 7r.
61. Wolfe to Barrington, 27 October. Ibid., f. 9r.
62. Wolfe to Barrington, 25 October. Egerton 3432, f. 9r; same to Lord George Henry Lennox, 6 November. *H.M.C.*, Bathurst 76, 11.
63. Wolfe to Barrington, 30 October. Egerton 3432, f. 11r.
64. Ibid., f. 11v.
65. Ibid., f. 12r.
66. Barrington to Wolfe, 1 November. W.O. 4/52, 359; 2 November W.O. 5/43, 451.
67. Wolfe to Barrington, 8 November. Egerton 3432, f. 13r.
68. Wolfe to his mother, November 1756. Beckles Willson, op. cit., 306.
69. Barrington to Wolfe, 13 November. W.O. 5/43, 478.
70. Thomas Whitmore of Apsley to Holdernesse, 11 November. S.P. 36/136, ff. 93–4r, Barrington to Holdernesse, returning letters of Thomas Whitmore and Lord Powis ('I am in hopes the High Sheriff will be able to quell the riots, without the assistance of the military power, which is at all times most desirable'), 13 November. S.P. 41/22.
71. Barrington to Kingsley, 16 November. W.O. 5/43, 484. Same to Earl of Home, 16 November. W.O. 4/52, 399.
72. Wolfe to Barrington, 15 November. Egerton 3432, f. 15r.
73. Lord Powis to Holdernesse, 24 November. Egerton 3440, f. 263v.
74. Barrington to Wolfe, 19 November. W.O. 5/43, 494.
75. Barrington to Holdernesse, 29 November. Egerton 3432, f. 17r.
76. Sir Robert Henley to Pitt, 20 December. S.P. 36/136, f. 153.
77. Wolfe to Barrington, 15 November. Egerton 3432, f. 15r.
78. Barrington to O.C. Cornwallis' Regiment (to Derby and Nottingham); same to O.C. Huske's Welsh Fuziliers (to Leicester); same to O.C. Effingham's Regiment (to Norwich), 18 November. W.O. 5/43, 486, 487, 488.
79. Barrington to Lt.-Col. La Fausille, 18 November. W.O. 4/52, 408. (General Wolfe is not to be confused with Lt.-Col. James Wolfe.) Barrington to Lord Egremont, 20 November. W.O. 4/52, 416.
80. Barrington to O.C. 3rd Dragoons; same to O.C. 24th Foot, 30 November. W.O. 5/44, 2, 3.
81. Same to O.C. 37th Foot, 2 December. Ibid., 5.
82. Same to O.C. 37th Foot, 18 December. Ibid., 37.

83. Same to O.C. 20th Foot, 13 December. Ibid., 24.
84. Same to O.C. 36th Foot, 31 December. Ibid., 58–9.
85. Same to O.C. 4th Foot, 2 December. Ibid., 6.
86. Same to O.C. 26th Foot, 30 December. Ibid., 52.
87. Barrington to W. Peters, Esq., at Padstow, 4 December; same to O.C. 26th Foot, 4 December. W.O. 4/52, 475, 476.

CHAPTER 8

1. See Chapter 5.
2. Barrington began to keep these appeals, probably for his own protection. (A few magistrates had written to him in 1756 but he had discarded their letters, and evidence for them exists now only in his replies to them.) In 1757 files began to be formed of magistrates' and officers' letters on riots. W.O. 1/973, 974, 976.
3. In such cases an officer would not do more than march to the scene, waiting for confirmation of his action from London.
4. [No title], 27 July 1757. Add MSS. 33047, f. 99. All dates in this chapter are 1757 unless otherwise stated.
5. Ibid.
6. 'State of the Army', n.d. Add MSS. 33047, f. 213.
7. R. Vyvyan to Barrington, 11 January. W.O. 1/974, 157; A. K. Hamilton Jenkin, *The Cornish Miner* (1962), 150.
8. Barrington to Mr Godolphin, 5 January. W.O. 4/53, 27.
9. Thomas Tyrwhitt to Thomas Hearne, 4 January. Ibid., 34.
10. Barrington to Godolphin, 5 January. Ibid., 27.
11. Barrington to Sir J. Molesworth, 15 March. Ibid., 347–8.
12. Barrington to O.C. 26th Foot, 15 March. W.O. 5/44, 172.
13. Tyrwhitt to O.C. Howard's (3rd Foot) at Plymouth; same to John Hearn at Padstow, 8 April. W.O. 4/53, 456, 457.
14. Barrington to O.C. 3rd regiment at Plymouth, 7 May. W.O. 4/51, 31. The report came directly to Barrington from the sheriff.
15. Captain Charles Campbell to Col. Howard at Plymouth, 2 May. W.O. 1/974, 153–4.
16. F. H. Thomas (J.P. at Penryn) to Barrington, 21 May. W.O. 1/973, 883.
17. Barrington to O.C. Kings Own Regiment of Foot (at Exeter), 10 May, W.O. 5/44, 298.
18. Barrington to O.C. invalids at Bristol, 14 January. W.O. 4/53, 62.
19. Wolfe to the Duke of Richmond, 19 January. *Unpublished letters of James Wolfe*, ed. P. L. Carver, reprinted from *University of Toronto Quarterly*, Vol. VIII, No. 1 (October 1938).
20. Barrington to Wolfe, 21 February. W.O. 4/53, 265; the order is contained in W.O. 5/44, 133.
21. See p. 105.
22. The troop tactics in these riots are discussed in Chapter 13.
23. Lt.-Col. La Fausille to Barrington, 9 April. W.O. 1/973, 662.
24. 19 June. W.O. 1/973, 709–12.
25. Barrington to Lt.-Gen. Sir John Mordaunt (Dorchester), to the Duke of

Marlborough (Barham Downs and Chatham), to Lt.-Gen. Campbell (Amersham), and to Lt.-Gen. Hawley (Salisbury), n.d. but apparently 24 June from position in the letter-book. W.O. 4/54, 158, 159.

26. 6 and 7 July. W.O. 5/44, 357–85, 388.
27. Ibid., 388–9.
28. Ibid., 388.
29. Ibid., 388.
30. Ibid., 390.
31. All on 21 June.
32. Burgoyne to Bedford (3.30 p.m.); Bedford to Barrington (5 p.m.), 31 August. W.O. 1/974, 39–43, 35. Barrington to Bedford (9 p.m.), 31 August. W.O. 4/54, 371.
33. Barrington to O.C. Royal Regiment of Horse Guards, 31 August. W.O. 5/44, 468.
34. Bedford to Holdernesse, 1 September. S.P. 36/138, ff. 1v.–2r.
35. Bedford to Barrington, 7 September (2.30 a.m.). W.O. 1/973, 105.
36. John Bullock to Bedford, n.d. Ibid., 109–12.
37. Royston to Barrington, 7 September. Ibid., 923–4.
38. Pitt to Barrington, 6 September. S.P. 44/189, 432–3.
39. Tyrwhitt to O.C. Royal Regiment of Horse Guards, 7 September. W.O. 5/44, 486.
40. Same to O.C. 1st Dragoons, 7 September. Ibid., 488.
41. Same to Bedford, 7 September; same to Royston, 8 September; same to Hardwicke, 8 September. W.O. 4/54, 411, 413, 416.
42. Tyrwhitt to Marlborough, 8 September. Ibid., 412.
43. See Map 1, p. 106.
44. E.g. the Bristol riots of August 1749. S.P. 44/187, 123.
45. See Chapter 6. By 1757 Holdernesse was Secretary of State for the Northern Department.
46. Hardwicke to Newcastle, 11 September. Add. MSS. 32874, f. 4. Same to Royston, 9 September. Add. MSS. 35351, ff. 407v–408r.
47. Royston to Hardwicke, 10 September. Ibid., ff. 410v.–411r.
48. Ibid., f. 410v.
49. Hardwicke to Newcastle, 19 September. Add. MSS. 32874, f. 147r.
50. Hardwicke to Royston, 18 September. Add. MSS. 35351, f. 417r. Barrington's letter, mentioned in Hardwicke's, is not entered in the War Office out-letter book, one of many gaps in the W.O. series discernible from extrinsic sources.
51. Barrington to Major Forbes at Richmond, 17 September. W.O. 4/54, 445, W.O. 5/44, 500.
52. Same to O.C. troop of Royal Regiment of Horse Guards at Twickenham, 17 September. Ibid., 500.
53. Tyrwhitt to O.C. 4th Dragoons, 6 September. Ibid., 486.
54. Barrington to O.C. 4th Dragoons at Hertford, 22 September. Ibid., 507.
55. Same to O.C. troops of 4th Dragoons at Ware, 22 September. Ibid., 504.
56. Same to O.C. 1st Dragoons, 28 September. W.O. 5/45, 26–7.
57. Same to O.C. 3rd Dragoon Guards, 29 September. Ibid., 32.
58. Same to O.C. 10th Dragoons at Petworth and Lewes, 23 September, Ibid., 1.

59. Same to O.C. troops of 10th Dragoons at Petworth and Canterbury, 6 October. W.O. 4/54, 510. The light troop was also sent for, 6 October. W.O. 5/45, 43.
60. Barrington to Arthur Onslow, 6 October. W.O. 4/54, 517. Same to O.C. troops of Royal Regiment of Horse Guards at Kingston, Richmond and Hounslow, 6 October. W.O. 5/45, 46.
61. Barrington to Sir Nicholas Carew, 6 October. W.O. 4/54, 517. The dragoons were ordered to help if required. Barrington to O.C. Inniskilling Dragoons, 6 October. W.O. 5/45, 44.
62. Barrington to Major Scott, 20 September. W.O. 4/54, 448.
63. Nathaniel Cholmley of Howsham to Newcastle, 14 September. Add. MSS. 32874, f. 46r.
64. Lord Irwin to Newcastle, 15 September. Ibid., f. 61r.
65. Henry Willoughly to D'Arcy, 15 September (sent by D'Arcy to Holdernesse, 16 September). Egerton 3436, f. 137.
66. Irwin to Holdernesse, 15 September. Ibid., f. 138. Same to Newcastle, 15 September. Add. MSS. 32874, f. 62r.
67. Holdernesse to D'Arcy, 17 September. Egerton 3436, ff. 139–40.
68. Same to Lord Mayor of York, 17 September. Ibid., ff. 140–1.
69. E.g. W. Osbaldeston to Newcastle, 16 September. Add. MSS. 32874, f. 88. See above p. 19.
70. Newcastle to Irwin, 19 September. Ibid., ff. 155–6.
71. Ancaster to Newcastle, 19 September. Ibid., ff. 157–8. Newcastle to Ancaster, 20 September. Ibid., f. 179r.
72. Wynn to Newcastle, 22 September. Ibid., f. 222v.
73. Ibid., f. 223r.
74. C. H. Lane to Holdernesse, 24 September. S.P. 36/138, f. 30r.
75. Dupplin to Newcastle, 24 September. Add. MSS. 32874, f. 265v.
76. Rockingham to Newcastle, 24 September. Ibid., f. 270v.–271r.
77. Dupplin to Newcastle, 24 September. Ibid., f. 265v.–266r.
78. Newcastle to Rockingham, 27 September. Ibid., f. 327v.
79. Mansfield to Newcastle. Ibid., ff. 318–20.
80. Newcastle to Wynn, 27 September. Ibid., f. 332r; Barrington to O.C. 4th Dragoons at Royston, 28 September. W.O. 5/45, 24.
81. Barrington to O.C. 1st Dragoons, 28 September. Ibid., 26–7.
82. E.g. Newcastle to Nathaniel Cholmley, 7 October. Add. MSS. 32874, f. 467; Holdernesse to Hutton, n.d. Egerton 3436, f. 185v.
83. It is mentioned in Rockingham to Newcastle, 17 October. Add. MSS. 32875, f. 156.
84. Newcastle to Hardwicke, 15 October; same to Earl of Coventry, 18 October. Ibid., ff. 121r., 174r.
85. L. Pilkington to Holdernesse, 22 November. Egerton 3436, f. 176r.
86. Barrington to O.C. 25th Foot, 26 November. W.O. 5/45, 173. 'The order was very expeditiously complied with, for the men were in Wakefield yesterday sevenight.' L. Pilkington to Holdernesse, 7 December. Egerton 3436, f. 181r.
87. Mayor and magistrates of Boston to Pitt, 2 November. S.P. 36/138, ff. 113–14. Pitt to Mayor of Boston, 4 November. S.P. 44/189, 465–6.
88. Pitt to Barrington, 4 November. Ibid., 463–4. Barrington to O.C. companies of 5th Foot at Leicester, and to O.C. troops of 10th Dragoons at

Northampton, 4 November. W.O. 5/45, 141–2.

89. Mayor of Boston to Pitt, 7 November. S.P. 36/138, ff. 129–30.
90. Pitt to Barrington, 11 November. S.P. 44/189, 477; Barrington to Pitt, 12 November. W.O. 41/23.
91. Gabriel Hanger of Driffield (near Cirencester) to Pitt, 6 November. S.P. 36/138, f. 128.
92. Pitt to Barrington, 8 November; same to Gabriel Hanger, 8 November. S.P. 44/189, 466–7.
93. *Manchester Mercury*, 14 June; *Gent. Mag.*, (1757), 285; Arthur Redford, *The History of Local Government in Manchester* 3 vols (1939–40), I, 143–4.
94. Barrington to O.C. 6th Dragoons at Northampton, 9 June. W.O. 5/44, 346.
95. Barrington to James Bailey (Mayor), 21 June. W.O. 4/54, 150. Same to O.C. company of invalids at Carlisle, 21 June. W.O. 5/44, 389.
96. See Chapter 13.
97. Barrington to O.C. 4th Dragoons at York, 17 November. W.O. 5/45, 157–8.
98. Same to O.C. companies of 25th Foot at Derby, 19 November. Ibid., 159–60.
99. Same to same at Derby, 19 November. Ibid., 161–2.
100. Barrington to James Bailey, 26 November. W.O. 4/55, 86.
101. James Bailey to Barrington, 23 December. W.O. 1/974, 29: Barrington to James Bailey, 28 December. W.O. 4/55, 174.
102. Francis Gildart to Barrington, 13 November. W.O. 1/974, 197.
103. Barrington to O.C. 25th Regiment at Derby, 19 November; same to O.C. Invalids at Manchester, 18 November. W.O. 5/45, 168, 165.
104. Barrington to O.C. companies of the 25th Regiment at Ashby and Derby, 19 November, W.O. 5/45, 166–7, 168. Same to Town Clerk of Liverpool, 19 November. W.O. 4/55, 69. Same to Sir Ellis Cunliffe, 25 November. Ibid., 82.
105. Francis Gildart to Barrington, 28 November. W.O. 1/974, 103–4.
106. W.O. 27/5.

CHAPTER 9

1. A good account is W. J. Shelton, *English Hunger and Industrial Disorders* (1973), chapters 1 and 3.
2. T. S. Ashton, op. cit., 21; E. L. Jones, op. cit., 143.
3. Barrington to Lord Burghersh, 25 January. W.O. 4/78, 337. Similar circumstances arose at Newcastle and Ipswich: Barrington to Sir Walter Blackett, 5 May; same to Major Skey, 7 May. W.O. 4/79, 288, 301. All dates are 1766 in this chapter.
4. Charles D'Oyly to O.C. Companies of 43rd Regiment, 14 and 18 February and 15 March. W.O. 5/54, 53, 54, 58, 92.
5. Barrington to O.C. 2nd and 3rd Dragoon Guards, 1st, 2nd, 3rd, 4th, 6th, 7th, 10th, and 11th Dragoons and 15th Light Dragoons, 2 and 3 May. W.O. 4/79, 274, 275.
6. D'Oyly to O.C. 1st Dragoons at Blandford, 24 February. W.O. 5/54, 62.
7. Barrington to O.C. 3rd Dragoons, 1 August. Ibid., 270.
8. Same to O.C. 2nd Light Dragoons, 8 August. Ibid., 278.
9. Shelton, op. cit., 34.
10. Barrington to O.C. Troops of 3rd Dragoons, 6 September. W.O. 5/54, 294.

11. Same to Lt.-Col. Bonham at Blandford, 6 September. W.O. 4/80, 252. Ottery is 20 miles, and Cullompton 26 miles from Lyme.

12. Charles D'Oyly to O.C. detachment of 43rd Foot, 20 September. W.O. 5/54, 308.

13. Same to Mayor of Tiverton, 20 September. W.O. 4/80, 288.

14. Same to O.C. 4th Dragoons at Worcester; to George Harris at Gloucester; to Samuel Sheppard at Hampton; all on 19 September. Ibid., 283, 284, 288.

15. Same to Charles Garth and James Sutton at Devizes; to Postmaster at Devizes, 22 September; to O.C. 13 Foot at Salisbury, 21 September. Ibid., 289, 290, 292.

16. 30 Geo. II, c. 1., 31 Geo. II, c. 1, 32 Geo. II, c.2.

17. Shelburne to the King; the King to Shelburne, 2 September. Fortescue, *Correspondence*, I, 384, 385; dated 1 September by L. B. Namier, *Additions and Corrections to . . . The Correspondence of King George the Third*, I, (Manchester 1937), 63.

18. The King to Seymour Conway, 20 September. Fortescue, *Correspondence*, I, 389; Seymour Conway to Newcastle, 21 September. Add. MSS. 32977, f. 120r; same to Lord President, 19 September. S.P. 44/142, 9–10.

19. Poor harvests were reported from Russia, Turkey, France, Spain, Portugal and Italy. Shelton, op. cit., 42.

20. Privy Council minutes, 24 September. P. C. 2/112, 46–8.

21. Privy Council minutes, 26 September. Ibid., 50–1; Seymour Conway to the King, 24 September, the King to Seymour Conway, 24 September. Fortescue, *Correspondence*, I, 397, 398; *London Gazette*, No. 10662, 23–7 September.

22. Newcastle to White, 27 September. Add. MSS. 32977, f. 170r.

23. Statement of Mr Farrer in Privy Council Minutes, 24 September. P.C. 2/112, 47.

24. Seymour Conway to the Duke of Marlborough and Lord Berkeley, 2 October. S.P. 44/142, 12–14.

25. Shelton, op. cit., 46–8.

26. Ibid., 99.

27. These movements are all summarised in Table V.

28. See above, Chapter 6. The units were 2nd Dragoon Guards (Colchester), 3rd (Manchester), 1st Dragoons (Canterbury), 2nd (Lewes), 3rd (Blandford), 4th (Worcester), 6th (Coventry), 7th (Northampton), 10th (Leeds), 11th (Stamford), and 15th Light Dragoons (Derby). W.O. 4/80, 293–4. Barrington to Seymour Conway, 25 September. S.P. 41/25.

29. Barrington to Royal Regiment of Horse Guards (York), to 1st Light Dragoons (Bridgend), to 2nd Light Dragoons (Epsom), and to officers commanding the same cavalry regiments as before, 24 September. W.O. 4/80, 319–20, W.O. 5/54, 318–19.

30. Same to O.C. 4th Foot (Plymouth), 8th and 35th (Chatham), 13th (Salisbury), 22nd (Dover Castle), 23rd (Carlisle, Whitehaven, Newcastle and Berwick) and 43rd (Winchester), 24 September. W.O. 4/80, 321, W.O. 5/54, 319.

31. Same to O.C. independent companies of invalids at Chester, Tilbury, Tynemouth, Landguard Fort, Pendennis, Plymouth, Carlisle, Hull, Portsmouth, Yarmouth, Bristol, Sheerness, Liverpool and Tenby, 27 September. W.O. 5/54, 320.

32. See above Chapter 6.
33. Barrington to Warde, 3 October. W.O. 4/80, 384.
34. Shelton, op. cit., 40.
35. A Draft, 2 October. Barrington MSS. H.A. 174: 1026/6c(4)
36. Memo., 'What may be done to reinforce troops in the West'. n.d. Ibid.
37. See Table 9.3.
38. Barrington to Suffolk, 1 October. Barrington MSS. H.A. 174: 1026/107, 11–12.
39. Same to Robert Nugent (Bristol) 4 October; to Samuel Sheppard (Hampton) 7 October. W.O. 4/80, 390, 403.
40. C. D'Oyly to Warde, 7 October; to Lord Bathurst (Cirencester) 7 October. Ibid., 402, 404–5.
41. C. D'Oyly to Warde, 16 October. Ibid., 417.
42. Same to same, 21 October. Ibid., 428–9.
43. Barrington to Warde, 3 November. Ibid., 476.
44. Same to William Dallaway, 9 November. Ibid., 492.
45. Same to Warde, 19 and 20 November. Ibid., 4/81, 31–2, 39.
46. Same to William How (Customs House, London), 6 October; C. D'Oyly to Edward Stanley, 22 October. W.O. 4/80, 399, 435.
47. Barrington to John Dodd (Swallowfield), 1 October. Ibid., 361.
48. *Gent. Mag.* (1766), 436–7, 491–3.
49. Ibid., 549, 598.
50. Edward Harvey to Major-General Parsloe, 29 September. W.O. 4/1044, 89. For a list of regiments intended to be reviewed by each general see Barrington's instructions to them of 6 October. W.O. 26/27, 325–9.
51. Mordaunt's (i.e. 10th) dragoons were at Leeds. There are no orders to them at this stage in the War Office letter-books, so their intervention must have been at the requisition of magistrates as a result of the general order of 25 September.
52. Edward Harvey to Major-General Keppel, 9 October. W.O. 4/1044, 94.
53. Same to Major-General Parsloe, to Lord Pembroke, and to Major-General Keppel, 22 October. Ibid., 97.
54. See Table 9.1.
55. Seymour Conway to W. Dallaway, 22 September. S.P. 44/142, 5.
56. Barrington to Shelburne, 24 September. W.O. 4/80, 314.
57. See *Calender of Home Office Papers of the Reign of George III, 1766–69* (1875), 124, for a list of pardons at special assizes.
58. Barrington to Thomas Nuttall, 31 October. Barrington MSS. H.A. 174: 1026/107, 13–14.
59. Barrington to E. Saxton, 8 January 1767. Ibid., 23–4.

CHAPTER 10

1. Sir John Fielding, *An Account of the Origin and Effect of a Police Set on Foot by His Grace the Duke of Newcastle in the year 1753, upon a Plan presented to his Grace by the late Henry Fielding, Esq.* (1758), iv–v.
2. *An Inquiry into the Causes of the late Increase of Robbers* (1751), xiv.
3. Tyrawley to Cumberland, February 1756. Egerton 3444, ff. 64–9.
4. Ibid., at f. 65r.

5. Barrington to the King, quoted in Shute Barrington, 154.

6. Ibid., 155–6.

7. Sandwich to Welbore Ellis, 7 and 25 October. S. P. 44/194, 130–1. 138. Halifax to J.P.s of East End, 19 October. S.P. 44/88, 114–15. Ellis to Constable of the Tower, 8 October, same to Lt.-Col. Ogilvie, 19 October, same to Captain Gore, 19 October. W.O. 4/73, 374, 421, 422. Same to O.C. Foot Guards at the Tower 8 and 26 October. W.O. 5/53, 232–3, 249; *Gent. Mag.* (1763), 515–16; *Public Advertiser*, 11, 13 and 19 October; Alfred Plummer, *The London Weavers Company 1600–1970* (1972), 321–2.

8. Walpole to Earl of Hertford, 20 May, 1765. *The Letters of Horace Walpole* (ed. Paget Toynbee), 16 vols (1903–5), VI, 241.

9. Walpole to Horace Mann, 25 May 1765. *Horace Walpole's Correspondence*, (ed. W. Lewis), 34 vols (1937–65), XXII, 301.

10. Extracted from *Gent. Mag.*, (1765), *London Chronicle, Lloyd's Evening Post*, and Horace Walpole's correspondence.

11. See Chapter 13.

12. Ellis to O. C. Guards at the Tower, 16 May. W.O. 4/77, 7, W.O. 5/53, 312–13: Same to Constable of the Tower, 16 May. W.O. 4/77, 8, W.O. 94/10, 489.

13. Ellis to the King, 6.30 [p.m.], 17 May. Fortescue, *Correspondence*, I, no. 62.

14. Ellis to Field Officer in Waiting for the three regiments of Foot Guards, 17 May. W.O. 5/53, 314–15.

15. Ellis to O. C. 11th Dragoons, 17 May. Ibid., 315.

16. Ellis to Field Officer in Waiting, 17 May. Ibid., 316. It is not clear from which point these soldiers were drawn: the Tower is most likely.

17. Ellis to the King, 6.30 [p.m.], 17 May, Fortescue, *Correspondence*, I, no. 62.

18. Ellis to Field Officer in Waiting for the 3rd Foot Guards, 17 May. W.O. 5/53, 318.

19. Ellis to O.C. 11th Dragoons; same to Gold Stick in Waiting, 17 May. W.O. 5/53, 319, 320: Halifax (at Bedford House) to the King, 17 May. Fortescue, *Correspondence*, I, no. 64. The orders cover the movement of cavalry; the movements of the Foot Guards (apart from the detachment of 50 men sent in the earlier part of the day) are not recorded in the letter-book at all. They probably marched from the Savoy and Somerset House on requisitions from magistrates.

20. Halifax to the King, 18 May, 9 p.m. Fortescue, *Correspondence*, I, no. 67.

21. Halifax to the King, 9 p.m., 17 May. Fortescue, *Correspondence*, I, no. 64.

22. Ellis to O.C. 11th Dragoons, 17 May. W.O. 5/53, 321.

23. Same to the King, 11.30 a.m., 18 May. Fortescue, *Correspondence*, I, no. 68.

24. Same to the Field Officer in Waiting, 17 May (in fact early on 18 May). W.O. 5/53, 316: Ellis to the King, 11.30 a.m., 18 May. Fortescue, *Correspondence*, I, no. 68.

25. Same to O. C. 11th Dragoons, 18 May, same to Field Officer in Waiting, 18 May. W.O. 4/77, 21, 16.

26. Halifax to the King, 11 a.m., 18 May. Fortescue, *Correspondence*, I, no. 65.

27. Ellis to O.C. Queens Dragoon Guards, 18 May. W.O. 5/53, 323.

28. Same to Mordaunt's Dragoons, 18 May. Ibid., 324.

29. Same to the King, 11.30 a.m., 18 May. Fortescue, *Correspondence*, I, no. 68.

30. Same to O. C. Elliot's Light Dragoons, 18 May. W.O. 5/53, 326.

31. Same to O. C. The Blues, 18 May. W.O. 4/77, 23.

32. Halifax to the King, n.d. Fortescue, *Correspondence* I, no. 72. L. B. Namier, *Additions and Corrections to ... The Correspondence of King George the Third* (Manchester, 1937), I, 28.
33. Edward Harvey to Ellis, 20 May. W.O. 4/1044, 26.
34. Cumberland to the King, 20 May. Fortescue, *Correspondence*, I, no. 75.
35. Ellis to Gold Stick in Waiting, 20 May. W.O. 4/77, 30.
36. Same to commander of these corps, 20 May. Ibid., 31, 32.
37. Same to Lord Mayor, 20 May. Ibid., 36–7.
38. Same to Gold Stick in Waiting, 20 May. Ibid., 38.
39. Same to O.C. Queen's Dragoon Guards at Islington, 20 May. Ibid., 43.
40. Same to O.C. 10th Dragoons, 20 May. Ibid., 43.
41. Same to Lord Granby, 20 May. Ibid., 40: Same to Duke of Northumberland, 20 May. W.O. 1/982, 144.
42. C. D'Oyly to Sir Charles Frederick, Ellis to O.C. Foot Guards at the Savoy and to Francis Matthews, 20 May. W.O. 4/77, 39, 41, 42.
43. Same to the King, 7.30 p.m., 21 May, Fortescue, *Correspondence*, I, no. 77.
44. Same to O. C. 15th Light Dragoons, 23 May, to Queen's Dragoon Guards, to 10th Dragoons, 29 May, and to 11th Dragoons, 4 June. W.O. 5/53, 331, 337, 345.

CHAPTER II

1. Lord Shelburne to Secretary at War, 26 January. S.P. 44/196, 195. All dates are 1768 in this chapter.
2. See G. Rudé, *Wilkes and Liberty, A Social Study of 1763 to 1774* (1962), 41–56; Shelton, op. cit., Part 2, Chapter 2.
3. *St. James' Chronicle*, 19–21 April.
4. Ibid., 23–6 April.
5. Horace Walpole, *Memoirs of the Reign of King George the Third*, ed. G. F. Russell Barker, 4 vols (1894), II, 126–7.
6. Ibid., III, 97.
7. Edmund Burke to Charles O'Hara, 11 April. *The Correspondence of Edmund Burke*, ed. Thomas J. Copeland, 9 vols (1958–70), I, 349.
8. 28 March. Fortescue, *Correspondence*, II, no. 599.
9. The King to Barrington, 28 March. Ibid., no. 600.
10. Thomas Whateley to George Grenville, 18 April. *The Grenville Papers: being the Correspondence of ... the Rt. Hon. George Grenville* (ed. W. J. Smith), 4 vols (1852–3), II, 268.
11. 9.37 a.m. Fortescue, *Correspondence*, II, no. 601 (a draft).
12. Weymouth to Barrington, 29 March. S.P. 44/142, 43.
13. 'Having yesterday consulted your Lordship ... ' Ibid.
14. Weymouth to Gold Stick, 29 March. Ibid., 44.
15. Barrington to the King. Fortescue, *Correspondence*, II, no. 602.
16. Same to Field Officer in Staff Waiting, 29 March. W.O. 5/55, 276.
17. Same to the King, 29 March. Fortescue, *Correspondence*, II, no. 603.
18. Weymouth to Northumberland, 29 March. S.P. 44/142, 42–3.
19. Barrington to O.C. 2nd or Queen's Light Dragoons, 4 April. W.O. 5/55, 278.
20. Same to same, 25 April. Ibid., 307.

21. Same to O.C. 25th Regiment, 20 April. Ibid., 302.
22. Same to O.C. 1st Light Dragoons, 27 April. Ibid., 303, 304.
23. Same to O.C. 2nd Light Dragoons, 27 April. Ibid., 307.
24. Same to O.C. 3rd Dragoons, 29 April. Ibid., 315.
25. Same to O.C. 2nd Dragoons, 29 April. Ibid., 315.
26. Same to O.C. 6th Dragoons, 10 May. Ibid., 326.
27. Same to O.C. Royal Regiment of Horse Guards, 10 May. Ibid., 329.
28. See Chapter 13.
29. See Chapter 3.
30. Fortescue, *Correspondence*, II, no. 607.
31. Northumberland to Weymouth and Shelburne, 13 April. S.P. 44/142, 51–2.
32. *St. James' Chronicle*, 19–21 April.
33. Barrington to Weymouth, 15 April. S.P. 44/142, 54.
34. Weymouth to Fielding, 15 April; same to Ponton, 17 April. Ibid., 56–8.
35. Such orders would go to the regiments held in reserve outside the capital.
36. Paper of the Adjutant-General, enclosed in Weymouth's to Northumberland, 19 April. S.P. 44/142, 61.
37. Lord Mayor to Weymouth, 19 April. Ibid., 65.
38. Fielding to Robert Wood, 28 April. Ibid., 114.
39. Weymouth to Northumberland, 25 April. Ibid., 71–2.
40. Robert Wood to Fielding, 9 June. Ibid., 138.
41. Barrington to Field Officer in Waiting, and to Gold Stick, 27 April. W.O. 5/55, 316.
42. Barrington MSS. H.A. 174: 1026/6c (1).
43. Ponton to Barrington, 29 April. W.O. 1/874, 41–2.
44. Barrington to Ponton, 29 April. W.O. 4/83, 354.
45. Edward Harvey to Colonel Cooper, 28 April. W.O. 3/24, 33.
46. Ponton to Wood, 3 May. S.P. 44/142, 118–19.
47. Weymouth to Barrington, 6 May. Ibid., 76–7.
48. Edward Harvey to Major-General Urmston, 7 May. W.O. 3/24, 35. Same to C.D'Oyly, 7 May: W.O. 1/874, 49.
49. Ponton to Weymouth; copies also went to Grafton, Shelburne and the Lord Chancellor, 9 May. S.P. 44/142, 78–9.
50. Wood to Ponton, 9 May. Ibid., 87.
51. See Chapter 13.
52. Fielding to Wood, 8 June. Ibid., 132–6.
53. Same to same, 15 June. Ibid., 147–50.
54. Wood to Barrington, 17 June. Ibid., 150.
55. Barrington to Weymouth, 18 June. Ibid., 152.
56. Fielding to Wood, 28 January, 1769. Ibid., 195.

CHAPTER 12

1. For a fairly adequate factual treatment of the events see J.P. de Castro, *The Gordon Riots* (1926). A more recent but popular account is Christopher Hibbert, *King Mob* (1959).
2. *P.H.*, XXI, 670, 671.
3. Lord Stormont to magistrates of Bow Street and Lichfield Street (a draft),

11.23 p.m., 2 June, 1780. S.P. 37/14, f. 142r. The letter was sent at 11.55. S.P. 37/20, f. 2r. All dates in this chapter are 1780.

4. Stormont to Charles Jenkinson, 2 June (a draft). S.P. 37/14, f. 144r.
5. Same to Major-General Wynyard, 3 June. S.P. 37/20, f. 13.
6. Cabinet minute (Stormont's Office) 11.45, 6 June. Fortescue, *Correspondence*, V, no. 3052. See Chapter 1.
7. Jenkinson to General Sir George Howard, 7 June. W.O. 4/110, 277–8.
8. Stormont to magistrates of Bow Street and Lichfield Street, 11.55 p.m., 2 June. S.P. 37/20, f. 2r. See above p. 148.
9. Same to Sir John Hawkins, 'past midnight', 2 June [i.e. in fact 3 June]. Ibid., f. 4r.
10. Same to Lord Mayor, 2.15 a.m., same to magistrates of Bow Street and Lichfield Street, 2 p.m., 3 June. Ibid., ff. 8r and 9r.
11. Stormont to Major-General Wynyard, 3 June. Ibid., f. 13.
12. Wynyard to Stormont, 3 June. S.P. 37/21, f. 1.
13. Mr Wright to Sir Stanier Porton, 3 June. S.P. 37/14, f. 150.
14. Hillsborough to Gold Stick, 3 June. S.P. 41/28.
15. Stormont to Secretary at War, 4 June. S.P. 37/20, f. 29r.
16. Same to same, 4 June. Ibid., f. 31r.
17. Same to same, 4 June. Ibid., f. 33.
18. Lewis to O.C. H. M. Forces in the Tower, 5 June. W.O. 5/62, 312–13.
19. Tower Entry Book, 5 June. W.O. 94/10, 513.
20. Jenkinson to General Craig, 5 June. W.O. 4/110, 260.
21. Jenkinson to O.C. Queen's Light Dragoons, 5 June. W.O. 5/62, 312. Same to Stormont, 5 June. W.O. 4/110, 261–2, S.P. 37/20, f. 45v.
22. See e.g. his letter of protest to Lord Stormont about the failure of magistrates to act, 6 June. W.O. 4/110, 265–7.
23. W.O. 34/103 and 104.
24. Stormont and Hillsborough to Amherst, 12.40 a.m., 5 June [i.e. 6 June]. S.P. 37/14, f. 171, W.O. 34/103, 19r.
25. *Ann. Reg.* (1780), 193.
26. Amherst to O.C. 16th Light Dragoons, 2 a.m., 6 June. W.O. 34/234, 1.
27. Amherst to O.C. 3rd Dragoon Guards at Colchester; same to O.C. 3rd Dragoons at Petworth; same to O.C. 4th Dragoons at Canterbury, 6 June. Ibid., 3–4. Later the same day more specific orders (from Jenkinson's office) ordered the 3rd Dragoons to Croydon, and the 3rd Dragoon Guards to Whitechapel, Islington, Tottenham Court, Marylebone, Lisson Green and Paddington. Jenkinson to O.C. 3rd Dragoons; same to O.C. 3rd Dragoon Guards, 6 June. W.O. 5/62, 318.
28. Extracted from W.O. 5/62, 321–3, 324.
29. Extracted from W.O. 5/97, 271, 272, 274, 276, 277, 278, 279 and W.O. 4/766, 130, 131, 132, 133.
30. See below pp. 184–5.
31. See Table 12.2.
32. Colonel Stuart to Lord Bute, June 3 (a misprint for 8), in *A Prime Minister and His Son*, ed. Hon. E. Stuart Wortley (1925), 182.
33. W.O. 34/234, 5, 6, 8, 11, 12, 13, 14.
34. See a list 'Disposition of Posts: Foot Guards', n.d., but apparently not before 8 June from position in file, W.O. 34/103, f. 208r.

35. Ibid., f. 203r., for the units; exact figures for the strength of each unit are not included, and do not appear to be available for 8 June. they are taken from a 'List of effective rank and file in and about London on 1st July'. W.O. 34/189, f. 80r.

36. Ibid.

37. Estimated.

38. A note of a 'Disposition of the Troops in and about London during the late Riots in the beginning of June 1780' (supplementing an interesting map in the Guildhall Print Room, showing the defences) has somewhat differing figures. The total of officers, N.C.O.s and men involved in the operation is there alleged to be 13,016. Guildhall Library MSS. 14,287. This carefully prepared list is however undated and clearly refers to the state of affairs a day or so after the suppression: it mentions the presence of the 18th and 52nd Foot, and the Stafford, Cambridge, Northampton and Buckingham regiments of militia, all of which, although ordered on or before 8 June, did not appear until later. For a printed version of the map see Philippa Glanville, *London in Maps* (1972), 136–7.

39. Twisleton to Amherst, 8 June. W.O. 34/103, f. 187r.

40. Place Papers. Add. MSS. 27828, f. 127.

41. Dean of the Arches to Jenkinson, 7 June. Add. MSS. 38344, f. 140r. Amherst to Jenkinson, 12.45 a.m. 7 June (i.e. 8 June). W.O. 34/234, f. 14.

42. Jenkinson to Mr Hatsell, 7 June. W.O. 4/110, 274.

43. *The Parliamentary Register; or History of the Proceedings and Debates of the House of Commons*, XVII, 724.

44. Clerke to Amherst, 7 June. W.O. 34/103, f. 61.

45. Bishop of St David's to Amherst, 8 June. Ibid., ff. 112, 113r.

46. Stormont to Amherst (two letters), 7 June. Ibid., ff. 56r and 95r.

47. *Public Advertiser*, 7 June.

48. William Howitt, *The Northern Heights of London* (1869), 355.

49. E.g. residents of Bartlett's Buildings, Holborn to Amherst, 8 June. W.O. 34/103, f. 224r.

50. *Ann. Reg.* (1780), 196.

51. *London Courant & Westminster Chronicle*, 10 June.

52. *Gent. Mag.* (1780), 295; General Roy to Matthew Cox (contractor), 7 June. W.O. 34/103, f. 96r. M. Lewis to Thomas Harley, 7 June. W.O. 4/110, 275–6: Same to Captain Stevenson, 9 June. W.O. 5/766, 135. John Boddington to Amherst, for provision of 100,000 musket cartridges from the Tower, 9 June. W.O. 34/103, f. 264r.

53. See below Chapter 13.

54. Hillsborough to Amherst, 7 June. W.O. 34/103, f. 69r.

55. Colonel Stuart to Lord Bute, 8 June, in *A Prime Minister and His Son*, ed. Hon. E. Stuart Wortley (1925), 182.

56. Twisleton to Amherst, 9 June. W.O. 34/103, f. 258v.

57. Townshend to Secretary of State, 9 June. S.P. 37/21, ff. 40r and 42.

58. Belford to Amherst, 10 June. W.O. 34/103, f. 282r.

59. Amherst to the King, 18 July. W.O. 34/194, f. 60r.

60. Debbieg to Governor and Company of the Bank of England 1 September. MP/H/13.

61. Daniel Booth to Debbieg, 21 September. Ibid.

62. Debbieg to Amherst, 9 June. W.O. 34/103, ff. 245–246r.
63. Ibid., f. 246r. Another 25 men were added on 12 June. Same to same, 12 June. Ibid., f. 352r. A further increase then brought the number to 169 by day and 195 by night. Report of Debbieg on the New River Guard, 16 June. W.O 34/104, f.92v.
64. Ibid., ff. 92–95v.
65. Ibid., f. 95.

CHAPTER 13

1. Barrington to Lt.-Col. Harvey, 27 August 1756. W.O. 4/52, 184.
2. W.O. 1/973, 974 and 976.
3. W.O. 34/103 and 104.
4. 'In compliance with the order of yesterday I am to acquaint you', etc., is a typical preamble to a report, e.g. Capt. S. Archer to Amherst, 12 June 1780. W.O. 34/103, f. 355r.
5. *P.H.*, XXI, 726–54.
6. See Chapter 1.
7. *London Chronicle*, 21–23 May, 1765, which also mentions a guard of foot guards, horse and horse-grenadier guards on duty under arms in St. James' Park ready for an instant alarm.
8. The following day cavalry was also placed at Lambeth, Hackney and St Marylebone. Welbore Ellis to the King, 21 May 1765, 7.30 p.m. Fortescue, *Correspondence*, I, no. 77.
9. Horace Walpole to the Earl of Hertford, 20 May 1765. *The Letters of Horace Walpole* (ed. Paget Toynbee), 16 vols (1903–5), VI, 241. See above Chapter 11.
10. *Gent. Mag.* (1765), 244.
11. Newcastle to Henry Pelham, 22 November 1727. S.P. 44/125, ff. 183–4.
12. 23 November 1727. W.O. 5/27, 315, 316.
13. Mayor and Corporation of Falmouth to Newcastle, 16 November 1727. S.P. 44/125, 186.
14. Samuel Fellows to Holdernesse, 30 August 1756. S.P. 36/135, ff. 289–91.
15. He had written on 25 August (9 p.m.) Ibid., ff. 256–7. His letter reached the Secretary of State's Office on the morning of the 27th and orders went from the War Office to Lt.-Col. Harvey of Cholmondeley's regiment (i.e. Inniskilling Dragoons) at Leicester on the same day. W.O. 5/43, 365–6.
16. Samuel Fellows to Holdernesse, 30 August 1756. S.P. 36/135, f. 289r.
17. Same to same, 5 September 1756. Ibid., f. 299r.
18. Who had been taken into custody earlier.
19. Samuel Fellows to Holdernesse, 7 September 1756. Ibid., ff. 305–6.
20. *London Chronicle*, 16–18 May 1765.
21. See below pp. 177–8.
22. *Public Advertiser*, 2 April 1768.
23. *Gazetteer and New Daily Advertiser*, 2 April 1768.
24. Egerton 3432, ff. 9–15. See above Chapter 8.
25. To Lord George Henry Lennox, 6 November 1756. *H.M.C.* Bathurst 76, 11.
26. Wolfe to Barrington, 27 October 1756. Egerton 3432, f. 9r.

27. His reputation in this respect has suffered after his repressive policy in Canada.

28. See above pp. 84–5.

29. Wolfe to Barrington, 30 October 1756. Egerton 3432, f. 12r. See also Barrington to Wolfe, 2 November 1756. W.O. 5/43, 451.

30. Royston to Hardwicke, n.d. but evidently early September 1757. Add. MSS. 35351, ff. 402v–403r.

31. Rockingham to Amherst, 8 June 1780. W.O. 34/103, f. 186r.

32. Report of Col. Lake, 12 June 1780. Ibid., f. 345r.

33. Report of Lt. Bygrave of the 16th Light Dragoons, 16 June 1780 (referring to events of 7 and 8 June). W.O. 34/104, f. 85r. The *Public Advertiser* for 9 June praised the firmness of the militia.

34. Philip Lloyd to C. Jenkinson, 20 June 1780. Add. MSS. 38214, f. 32v.

35. Ibid.

36. Sir Richard Worsley (O.C. South Hants Militia) to Amherst, 9 June 1780. W.O. 34/103, f. 239r.

37. Twisleton to Amherst, 9 June 1780. Ibid., f. 258r.

38. Report of Lt.-Col. Hulse, 8 June 1780. Ibid., f. 174r.

39. *London Evening Post*, 6–8 June 1780.

40. E.g. Barrington to Col. Watson, 11 June 1768; he had heard of the good behaviour of the troops and was glad 'particularly that the disturbance was so easily quelled, and that you were able to seize so many of the ringleaders'. W.O. 4/83, 440.

41. *Public Advertiser*, 27 August 1766.

42. H. Ibbetson to Holdernesse, 27 October 1753. Egerton 3436, f. 35r.

43. *Manual of Military Law*, 9th ed. (1969), Part II, Section V. Modern official writings on the subject for the training of officers are 'classified' and not available to the public.

44. Ibid., 502.

45. Report of Ensign J. Gascoyne, Coldstream Guards, 5 June. W.O. 34/103, f. 14r.

46. Report of Lt. T. Thoroton, Coldstream Guards, 5 June. Ibid., f. 20r.

47. Report of Lt. G. Calvert, Coldstream Guards, 6 June. Ibid., f. 24r.

48. Report of Ensign Charles Gould, 4 June. Ibid., f. 13r.

49. Report of Lt. Henry Fanshawe, 1st Guards, n.d. Ibid., f. 18.

50. S.P. 44/134, 1. Upon the shooting of one of the rioters a verdict of wilful murder against the soldiery (contrary to the coroner's ruling) was stubbornly returned by a jury evidently packed with warren-diggers. Ibid., 3.

51. Henry Pelham to O.C. Troops of the Royal Regiment of Horse Guards at Northampton, 24 June 1727; same to troops of the same regiment at Towcester, 24 June 1727. W.O. 5/27, 205–6.

52. Halifax to Welbore Ellis, 22 March 1765. W.O. 1/872, 117–18. Welbore Ellis to Halifax, 23 March 1765. S.P. 41/25.

53. F. W. Hamilton, *The Origin and History of the First or Grenadier Guards*, 3 vols (1874), II, 196.

54. i.e. Saunders Welch.

55. Welbore Ellis to the King, 11.30 a.m., 18 May, 1765. Fortescue, *Correspondence*, I, no. 68.

56. Horace Walpole to Earl of Hertford, 20 May 1765. *The Letters of Horace*

Walpole, ed. Mrs Paget Toynbee, 16 vols (1903–5), VI, 239–40: See also John Entick, *A New and Accurate History and Survey of London, Westminster, Southwark, and Places Adjacent*, 3 vols (1766), III, 257.

57. Ibid., 240.
58. Horace Walpole, Memoirs of the Reign of King George the Third, ed. G. F. Russell Barker, 4 vols (1894), II, 112.
59. *London Chronicle*, 16–18 May, 1765.
60. *Gent. Mag.* (1765), 244–5.
61. F. W. Hamilton, op. cit., II, 194.
62. Royston to Hardwicke, 10 September 1757. Add. MSS. 35351, ff. 410v–411r.
63. Ibid.
64. Report of Lt. Fanshawe, 1st Guards, 5 June 1780. W.O. 34/103, f. 18r.
65. Report of Capt. Albemarle Bertie, 1st Guards, 12 June 1780. Ibid., f. 360r.
66. i.e. but not with drawn swords.
67. Report of Cornet Hinde of 16th Dragoons, 9 June 1780. Ibid., f. 270. See below pp. 180–1 for what occurred subsequently.
68. The relative merits of cavalry and infantry in suppressing riots are discussed below pp. 181–2.
69. i.e. Cumberland.
70. 8 September 1756. W.O. 4/52, 217.
71. *Gazetteer and New Daily Advertiser*, 5 June 1780. *The Gentleman's Magazine* reported on the same incident, 'but such was the humanity of the commanding officer, that he restrained his men from firing upon them, as they appeared to him wholly unarmed'. 268.
72. Lt. William Read to Barrington, 15 November 1757. W.O. 1/973; 899–905; *Manchester Mercury*, 15 November; Whitworth's *Manchester Advertiser*, 22 November.
73. Lt.-Col. Duncombe to Holdernesse, 10 March 1761. Egerton 3436, ff. 381r–382r.
74. Ibid., f. 382r.
75. Holdernesse to Lord Ligonier, 12 March 1761. S.P. 44/139, 9.
76. Ibid.
77. Barrington to Lt.-Gen. Whitmore, 13 and 14 March 1761. W.O. 4/63, 567, 579.
78. See Chapter 2.
79. See above pp. 169–70.
80. *Public Advertiser*, 19 October 1763.
81. *Gent. Mag.* (1763), 516.
82. *Public Advertiser*, 19 October 1763.
83. Welbore Ellis to Lt.-Col. Ogilvie, 3rd Foot Guards at the Tower, 19 October 1763. W.O. 4/73, 421.
84. Shelburne to Secretary at War, 26 January 1768. S.P. 44/196, 195.
85. 17 April 1768. S.P. 44/142, 57–8. A similar letter was sent to Sir John Fielding. Ibid., 56–7.
86. It was later published by Wilkes himself in the *St. James' Chronicle*, 8–10 December 1768.
87. *Gazetteer & New Daily Advertiser*, 11 May 1768.
88. *R. v. Gillam (1768)*. Ann. Reg., 228–9.

89. Ibid. Testimony of Robert Allen (a peace officer, not related to the youth who was shot) whose sympathies lay with the crowd; it can be contrasted with the outburst of one of the guardsmen earlier that day: 'We are all ready to fire on our enemies the French and Spaniards but never will on our own countrymen.' *Gazetteer & New Daily Advertiser* 11 May 1768.

90. This is corroborated by another witness who heard a sergeant say that the firing was 'chiefly over the heads of the mob'. Testimony of James Earle in *R. v. Gillam*. T. S. 3213, box 920.

91. There seems to be no agreement about the numbers killed. Rudé accepts a figure of eleven, relying on Burke's estimate.

92. 'Return of the men which were Hurt or wounded in St.George's Fields by the Mob, during the late Disturbances.' Barrington MSS. H.A.174: 1026/6c (1).

93. Testimony of James Darbyshire in *R. v. Gillam. Ann. Reg.* (1768), 231.

94. The miners of Cornwall, a constant thorn to Secretary of State and army, regularly rioted. Three were shot dead by a force of invalids from the Plymouth garrison in 1773. Deputy Mayor to Barrington, 9 February 1773. W.O. 40/16. Such incidents were not common in the years 1769–79; also they occurred in provinces distant from London.

95. See above p. 175.

96. Report of Lt. David Howell, 6 June. W.O. 34/103, f. 31r.

97. Report of Cornet Hinde, 9 June. W.O. 34/103, f. 270v.

98. Report of Capt. John Woodford, 7 June. W.O. 34/103, f. 103. (As a guardsman Woodford was a captain in the Guards and a lieut.-colonel in the army.)

99. Ibid., f. 103v.

100. See above pp. 27–8.

101. See above p. 175.

102. Lord Townshend to Amherst, 6 June 1780. W.O. 34/103, f. 26r.

103. Stormont and Hillsborough to Amherst, 12.40 a.m., 6 June 1780. Ibid., f. 19r.

104. Mr and Mrs Wilmot (Bloomsbury Square) to Amherst, 7 June. Ibid., f. 64r.

105. Add. MSS. 23653, 1–9.

106. Report of Capt. Gardner (Queen's Light dragoons), 13 June. W.O. 34/104, f. 8v.

107. Report of Col. Sir John Wrottesley, 8 June. W.O. 34/103, ff. 193–4.

108. Ibid.

109. *Gent. Mag.* (1780), 268.

110. Ibid.

111. From a newspaper cutting in the Place Papers. Add. MSS. 27828, f. 127r.

112. N. Wraxall, *Historical Memoirs of My Own Time*, 2 vols (1815), I, 333.

113. G. T. Kenyon, *Life of Lloyd, First Lord Kenyon* (1873), 64.

114. *Morning Post*, 12 June.

115. *London Courant*, 7 June.

116. Barrington to Jenkinson, 9 June 1780. Add. MSS. 38214, f. 11v.

117. 7 June 1780. W.O. 4/110, 287. The Adjutant-General was Lt.-Gen. William Amherst, brother of the Commander-in-Chief.

118. Amherst to O.C. Troops at Lambeth and Southwark, 6 June. W.O. 34/234, 1.

119. Place Papers. Add. MSS. 27828, f. 127r.

120. This was the subject of a contemporary painting (reproduced by de Castro,

op. cit., and as a cover to the Penguin edition of Dorothy George's *London Life in the Eighteenth Century* (1966)) which clearly shows the members of the Association firing in pairs, not in volleys.

121. Place Papers. Add. MSS. 27828, f. 127r.

122. Twisleton to Amherst, 8 June. W.O. 34/103, f. 198r.

123. Lt. Wilmot to his parents (sent on 14 June by Mrs Wilmot to Amherst), 8 June. W.O. 34/125, f. 115r.

124. Copy garrison orders, 7 June. W.O. 94/59, f. 59 (4).

125. Belford to Amherst, 6 June. W.O. 34/103, f. 30r.

126. Ibid., 30v.

127. Amherst to John Boddington at the Tower, 7 June. W.O. 34/234, 8.

128. Worsley to Amherst, 7 June. W.O. 34/103, f. 67r.

129. John Boddington to Morse, 8 June. Ibid., f. 149r.

130. Copy orders of 7 June. Ibid., f. 38r.

131. Hillsborough to Amherst, 7 June. Ibid., f. 69r.

132. Wraxall, op. cit., 334.

133. Ibid., 332.

Bibliography

A   MANUSCRIPT SOURCES

Public Record Office

State Papers: S.P.	35/10, 60.
	36/1, 4–6, 50, 51, 61, 113, 123, 135–8.
	37/4, 6–11, 13, 14, 20, 21.
	41/6, 12, 19, 22–6, 28, 33.
	42/48.
	44/25, 88, 125, 129, 131, 132, 134, 139, 141, 142, 187, 189, 194, 196, 197, 232.
War Office Papers: W.O.	1/678, 680–2, 825, 870, 872, 874, 877, 890, 973, 974, 976, 982, 986, 1007, 1009, 1137.
	3/4, 24.
	4/20, 28, 29, 32, 34–6, 49, 51–5, 63, 73, 76–81, 83, 84, 90, 91, 105–8, 110, 1044.
	5/27, 30–4, 39, 41, 43–5, 52–5, 58, 61, 62, 96, 97, 766.
	26/27.
	27/5, 12, 13.
	30/54, 58, 81, 111.
	34/103, 104, 109, 125, 156, 164, 186, 189, 191, 194, 203, 231, 234, 241, 244.
	40/17.
	72/8.
	94/10, 48, 58, 59.
Home Office Papers: H.O.	50/462.
	51/151.
Privy Council Papers: P.C.	2/112.
	4/2.
Treasury Solicitors' Papers: T.S.	11/1408/443.
	11/2696/818.
	11/3213/920.
	11/3467/946.
	11/3707/995.
	11/5728/1116.
	11/5956/1128.

Chatham Papers: P.R.O.   30/8/18.
                                30/8/48.
                                30/8/76.
Maps and Plans: MP/H/13.
Admiralty Papers: Adm.   1/4127, 4328.
                                2/1167.

British Museum

Hardwicke MSS. Add. MSS.35351, 35415, 35893.
Holderness MSS. Egerton   3430, 3432, 3436–40, 3444.
Liverpool MSS. Add. MSS. 38,214, 38,307, 38,344, 38,564.
Newcastle MSS. Add. MSS.32,695, 32,867, 32,868, 32,871, 32,873–5.
                                  32,977, 32,989, 32,997, 33,047, 33,049.
Place MSS. Add. MSS.   27,828.

Guildhall Library

Guildhall MSS. 14,287.

Suffolk Record office (Ipswich)

Barrington MSS. H.A.174: 1026/3a, 6a(2), 6c(1), 6c(3), 6c(4), 7, 107.

B   NEWSPAPERS AND PERIODICALS

Annual Register.
Gentleman's Magazine.
Gazeteer and New Daily Advertiser.
Ipswich Journal.
Kentish Post.
Lloyd's Evening Post.
London Chronicle.
London Courant and Westminster Journal.
London Evening Post.
London Gazette.
Manchester Mercury.
Mist's Weekly Journal.
Morning Post.
Public Advertiser.
St. James Chronicle.
Westminster Journal.
Whitehall Evening Post.

C PARLIAMENTARY AND LEGAL SOURCES

John Almon, ed., *The Parliamentary Register . . . 1774–1780* (1775–80).
William Cobbett, ed., *Cobbett's Parliamentary History of England*, 36 vols (1806–20).
John Debrett, ed., *The History, Debates, and Proceedings of Both Houses of Parliament . . . 1743 to . . . 1774* (1792).
T. B. Howell, *A Complete Collection of State Trials and Proceedings for High Treason and other Crimes and Misdemeanours*, 21 vols, continuation by T. J. Howell, 12 vols (1817–26).
Sir Matthew Hale, *The History of the Pleas of the Crown*, 2 vols (1800).
Journals of the House of Commons.
Manual of Military Law (9th ed., 1968).
The Queen's Regulations for the Army (1961).
Statutes at Large.
John Wright ed., *Sir Henry Cavendish's Debates of the House of Commons, During the Thirteenth Parliament . . . Commonly Called the Unreported Parliament . . . 1768–1771*, 2 vols (1841–3).

D CONTEMPORARY PUBLICATIONS

John Adolphus, *The History of England from the Accession of King George the Third, to the Conclusion of Peace in the Year 1783*, 3 vols (1802).
Anon., *The Cadet, a Military Treatise* (1762).
Anon., *Standing Orders for the Light Horse Volunteers of London and Westminster* (1805).
[Army Lists]. *A List of the Officers of the Army and of the Corps of Royal Marines* (from 1754).
Sir William Blackstone, *Commentaries on the Laws of England*, 4 vols (Oxford, 1773).
Humphrey Bland, *A Treatise of Military Discipline* (1727).
Richard Burn, *The Justice of Peace, and Parish Officer* (1755).
Henry Chamberlain, *A New and Compleat Survey of the Cities of London and Westminster, the Borough of Southwark, and Parts Adjacent . . . to the Year 1770* (1771).
John Chamberlayne, *Magnae Britanniae Notitia; or the Present State of Great Britain*, 17 vols (1708–55).
[Patrick Colquhoun], *A Treatise on the Police of the Metropolis* (1796).
The Court and City Kalendar (1745–69).
The Court and City Register (1742–1814).
Campbell Dalrymple, *A Military Essay, Containing Reflections on the Raising, Arming, Cloathing, and Disciplining of the British Infantry and Cavalry* (1761).
M. Dalton, *The Countrey Justice, Containing the Practice of the Justices of the*

Peace out of their Sessions (1635).

Daniel Defoe, *A Tour through the Whole Island of Great Britain, Divided into Circuits or Journies,* 2 vols (1962).

Sir Thomas de Veil, *Observations on the Practice of a Justice of the Peace* (1747).

Charles Dupin, *View of the History and Actual State of the Military Force of Great Britain,* 2 vols (1822).

John Entick, *A New and Accurate History and Survey of London, Westminster, Southwark, and Places Adjacent,* 3 vols (1766).

Henry Fielding, *An Enquiry into the Causes of the Late Increase of Robbers* (1751).

Sir John Fielding, *An Account of the Origin and Effects of a Police, Set on Foot by His Grace the Duke of Newcastle in the Year 1753* (1758).

[James Glenie], *A Short Essay on the Modes of Defence Best Adapted to the Situation and Circumstances of this Island. . . . By an Officer* (1785).

Francis Grose, *Advice to the Officers of the British Army* (1782).

P. J. Grosley, *A Tour to London; or, New Observations on England, and its Inhabitants,* trans. T. Nugent, 2 vols (1772).

G. Hanger, *Military Reflections on the Attack and Defence of London* (1795):

Walter Harrison, *A New and Universal History, Description, and Survey of the Cities of London and Westminster* (1775).

[J. Hewitt], *A Guide for Constables and All Peace Officers, in the Due and Lawful Exercise of their Office* (1779).

J. Hewitt, *A Journal of the Proceedings of J. Hewitt, Mayor, and One of His Majesty's Justices of the Peace for the City and County of Coventry, in the Year 1756, in the Suppressing of Riots and Tumults* (1779).

Robert Hinde, *The Discipline of the Light Horse* (1778).

[Thomas Holcroft], *A Plain and Succinct Narrative of the Late Riots and Disturbances in the Cities of London and Westminster, and Borough of Southwark . . . by William Vincent* (1780).

John Impey, *The Office of Sheriff, Shewing its History and Antiquity* (1786).

Sir William Jones, *An Enquiry into the Legal Mode of Suppressing Riots* (1780).

General R. Kane, *A System of Camp Discipline* (1757).

William Lambarde, *Eirenarcha: or of the Office of Justice of Peace, in Foure Bookes* (1599).

[Charles Lennox, 3rd Duke of Richmond], *An Answer to a Short Essay* (1785).

William Maitland, *The History and Survey of London from its Foundation to the Present Time,* 2 vols (1756).

W. Marshall, *A Review of the Reports to the Board of Agriculture* (1815).

William Morgan and John Ogilby, *Ogilby and Morgan's Book of the Roads* (1745).

William Morgan and John Ogilby, *The Traveller's Pocket Book,* (1759).

W. Nelson, *The Office and Authority of a Justice of Peace* (1718).

[John Ogilby], *England and Wales, or Ogilby Improved* (1720).

John Ogilby, *Mr Ogilby's Tables of his Measur'd Roads* (1676).

John Ogilby and William Morgan, *Mr Ogilby's and Mr Morgan's Pocket Book of the Roads* (1680).

Philonomos, *The Right Method of Maintaining Security in Person and Property to all the Subjects of Great Britain, by a Vigorous Execution of the Present Laws of the Land . . . with a Short View of the Consequences Attending a Military Force* (1751).

Malachy Postlethwayt, *The Universal Dictionary of Trade and Commerce,* 2 vols (1774).

John Rocque, *A Plan of the Cities of London and Westminster, and Boroughs of Southwark, with the Contiguous Buildings; from an Actual Survey* (1746).

The Royal Kalendar (1767–1893).

Rules and Articles for the Better Government of His Majesty's Horse and Foot Guards and All Other His Forces in Great Britain and Ireland, Dominions Beyond the Seas, and Foreign Parts, for the 24th of March, 1753 (1753).

Thomas Simes, *The Military Guide for Young Officers, Containing a System of the Art of War* (1776).

Thomas Simes, *The Military Medley* (1768).

George Smith, *A Universal Military Dictionary* (1779).

Saunders Welch, *Observations on the Office of Constable* (1754).

Gilbert White, *The Natural History and Antiquities of Selborne* (1789).

James Wolfe, *General Wolfe's Instructions to young Officers* (1780).

Arthur Young, *A Six Months' Tour through the North of England* (1771).

E   PUBLISHED CORRESPONDENCE, MEMOIRS, BIOGRAPHIES ETC.

Shute Barrington, *The Political Life of William Wildman, Viscount Barrington, Compiled from Original Papers* (1815).

Historical Manuscripts Commission, *Bathurst MSS. 76.*

Bedford. *Correspondence of John, Fourth Duke of Bedford,* ed. Lord John Russell, 3 vols (1842–6).

John Brooke, *King George III,* (1972).

Burke. *The Correspondence of Edmund Burke,* ed. Thomas J. Copeland, 9 vols (Cambridge, 1958–70).

Burke. *Correspondence of the Right Honourable Edmund Burke; 1744 . . . 1797,* ed. Fitzwilliam and Bourke, 4 vols (1844).

Calendar of Home Office Papers of the Reign of George III, 1766–69 (1875).

Calvert. *The Journals and Correspondence of General Sir Harry Calvert,* ed. Sir H. Verney (1853).

Sir James Campbell, *Memoirs of Sir James Campbell of Ardkinglas,* 2 vols (1832).

J. F. Crosthwaite, *Brief Memoir of Major General Sir John George Woodford, K.C.B., K.C.H.* (1881).

Sir H. Ellis, *Letters Illustrative of English History,* 4 vols (1827).

Francis. *Memoirs of Sir Philip Francis, K.C.B., with Correspondence and*

Journals, ed. Joseph Parkes and H. Merivale, 2 vols (1867).

George III. *The Correspondence of King George the Third from 1760 to December 1783*, ed. Sir J. Fortescue, 6 vols (1927–8).

Grafton. *Autobiography and Political Correspondence of Augustus Henry, third Duke of Grafton*, ed. Sir W. R. Anson (1898).

Grenville. *The Grenville Papers: being the Correspondence of . . . the Right Hon: George Grenville*, ed. W. J. Smith, 4 vols 1852–3.

Samuel Hoare, *Memoirs of Samuel Hoare*, ed. F. J. Pryor (1911).

G. A. Jacobson, *William Blathwayt, a Late Seventeenth Century Administrator* (New Haven, 1932).

Jones. *The Letters of Sir William Jones*, ed. G. Cannon (Oxford, 1970).

J. H. Jesse, *Memoirs of the Life and Reign of King George the Third* (1867).

G. T. Kenyon, *Life of Lloyd, First Lord Kenyon* (1873).

R. Leslie-Melville, *The Life and Work of Sir John Fielding* (1934).

J. C. Long, *Lord Jeffrey Amherst, a Soldier of the King* (New York, 1933).

L. S. Mayo *Jeffrey Amherst: a Biography* (New York, 1916).

North. *The Correspondence of King George the Third with Lord North from 1768 to 1783*, ed. W. Bodham Donne, 2 vols (1867).

Osborn. *The Letters of Sarah Byng Osborn, 1721–1773*, ed. John McClelland (1930).

T. Percival, *Biographical Memoirs of T. B. Bayley* (1802).

F. A. Pottle, *James Boswell. The Earlier Years, 1740–1769* (1966).

Historical Manuscripts Commission, *12 V Rutland MSS*.

Historical Manuscripts Commission, *15 V.F.S. Savile Foljambe MSS*.

Shelburne. *Life of William, Earl of Shelburne*, 3 vols (1875–76).

Walpole. *Horace Walpole's Correspondence*, ed. W. S. Lewis, 34 vols (1937–65).

Walpole. *The Last Journals of Horace Walpole during the Reign of George III from 1771–1783*, ed. A. Francis Stuart, 2 vols (1910).

Walpole. *The Letters of Horace Walpole, Fourth Earl of Orford*, ed. Paget Toynbee, 16 vols (1903–5).

Walpole. *Memoirs of the Reign of King George the Third*, ed. G. F. Russell Barker, 4 vols (1894).

Walpole. *Memoirs of the Last Ten Years of the Reign of George the Second*, ed. Henry Fox, 3 vols (1847).

Wilkes. *The Correspondence of the Late John Wilkes, with his Friends*, ed. John Almon, 5 vols (1805).

Beckles Willson, *The Life and Letters of James Wolfe* (1909).

Wolfe. *Wolfe to the Duke of Richmond. Unpublished Letters*, ed. P. L. Carver (1938).

James Woodforde, *The Diary of a Country Parson: the Reverend James Woodforde, 1758–1802*, 5 vols (1924–31).

Hon. E. Stuart Wortley ed., *A Prime Minister and his Son* (1925).

Sir N. Wraxall, *Historical Memoirs of my own Time*, 2 vols (1815).

F   MONOGRAPHS AND BACKGROUND STUDIES

W. M. Acres, *The Bank of England from Within 1694–1900*, 2 vols (1931).

W. Albert, *The Turnpike System in England, 1663–1840* (1972).

F. H. Allport, *Social Psychology* (Cambridge, 1924).

Gilbert Armitage, *The History of the Bow Street Runners, 1729–1829* (1912).

T. S. Ashton, *Economic Fluctuations in England 1700–1800* (1959).

T. S. Ashton, *An Economic History of England: the Eighteenth Century* (1955).

C. T. Atkinson, *History of the Royal Dragoons, 1661–1934* (Glasgow 1934).

Corelli Barnett, *Britain and Her Army, 1509–1970* (1970).

Max Beloff, *Public Order and Popular Disturbances, 1660–1714* (1938).

B. R. Berelson and G. Steiner, *Human Behaviour: an Inventory of Scientific Findings* (New York, 1964).

Sir Walter Besant, *The Survey of London*, 10 vols (1902–12).

Howard L. Blackmore, *English Military Firearms* (1961).

E. S. Bogardus, *Fundamentals of Social Psychology* (New York, 1950).

John Brooke, *The Chatham Administration, 1766–1768* (1956).

Ian Brownlie, *The Law Relating to Public Order* (1968).

Richard Cannon, *Historical Records of the British Army, Comprising the History of every Regiment in His Majesty's Service*, 71 vols (1834–50).

J. D. Chambers, *Nottinghamshire in the Eighteenth Century: a Study of Life and Labour under the Squirearchy* (1932).

J. D. Chambers and G. E. Mingay, *The Agricultural Revolution: 1750–1850* (1966).

J. H. Clapham, *An Economic History of Modern Britain*, 3 vols (Cambridge 1926–38).

C. M. Clode, *The Military Forces of the Crown*, 2 vols (1869).

G. D. H. Cole and R. Postgate, *The Common People, 1746–1946* (1946).

W. H. B. Court, *A Concise Economic History of Britain from 1750 to Recent Times* (Cambridge, 1954).

T. A. Critchley, *The Conquest of Violence* (1971).

E. E. Curtis, *The Organization of the British Army in the American Revolution* (New Haven and London, 1926).

W. H. R. Curtler, *The Enclosure and Distribution of our Land* (Oxford, 1920).

H. C. Darby, *The Draining of the Fens*, 2 vols (Cambridge, 1940).

F. O. Darvall, *Popular Disturbances and Public Order in Regency England* (1934).

J. P. De Castro, *The Gordon Riots* (1926).

Lord Ernle, *English Farming, Past and Present* (1961).

Samuel E. Finer, *The Man on Horseback. The Role of the Military in Politics* (1962).

Sir John Fortescue, *A History of the British Army*, 13 vols and 6 atlases (1899–1930).

J. F. C. Fuller, *British Light Infantry in the Eighteenth Century* (1925).

M. D. George, *London Life in the Eighteenth Century* (1966).

E. W. Gilboy, *Wages in Eighteenth Century England*, (Cambridge, Mass., 1934).

C. Gill and Asa Briggs, *History of Birmingham*, 2 vols (1952).

Philippa Glanville, *London in Maps* (1972).

H. C. Gordon, *The War Office* (1935).

Sir F. W. Hamilton, *The Origin and History of the First or Grenadier Guards*, 3 vols (1874).

J. L. and B. Hammond, *The Town Labourer 1760–1832* (1925).

J. L. and B. Hammond, *The Village Labourer* (1932).

W. Hasbach, *A History of the English Agricultural Labourer* trans. Ruth Kenyon (1966).

C. Hibbert, *King Mob* (1959).

E. J. Hobsbawm, *Labouring Men. Studies in the History of Labour* (1964).

Sir William Holdsworth, *A History of English Law*, 17 vols (1903–72).

A. K. Hamilton Jenkin, *The Cornish Miner* (1927).

E. L. Jones, *Seasons and Prices: the Role of the Weather in English Agricultural History* (1964).

W. H. R. Jones, *Bradford on Avon; a History and Description* (Bradford-on-Avon, 1907).

D. L. Keir and F. H. Lawson, *Cases in Constitutional Law* (Oxford, 1928).

D. L. Keir, *The Constitutional History of Modern Britain*, (1960).

Gustave Le Bon, *The Crowd. A Study of the Popular Mind* (1896).

W. E. H. Lecky, *A History of England in the Eighteenth Century* 8 vols (1878–90).

W. M. Lee, *A History of Police* (1901).

E. M. Lloyd, *A Review of the History of Infantry* (1908).

E. S. Lindley, *Wotton under Edge: Men and Affairs of a Cotswold Wool Town* (1962).

S. Maccoby, *The English Radical Tradition, 1763–1914* (1952).

W. McDougall, *The Group Mind. A Sketch of the Principles of Collective Psychology* (Cambridge 1920).

P. Mantoux, *The Industrial Revolution in the Eighteenth Century* (1928).

Dorothy Marshall, *Eighteenth Century England* (1962).

F. C Mather, *Public Order in the Age of the Chartists* (Manchester, 1959).

Sir Lewis Namier and John Brooke, *Charles Townshend* (1964).

Sir Lewis Namier and John Brooke, *The History of Parliament. The House of Commons, 1754–1790*, 3 vols (1964).

A. Neuberg, *Armed Insurrection* (1920).

J. S. Omond, *Parliament and the Army, 1642–1904* (1933).

Vivian Ogilvie, *The English Public School* (1957).

L. S. Penrose, *On the Objective Study of Crowd Behaviour* (1952).

Hugh Phillips, *Mid-Georgian London* (1964).

Alfred Plummer, *The London Weavers' Company 1600–1700* (1972).

E. A. Pratt, *A History of Inland Transportation in England* (1912).

L. Radzinowicz, *A History of English Criminal Law*, 4 vols (1948–68).

Arthur Raistrick, *Dynasty of Ironfounders. The Darbys and Coalbrookdale*, (1953).

Arthur Redford, *The History of Local Government in Manchester*, 3 vols (1939–40).

Charles Reith, *The Police Idea: its History and Evolution in England in the Eighteenth Century and After* (1938).

Howard Robinson, *Britain's Post Office. A History of Development from the Beginnings to the Present Day* (1935).

H. C. B. Rogers, *The Mounted Troops of the British Army, 1066–1945* (1959).

Pat Rogers, *Grub Street: Studies in Subculture* (1972).

L. T. C. Rolt, *The Aeronauts. A History of Ballooning, 1783–1903* (1966).

George Rudé, *The Crowd in History* (New York, 1964).

George Rudé, *Hanoverian London: 1714–1808* (1971).

George Rudé, *Paris and London in the Eighteenth Century: Studies in Popular Protest* (1969).

George Rudé, *Wilkes and Liberty. A Social Study of 1763–74* (1962).

R. E. Scouller, *The Armies of Queen Anne* (Oxford, 1966).

Samuel Seyer, *Memoirs, Historical and Topographical of Bristol and its Neighbourhood, from the Earliest Period down to the Present Time*, 2 vols (Bristol, 1821–3).

W. J. Shelton, *English Hunger and Industrial Disorders* (1973).

N. J. Smelser, *Social Change in the Industrial Revolution* (1959).

N. J. Smelser, *Theory of Collective Behaviour* (1962).

E. P. Thompson, *The Making of the English Working Class* (1963).

M. A. Thomson, *A Constitutional History of England, 1642–1801* (1938).

M. A. Thomson, *The Secretaries of State, 1681–1782* (1968).

A. S. Turberville, ed., *Johnson's England*, 2 vols (Oxford, 1933).

Alfred Vagts, *A History of Militarism* (1959).

A. P. Wadsworth and Julia Mann, *The Cotton Trade and Industrial Lancashire, 1600–1780* (1931).

G. G. Walker, *The Honourable Artillery Company, 1537–1947* (1954).

J. Steven Watson, *The Reign of George III, 1760–1815* (1960).

Robert F. Wearmouth, *Methodism and the Common People of the Eighteenth Century* (1945).

S. and B. Webb, *English Local Government from the Revolution to the Municipal Reform Act*, 9 vols (1906–29).

J. R. Western, *The English Militia in the Eighteenth Century* (1956).

Basil Williams, *The Whig Supremacy* (1962).

E. N. Williams, *The Eighteenth Century Constitution* (Cambridge, 1960).

Charles Wilson, *England's Apprenticeship* (1603–1763).

Peter Young and J. P. Lawford, ed., *History of the British Army* (1970).

G ARTICLES

Olive Anderson, 'The Constitutional Position of the Secretary at War, 1643–1855', *Journal of the Society of Army Historical Research*, XXXVI (1958), 165.

Anon., 'On the Suppression of Riots by Military Interference', *Law Magazine, or Quarterly Review of Jurisprudence*, IX (February–May 1832), 66.

Edwin Gay, 'Arthur Young on English Roads', *The Quarterly Journal of Economics*, XLI (1927), 545.

Olive Gee, 'The British War Office in the Later Years of the American War of Independence', *Journal of Modern History*, XXVI (July 1954), 11.

R. B. Rose, 'Eighteenth Century Price Riots and Public Policy in England', *International Review of Social History*, VI, No. 2 (1961), 277.

Hans Speier, 'Militarism in Eighteenth Century England', *Social Research*, III (1936), 309.

E. P. Thompson, 'The Moral Economy of the English Crowd in the Eighteenth Century', *Past and Present* (February 1971).

H UNPUBLISHED STUDIES

I. F. Burton, *The Secretary at War and the Administration of the Army during the War of the Spanish Succession* (unpublished Ph.D. thesis, London, 1960).

Index

DATE DUE

HIGHSMITH 45230